AF575580

RED, WHITE & NEW:

Tales of Young Russian Americans

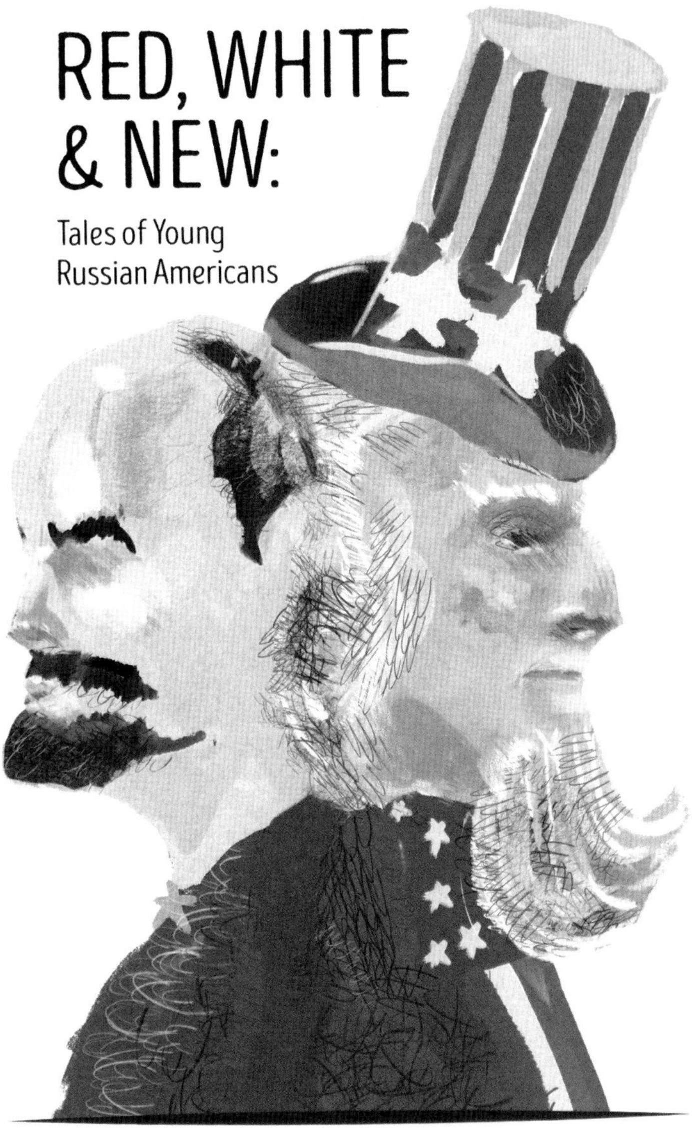

Edited with an Introduction by

ARIEL KIRMAN

Copyright © 2021 Ariel Kirman

Little Creek Press®
A Division of Kristin Mitchell Design, Inc.
5341 Sunny Ridge Road
Mineral Point, Wisconsin 53565

Book Design and Project Coordination:
Little Creek Press and Book Design

Cover art by Sebastian Cudicio

First Printing
October 2021

All rights reserved

No part of this book may be used or reproduced
in any manner whatsoever without written
permission from the publisher.

Printed in the United States of America

For more information or to order books,
www.littlecreekpress.com

Library of Congress Control Number: 2021919846

ISBN-13: 978-1-955656-09-2

This book is dedicated to my grandparents,
who gave up the world they knew to create
the world I know. *Spasibo.*

Ida & Vladimir Kirman
Emilia & Alex Krasilovsky

TABLE OF CONTENTS

INTRODUCTION

I have never been to Russia, but there is something Russian about me. I am the child of immigrants. My parents were born in the former Soviet Union in the 1970s and came to America as children at age eight. Their parents—my grandparents—gave up the lives they had for a journey across worlds so that my parents could have better futures. My parents' and grandparents' journey took them by train across the Iron Curtain, to Vienna and then to a suburb of Rome, where they waited three months for their asylum bid to be granted. They arrived in America as refugees—without money, language, or a clue about their new homeland. The story of how they adapted to their new world, while keeping one foot in the old one, has always fascinated and inspired me. I decided to write a book to study the immigration experience of those who, like my parents, came to America from the former Soviet Union as children. There are lessons in their life stories that go far beyond the Russian immigration experience. They are universal stories of change and hardship; of being excluded as an "other" and of yearning to be accepted; of fear and courage; of starting with rags and looking for riches; of the rift between new ways and old; and of many rebirths—ethnic, cultural, and religious, among others. And they are stories of America and the American dream, from a perspective that most of us don't get to see.

THE "IN-BETWEEN" PEOPLE, AKA "GENERATION 1.5"

A few years ago, I noticed something interesting. Some days my parents were "just Americans." They would speak English to each other and act in ways utterly indistinguishable from other Americans their age. But on other days, they seemed more Russian. Not completely so, but as with a ray of sunshine struggling through the clouds, I could catch it in brief glimpses. Sometimes it would be the occasional lapse into Russian among themselves (maybe as a means to conceal something from my brother or me). Sometimes, it was a story about life in the "old country" or life as a new immigrant. These stories of hardship, discrimination, and struggle often came with a warning. "Don't be spoiled," they seemed to be saying. "You have to appreciate what you have and how few people around the world have it." (I could fill in the obligatory "So go do your homework" at this point.) Of course, there was detail about the struggles that they and their parents and grandparents had overcome in coming to America. These were life lessons my brother and I grew up on in New York. But I saw their dual Russian-American identity most clearly at the occasional family gathering when grandparents were at the table. My grandparents—whom I call "Baba" (grandma) and "Deda" (grandpa)—find it easier to speak in Russian and sometimes struggle to express themselves in English fully. So my parents would pivot from speaking Russian to their parents and then English to us, often translating what Baba and Deda had just said. They were a bridge spanning a cultural and linguistic divide.

Some scholars use the term "Generation 1.5" when describing the experience of young immigrants like my parents, who fall somewhere between first-generation adult immigrants and their U.S.-born second-generation children.[1] The experiences of Gen 1.5'ers straddle two worlds and two cultures. They are tasked with the challenge of navigating their new country while keeping some part of their old country in their lives. As I learned in compiling this book, a person's immigration

1 In work dating back to the 1960s, the sociologist Rubén Rumbaut described Cuban-American child immigrants as being one-and-a-half generation (later changed to Generation 1.5). Rubén Rumbaut, "Ages, Life Stages, and Generational Cohorts: Decomposing the Immigrant First and Second Generations in the United States," International Migration Review, Vol. 38, No. 3., Conceptual and Methodological Developments in the Study of International Migration (Fall 2004), 1160–1205.

story means so much more than the physical aspect of moving from one country to another. Even more significantly, it also means the resettlement process—adapting to the new country, especially in those early years when the new country can also feel so alien. And this Janus-like quality, in which the Gen 1.5'ers are looking in two directions, applies not only to countries but also to people. It is fascinating to observe the dual roles that Gen 1.5'ers play with their parents and grandparents. They are children and still need their parents to guide them, but in this new environment, with their superior cultural and language fluency, the Gen 1.5'ers are also their parents' guides.

Why study this particular cohort? The easy answer might be that this story starts close to home. I grew up on Russian stories (immigration and others), and this was familiar ground in many ways. But the real reason lay elsewhere. I considered writing a more general interest book, profiling stories from immigrants from around the world. By contrast, a focus on Russian (or ex-Soviet, as discussed below) is narrower. But I ultimately opted for depth over breadth. I have a deep interest in immigration more generally, but I was seeking an "Archimedean point" from which I could begin to study the topic. By studying one cohort more deeply—which, as you will soon see, is remarkably diverse in so many unpredictable ways—I thought I could gain a deeper understanding, which could identify common themes and lessons about immigrants more broadly. After two years of research, preparation, conversations, interviews, and editing 20 stories here, I feel vindicated in the choice. Yet, if this experience has taught me anything, it is that these stories are not enough. By the end, I wanted to include another 20 stories, knowing that our understanding of the collective American immigration saga grows with each narrative.

Why focus on children (in my case, those who came to the U.S. between the ages of three and fifteen)? On some level, this again presented the depth versus breadth question. Trying to understand a group that numbers hundreds of thousands of people, let alone in a book this size, requires narrowing. A focus on the Generation 1.5 cohort accomplishes that, but thankfully not at the expense of narrowing the intellectual inquiry at hand. In fact, it does the opposite; it widens the exploratory lens by making us focus on the parts of the immigration story often overlooked. We often think about "immigrants" and "children of immigrants," but rarely do we think about those who are both. Unlike their parents, the Gen 1.5'ers do not make the decision to immigrate, yet they often shoulder the biggest burden to make that immigration a success. At a time when others are playing with teddy bears or baseballs, they are thrown into a new and often cold environment—with meager language skills, few friends, no money, and little parental help—and told, "Go!" They struggle and adapt and often pull their parents and grandparents along for the ride. They feel immense pressure to succeed, keenly aware of their parents' sacrifices to bring them to America. They are a treasure trove of complex identity, which I was eager to explore.

"RUSSIAN" IMMIGRATION: A DRAMA IN SEVERAL ACTS

Every story needs a setting of the scene, a backdrop to the unfolding drama. Russian immigration to America has a long history. The period between 1881 and 1914 saw a large-scale departure from the czarist empire and was part of the largest influx of immigrants in American history. The first decade after the Russian Revolution in 1917—when the Soviets were still consolidating power and exiling their political opponents—also saw a wave of immigration, much of it motivated by political opposition to the new Soviet regime. And there was a trickle that managed to leave in the confusion of the immediate aftermath of World War II. All of this was prehistory to the immigration stories in this book, which really began in the 1960s and 1970s.

During the post World War II Soviet era, emigration was severely restricted. Yet the U.S.S.R. occasionally lifted restrictions, and there were several waves of immigration that permitted Soviet citizens, mostly Jews, to leave. Since about 1970, it is estimated that over 400,000 Jews from the former Soviet Union have come to America, the largest wave of Jewish immigration to America since the 1920s.[2] Immigration can sometimes be understood as a combination of two factors: those that drive people from their homelands (the "push") and the traits that make foreign lands enticing (the "pull"). And while each family sought a new life in America for unique reasons, Russian immigration

2 Annelise Orleck, *The Soviet Jewish Americans* (Brandeis University Press, 1999), 2.

to the United States can best be understood as three, albeit sometimes overlapping, waves of "push and pull factors."[3]

The first wave began shortly after Israel's Six-Day War in 1967, peaking in 1971/1972 before turning into a trickle. The 1967 Six-Day War triggered renewed Jewish pride among the Jews of the Soviet Union. With the rise of a Soviet Jewry movement, both inside the Soviet Union—where it included letter-writing campaigns and hunger strikes—and in the West, the Soviets allowed a limited number of Jews to leave to Israel for "family reunification" reasons. During this period, those who left the U.S.S.R. were often willing to publicly express solidarity with Israel or Jewish religious practices. In many cases, they were willing to protest the treatment of the Jews in the Soviet Union. Many of these immigrants came from the peripheral areas of the U.S.S.R., such as the Baltic states (Lithuania, Latvia, and Estonia), Moldova, Uzbekistan, and Georgia, where Jews had assimilated less than in the Slavic heartland and the larger cities and were thus more religious and more willing to express Jewish pride. Anti-Semitism was officially not permitted in the U.S.S.R., but in practice, it was widespread and grew after the 1967 Six-Day War. After Israel's swift defeat of its Arab client states, the U.S.S.R. severed relations with Israel, increased its political and military support for the Arab states, outlawed Zionism, and unleashed a wave of anti-Israel ("anti-Zionist") and anti-Semitic propaganda. Most of the immigrants from this wave went to Israel, not the United States.

That choice of destination began to change dramatically with the second wave, which began around 1975 (and picked up steam in 1977) and lasted to 1981 when the aftermath of the invasion of Afghanistan and the boycott by the U.S. of the 1980 Moscow Olympics led to a colder Cold War climate that shut down immigration. The "Free Jewry" movement—with its famous slogan, "Let My People Go," powerfully evoking the story of Exodus—had begun during the first wave but was picking up steam in the West in the mid-1970s, with Jewish establishment groups, like the American Jewish Committee and

3 Since immigration was a continuous phenomenon, there is no universal demarcation of "waves" by historians, who have chosen to focus on different starting points and end points. For example, Orleck, Id., uses four waves, and her starting point is 1967. In contrast, others focus on three waves and start with the Russian Revolution in 1917. See, Dennis Shasha and Marina Shron, Red Blues: Voices from the Last Wave of Russian Immigrants (Holmes & Meier, 2002).

the World Jewish Congress (some feeling remorse for their inability to save Jews during the Holocaust), and grassroots groups like the Student Struggle for Soviet Jewry, leading the way. There were marches and protests. In some synagogues during the High Holy Days, there were empty chairs on the dais with the names of Soviet "prisoners of conscience." By the early 1970s, the issue had also become wrapped up in Cold War politics. Several politicians, most notably Senator Henry "Scoop" Jackson, Democratic Senator from Washington, advocated for confrontation with the Soviet Union rather than détente. In 1974, at Senator Jackson's urging, Congress passed into law the Jackson-Vanik Amendment to the Trade Act of 1974, which tied the Soviet Union's "most favored nations" status to reducing restrictions on immigration of Soviet Jews. This led to increased Soviet Jewish immigration in the late 1970s, including that of my parents, who came to the U.S. in 1979.

During this wave, Jewish immigrants started to increasingly choose the U.S. over Israel as a destination. For example, in the first half of the 1970s, 92.5 percent of such immigrants went to Israel, with most of the rest coming to America. By 1976 and 1977, only 50 percent went to Israel, and by 1979, only one-third did.[4] Why did so many refugees change their preferred destinations from Israel to America? Historians have posited a few possible explanations. First, the second wave saw many more Jews from more assimilated backgrounds, including from the large cities of Moscow and Leningrad (now St. Petersburg) and the more "Russified" cities of Ukraine, such as Odessa and Kharkov,[5] where my mother and father are from, respectively. With many of those most closely identifying with Israel and Judaism having left in the first wave, fewer such people remained. In many cases, the Jews of the second and third waves had a more assimilated Jewish identity, even though, as we will see below, they still preserved a sense of Jewish belonging, and anti-Semitism was *the* key driver for exit and, in many cases, the key driver. They espoused more universalist notions of freedom, which went beyond the Zionist ideals of the first wave. They also more

4 Mark Tolts, "A Half Century of Jewish Emigration from the Former Soviet Union: Demographic Aspects," (Paper presented at the Project for Russian and Eurasian Jewry, Davis Center for Russian and Eurasian Studies, Harvard University, on November 20, 2019). https://daviscenter.fas.harvard.edu/sites/default/files/files/2021-04/Tolts%20M.%20A%20Half%20Century%20of%20Jewish%20Emigration%20from%20the%20Former%20Soviet%20Union%20-%20Harvard4%20_0.pdf.

5 I use Kharkov, which is the spelling that was in place when my father was born there in 1970 and left there in 1978. Today, in a separate Ukraine, the city is known as Kharkiv.

explicitly cited better futures and opportunities for their children as a reason for immigration. Added to this, following the Yom Kippur War in 1973, a sense of insecurity and fear was another big motivator for many to stay away from Israel. With its constant conflict, even between major wars, Israel was perceived as a dangerous place for those serving in the military. This concern was hard to ignore in a nation devastated by World War II. That concern grew even more after the U.S.S.R.'s own army got bogged down for a decade in Afghanistan, starting in late 1979. In addition, under pressure from the American Jewish community, several Soviet refugee aid agencies, most notably HIAS (Hebrew Immigrant Aid Society) in 1976, changed their policies—which previously permitted help only to those going to Israel—to now be able to work with refugees seeking to come to the U.S.[6]

During Soviet times, exit visas were granted to go to Israel even when, as was the case during the second wave, most of the refugees went to America. During the Cold War, the Soviets would simply never admit that their own citizens would ever vote with their feet to leave the "Soviet socialist paradise" to emigrate to the decrepit and corrupt West that Soviet propaganda has spent years denigrating. So a Kabuki dance arose during these years. The Soviets issued exit visas to go to Israel, but the Jewish emigrants would then divert to Vienna and then Italy, where the U.S. government and aid agencies were set up to receive asylum applications based on religious persecution. This was known as "dropping out." Meanwhile, inside the Soviet Union, the process of requesting exit papers was complicated and fraught with risk. First, the would-be emigrant would need to receive a "vyzov" or invitation from a family member in Israel,[7] and the Jewish Agency in Israel would have to facilitate this. Then came a long process of seeking Soviet documentation and permission, which often led to awkward confrontations with work colleagues and neighbors, some of whom branded the would-be emigrant a traitor (or "parasite" in the parlance of the day). Many were immediately fired. The OVIR (Office of Visas and Registrations) could take months or years, in some cases, to process exit papers, with applicants and their families living in limbo. A few unlucky ones, who were refused for security or ideological

---

6 Orleck, 62.

7 Many immigrants found work-arounds, sometimes by finding someone with the same last name.

reasons, became known as "refuseniks" or "prisoners of Zion." Several contributors to this book fell into this category, with one having his family denied exit for five years because of his father's former security clearance. Even if all went well, the Soviets tore up your passport at the border, making emigrants stateless. It would take two or three months, in that pre-computer age, to process the asylum applications in Italy, during which time the families lived in Italy with the help of agencies such as HIAS and others. For many contributors in this book, these months were a formative experience—their first view of the West, with all the wonders and shock that brought forth. In later years, emigrants would simply board planes from Moscow or Kiev and dispense with this Kabuki theater.

The third immigration wave began in 1987, with the liberalization program initiated by Gorbachev, and accelerated with the dissolution of the U.S.S.R. in late 1991. It was the largest of the movements, which on some level is not surprising given the loosening of strictures on emigration in the former Soviet states. On the back of his "glasnost" and "perestroika" reforms, Gorbachev began to loosen immigration restrictions in 1987, but once the U.S.S.R. dissolved in December 1991, the gates were opened as they had never been during Soviet times. In those years immediately before and after the collapse of the U.S.S.R., the countries of the former Soviet Union, or F.S.U., in many cases went through periods of upheaval—economic instability, ethnic strife, and resurgent anti-Semitism as previously suppressed forces (nationalism and religion) were permitted more expression. In some places, the after-effects of the 1986 Chernobyl nuclear explosion also drove emigration. Most of the Jews leaving during this period preferred to come to the U.S., but the U.S. had largely shut its doors, with an unofficial quota of 40,000 per year and with priority given to those who had close relatives in the U.S. From 1991–1996, the U.S. ranked second (after Israel) as a destination. From 1997–2001, Germany took more F.S.U. immigrants than the U.S., and after September 11, 2001, the U.S. effectively ceased to be a major destination for immigrants from the F.S.U.[8] Even so, over 300,000 F.S.U. immigrants did make it

8 Mark Tolts, 'A Half Century of Jewish Emigration from the Former Soviet Union: Demographic Aspects,' paper presented at the Project for Russian and Eurasian Jewry, Davis Center for Russian and Eurasian Studies, Harvard University,' November 20th, 2019.

to the U.S. during the period 1989–2018.[9] A majority (over one million immigrants) ended up going to Israel, where they triggered a large demographic and social transformation of Israeli society.

STORYTELLING: A NOTE ON METHODOLOGY

There is a vast social science and historical literature, both quantitative and qualitative, devoted to Russian and Soviet immigration — books, studies, annual reports from Jewish agencies, and various cultural studies focused on topics such as acculturation and adolescent development in immigrant communities.[10] This book, while taking a different approach, benefits from this prior work. I spent many months educating myself on the issues that scholars and social scientists have written about to target contributors and guide them to issues I wanted to explore. I also picked participants along my chosen age spectrum (ages 3–15) to see how age at arrival influences acculturation. I distilled my research into a question guide (see Appendix), which I shared with all of the contributors. I had 85 questions spread over six distinct categories and several sub-categories. But I was clear that these were suggestions only, and ultimately each contributor wrote the story they wanted to write.

In picking contributors, I sought diversity—the area of the former Soviet Union they hailed from; where they landed in America; gender; what they did for a living; when they left (how old they were, but also which decade, especially whether during Soviet times or after); how their parents adapted; their level of religious observance; their views on dual-Russian identity; and so on. On some level, I accomplished this. I could have filled this book five times over with just immigrants who came from Ukraine to Brighton Beach in Brooklyn (known as "Little Odessa"), but I made a determined effort to also find people who landed in other places. The Soviet immigrant community is geographically dispersed but with a few large concentrations. The New

---

9 Ibid.

10 For studies of Soviet immigrant trends, such as age, income and synagogue membership, see e.g., Rita J. Simon, Julian Simon, and Jim Schwartz, *The Soviet Jews Adjustment to the United States* (Council of Jewish Federations, 1982); Barry Kostin, *The Class of 1979: The "Acculturation" of Jewish Immigrants from the Soviet Union* (North American Jewish Data Bank, CUNY Graduate School and University Center, 1990). For an example of qualitative observational studies, see Steven J. Gold, *Refugee Communities: A Comparative Field Study* (Newburn Park, Calif., 1992).

York metropolitan area (including New Jersey) has five to six times the number of Soviet immigrants as the next largest area, with Los Angeles, San Francisco, Chicago and Boston being the next most common.[11] But I wanted to also cover some of the other areas where immigrants landed, like Miami, Denver, and Baltimore. But in other ways, the space limitations meant that I could not explore all the combinations that I wanted. For example, I would have liked to include more people from the smaller Soviet republics, people with blue-collar jobs, or more non-Jews. But there are simply too many variables to combine in too few stories, so a fuller treatment will need a follow-up effort.

The sample is also a bit skewed toward those willing to write a long essay, which is an increasing challenge in a busy world, and a few decided not to participate for that reason. In five cases, I did interviews and worked with the contributor on editing a Q&A format. I also discovered that the task proved too emotional for a few would-be contributors who chose to stop mid-stream, the memories being difficult. While I edited each essay multiple times, I tried to preserve each writer's original style and voice because that is part of the story.

I found the participants in different ways. I wrote to Jewish agencies in various cities. I cold emailed a number of people I found on the Internet. I used my parents' network. I advertised on social media, and I followed leads given by other contributors. I realize that even this combination of methods did not yield a perfectly representative sample, but I was ultimately happy with the medley group I collected.

A note on terminology: I use "Russian" in the title of this book and elsewhere in some places when referring to the subject matter here, and do so even though what I most often mean is "Soviet" or "ex-Soviet." Although they are often together considered as one group, according to the U.S. Census Bureau, a majority of the immigrants who came from the U.S.S.R. came not from Russia itself but from one of the other 14 Soviet republics (now countries) such as Ukraine, Uzbekistan, Latvia, Georgia, and so on.[12] But I sometimes simplify for several reasons. First, the word "Russian" is more universally recognizable, especially among younger readers who were not alive when the Soviet Union dissolved in 1991 (anyone under 30). Also, in most parts of the former Soviet

---

11 Orleck, 131.

12 https://data.census.gov/cedsci/table?tid=ACSDT5Y2019.B05006.

Union, Russian culture and language were the dominant culture and language. The Soviets tried to create a "Soviet" culture, which itself was heavily Russified. For example, both my parents—my father is from Kharkov, Ukraine, and my mother from Odessa, Ukraine—grew up speaking Russian and not Ukrainian. If I asked them to describe where they are from, they might give me different answers on different days. Sometimes they may say Ukraine or, other times, the former Soviet Union. Still, other times, they might say they were "Russian Jews living in Ukraine." But others who lived outside of Russia, in one of the other republics of the Soviet Union, have stronger feelings (sometimes nationalist ones) to not refer to themselves as "Russian" but rather Latvian, Georgian, Ukrainian, or whatever, and especially after the Soviet Union's collapse in 1991. For this reason and accuracy, in most places, I use "Soviet" and "ex-Soviet." And, of course, each of the contributors self-identifies in their essays.

The "nationality" issue is also particularly interesting with respect to Jewish immigrants, who constitute the vast majority of this book's contributors. In Soviet times, the fifth line of the Soviet passport read, "Nationality," and Jews were required to identify "Jew" *(evrei)* as their nationality, regardless of whether they lived in Russia, Ukraine, Georgia, or elsewhere. Jews were therefore not viewed as Russian, or Ukrainian, or Georgian as other residents of those republics were. Many Jews adopted this nomenclature of the Soviet authorities. It was common to say "Russian" to distinguish a non-Jewish Russian from a Jewish one (as in "Oh, he married a Russian," which meant he married an ethnic Russian, and not a Jew). For some, therefore, seeing the word "Russian" in the book title may feel alien as a descriptor of their identity, while others are comfortable with it. Ironically, many scholars have observed that the fifth line on the Soviet passport, which served as the basis for anti-Semitism in university admissions, job hiring, and many other areas of life, also served as a way to preserve Jewish identity among a people who had largely been forced by the authorities to forgo it. Unlike during czarist times, Jews in the Soviet Union did not live in ghettos or shtetls but were interspersed among their non-Jewish neighbors (albeit concentrated in big cities and certain central Asian republics). So a regime that tried to stamp out Judaism ended up literally stamping it in, at least enough to allow many Soviet Jews to rekindle that attenuated identity in America.

THE STORIES AND THE LESSONS

When I began this project, I thought I knew a lot about immigration and this cohort of immigrants in particular. After all, I grew up in a household with two parents who fit the bill and grandparents who regale us with story after story about the "old country." But like Socrates, I feel that I know less now than when I began, as I have discovered new dimensions of inquiry that I didn't even know existed. From a distance, it is easy to stereotype any group: Russian immigrants are all educated, or are engineers (or criminals), or live in Brighton Beach, or all like flashy clothes, and so on. But I discovered a world of diversity of experiences related to immigration, acculturation, and identity that I did not expect.

Some of the contributors view themselves as totally American, with nary a memory of the old country. Most of those who feel this way either came to America before age five or lived in a very assimilated community, or both. Others have feet firmly planted in both countries, with Russian music, literature, language, and food and drink (especially vodka!) a big part of their lives. And others are in between. Some married fellow immigrants, while others did not. Some decided to transmit their Russian immigrant culture to their children, while others chose not to. I interviewed one person whose family missed Russia so much that they went back to the U.S.S.R., although they did return to the U.S. soon after. Some felt the pressure to pursue careers in law, medicine or business, feeling the unspoken (and often spoken) expectation of their parents and grandparents. "We did it for you," the older generation seems to be saying, "so go get a good job." Others took up their passions and became artists, musicians, and writers. Some discovered their Judaism (one became "ba'al teshuva," which refers to someone moving from secular to religious observance). Others rejected the religion.

But I was also fascinated to see how many common themes emerged. I was impressed by the clarity of the contributors' memories of their prior life in the old country and the immigration journey itself.

This book is definitely about both departures and arrivals. Most of the contributors had a good sense of the reason why their parents decided to leave. Most cited anti-Semitism, and a few added the potential for better lives for the kids. Still, it was also clear that most parents sheltered their children from the harshness of Soviet life. The memories are a combination of direct recollection and what the contributors learned "around the dinner table." Curiously, and a bit surprising to me, almost no one cited ideological opposition to communism as the main reason for leaving. Saying goodbye, especially when close family was being left behind (often grandparents or aunts and uncles, but in one case, a 10-year-old contributor was saying goodbye to her mom and brother) was a painful experience for many. There was no return expected, so the goodbyes were viewed as being forever. Many remembered that their Soviet passports were cut to pieces at the border. A few remembered their teddy bears being decapitated as aggressive, or maybe just vindictive, customs officers searched for contraband.

For most, the ones who went to Vienna and then lived in Italy for three months while petitioning for refugee status, those few months are seared into their brains. They provide the "before" and "after" for their young lives, a line of demarcation between two fundamentally different existences. I should not have been surprised when these kids had such pivot points. For me, the difference between age seven and eight may be on a fuzzy continuum of stability. For them, it might be an interplanetary-like transformation. Many described their amazement at their first impression of the West. For many it was in Vienna, and often these stories revolved around food in grocery stores. Kids who had only known long lines and empty shelves were now staring at row after row of all manner of delicacies, with no one grabbing them. My eight-year-old father was amazed to see cellophane-wrapped bread in a Viennese supermarket. The whole idea that bread would need to be preserved and left on a shelf was alien to him. Another contributor was amazed to see chocolate rabbits on the shelves and sausages hanging from the ceiling.

Learning English, playing in the street, selling goods in the open-air market, visiting sights, and waiting for the U.S. Government to clear their refugee status were common experiences that most contributors had while living in Italy, although they all differed in significant details. Some of the contributors describe discovering their Judaism en route to America. My father had heard the word "Jewish" in Ukraine but did not know what it meant. But at a Passover Seder while in Italy, he was told the whole story, including that his family had conducted Passover Seders every year even when in the U.S.S.R. They waited to conduct Seders until he went to sleep out of fear that he might—as a young child—tell his friends and get the family in trouble. A number of contributors had their own version of a similar story.

The story of their arrival in America and how they and their parents adjusted had some common themes and vast differences. Those who ended up living in areas with a heavier concentration of Russian immigrants tended to grow up with more Russian friends and cultural interactions. Those who grew up in smaller towns or cities with a smaller Jewish population were required to assimilate more. My mother's parents, who lived in a town in New Jersey with few first-generation immigrants, learned English more quickly than my father's parents, who lived in Queens, New York, and were surrounded by Russian friends. Especially in those smaller communities, the role played by volunteer Jewish families, who were assigned to "adopt" the new arrivals and show them the ropes, was a heartwarming part of the story I read over and over. These volunteer families brought the new arrivals to the local synagogue, brought them home for dinner (including Shabbat and Thanksgiving), helped them navigate the medical and social service systems, and gave them bags full of hand-me-down clothing. My mother's family was assigned such a family (a mother-daughter duo) who helped them in innumerable ways, and they keep in touch to this day.

A related theme is the help that the immigrant families received in the early years from the organized Jewish community—HIAS, NYANA, Jewish Family and Children's Services, JCCs, Jewish federations, and local synagogues, among others—as well as from the government (welfare, housing assistance, language training, etc.). Many contributors willingly acknowledge it and are grateful for it. In most cases, this was temporary, often just a few months, and the parents took jobs (however low-paying) to be independent and start making their way in the world. When I founded a small charity, called Diaper Essentials for New Americans (www.DENA.charity), focused on donating diaper bags and essential baby supplies to immigrant mothers, it was a proud moment for me to partner with HIAS and repay, in a small way, the help HIAS gave my parents when they first arrived to America.

In this book, the question of assimilation is central. Many factors, including age, geography, and socioeconomic issues played into a family's ability to adjust to their new environment. Rarely did the parents adapt as well as the children did. Most of the parents took jobs far lower down the socioeconomic hierarchy than they had in the U.S.S.R. or that they were educated for. Former factory managers became taxi drivers. Former artists became store clerks. One contributor's father went from working on rocket engines to fixing car engines. They needed to make ends meet. This was part of the sacrifice that the parents willingly made for their children. But other parents made their way up the professional ladder and became computer programmers and business owners. Many of the contributors specifically note how happy their parents are to be in the U.S., even when they had to accept some measure of downward social, if not necessarily economic, mobility and forfeiture of professional status. Cultural capital is hard to replace for adult immigrants, and most parents, even when they succeeded financially, were never able to feel culturally full at home in America. A few contributors described how, as their parents have gotten older, they have reverted to watching TV or reading books and newspapers in Russian.

In most cases, the children had to make their way through the acculturation maze on their own. They learned English quickly (remarkably, almost everyone did so by watching TV, cartoons in particular). Many encountered bullying in school, including Cold War-era taunts. It was not uncommon to be called a "dirty Jew" or a "Russian commie." In a role reversal, they had to act as the parent figure to their parents and grandparents, often helping the older generation, who did not speak English as well as they did, to navigate through various forms and bureaucracies. But they largely did succeed, just as their parents had hoped. Most of the contributors went to college and pursued their career dreams. Scholars have identified different types of acculturation models, organized around how much of the old and new identity the person retains. All of the contributors in this book successfully adapted to the new country, but they vary in the extent to which they retained a Russian identity. And while there was a lot of parental pressure to succeed academically and professionally, there was not as much pressure to do things "the Russian way." In other words, having sacrificed to bring their kids to the new world, the parents seemed to be letting the kids adapt to it without too much pressure to cling to the old one. Even so, many of the contributors grew up surrounded by Russian customs and adopted many of them anyway, even without the parental pressure. This conclusion left me wondering whether other ethnic immigrant experiences—Mexican, Korean, Pakistani or Somali, for example—strike the same balance between new and old, or whether the Russian cohort is unusual in this regard.

ARE ALL HAPPY (IMMIGRANT) FAMILIES ALIKE?

Tolstoy famously wrote in his opening for *Anna Karenina* that all happy families are alike, while each unhappy family is unhappy in its own way. When I consider the cohort I studied through the stories in this book, I think a better way to put it is that all families are both happy and unhappy in their own way. The Russian immigration stories you are about to read are of challenge and triumph, of adversity and success. There is unhappiness here mixed in with joy. They share much in common, but they are all complex and unique. I did not want to reduce them to a statistical study. I wanted to show the contributors as human beings so that readers, especially those who may not have much contact with this cohort of immigrants (or immigrants more generally), can see up close how the hopes and dreams of newly arrived Americans take shape. If there is one thing that most of them have in common, it is gratitude to their parents and America for the life they have been able to have due to America opening its arms to them. They remember the exact arrival date—not as July 1978, but as July 12, 1978—and some celebrate it as a personal Independence Day. When I read what one contributor wrote in the pages ahead: "I swell with pride when I have the opportunity to tell my tale, and I wear my identity of being a Russian-speaking, Latvia-born, fiercely proud Jewish woman that loves America proudly and loudly," I am the one swelling with pride.

Too often, as we read the press, we view immigrants as a monolith. They are either all good or all bad, all saints or all criminals. Soviet immigrants are no exception. They have been typecast as educated, smart and successful, and also as money-hungry, rude, and dishonest. Unfortunately, once you add politics to an issue, all you have in the end is politics. If more Americans viewed immigrants as real people with the same fears and desires as all of us, that would humanize our approach to the topic. This book is the story of a people, but it is also about 20 specific people (and their families). If this book were about Dominican immigrants or Indian ones, I suspect that it would be at once recognizable and foreign to readers of this book. Some of the concerns in those other communities, such as poverty, discrimination, and acculturation, would surely be similar, but I suspect they would have their own tales of why they left their home countries, how they got here, and what pressures they faced in the tug-of-war between generations and between the respective pulls of the old country and the new one. In other words, I hope there is more room for books like this one.

Ariel Kirman
New York, 2021

ELINA MOYN

My Story and Evolution: Assimilation and Back

NOW

I think about who I am now, what I have, and where I came from. In some ways, it doesn't seem real. If my parents didn't dare to emigrate from Latvia, what life would I have? Would I be here, living in Denver, a vice president of global operations of a successful company by my early thirties? Probably not. Would I own my own home, drive a nice car? Travel the globe? Doubtful. Would I have every opportunity in the world to succeed? And most importantly, would it be possible for me to be an openly and fiercely proud Jewish woman? I know for a fact that those things would not be within my reach if I didn't live in the United States of America. The life I have is simply because my parents pursued and achieved the American dream.

The wave of nausea hit me hard. "Papa, I'm not feeling good." And then it happened. I threw up on the airplane, smack in the aisle just as we landed. Welcome to America. Nice first impression.

I was six years old and one month exactly. The date was July 17, 1992. My parents, brother, grandmother, and I emigrated from Riga, Latvia, which in 1992 was fresh out of the clutches of the former Soviet Union. The U.S. Embassy picked the destination for us—Denver, Colorado. We had no family there, knew no one. Looking at the map,

I was convinced that the mountains here were volcanic. It's funny the things you worry about as a kid. We are in the U.S. because we were granted the status of refugees. My parents were desperate to break away from the historically reliable and systemic degradation of Jews in the USSR.

Back in Latvia, we were sub-citizens. You were threatened, sometimes punished, and many times ridiculed just because you were a Jew. You were strongly advised to hide your Star of David necklace under your shirt. Perhaps better not to go to synagogue. Chances of getting into a top university with perfect grades? "Good luck with that, Jew. Stay in your lane." Our passport nationality didn't say "Latvian," even though that was our birthplace. The stamp was "Jewish." I was only six years old before our departure, so thankfully no one spit in my face for my identification. My brother was 12 and was often called derogatory names, so he was familiar with antisemitism by that young age. My parents had a lifetime of wildly unfair and inappropriate treatment, but I guess it was better than what their parents went through. Some of my family was murdered (possibly buried alive) in a mass grave. Still, others were burned alive in a Riga synagogue. It is nearly impossible to trace the tragic deaths of most of my family, some of whom were given up to the Nazis by their own Lithuanian neighbors. To her dying day, my grandmother clutched the black and white photo of the mass grave memorial where some of her family was thought to be executed. She would describe over and over again her escape from Riga via livestock train, and the Latvians shooting from the rooftops at the Jews running for their lives. She said correctly that the Jews were being hunted like animals. There are so many horror stories from the Second World War, not unique to my family. I guess we were lucky because some family survived. Far too many did not. My parents didn't want my brother and me to live in the volatile, dangerous, degradation-filled, short-on-food, wildly corrupt world they grew up in. The collapse of the Soviet Union meant that the option of escape could become a reality.

My parents started the application process in 1989. The crumbling of the USSR and impending independence of Latvia meant a liberalized emigration policy, and they jumped right on it. Of course, there was the fear of a rejected application and the occasional "You better keep quiet about this, or you're going to lose your job, or worse." Mom and dad sent our application to Washington D.C. About a year later, we were invited for an interview at the U.S. Embassy in Moscow.

I still remember taking the night train with my family, seeing Red Square for the only time. It was spectacular. I vaguely remember the interview, but know that the same evening, we had to return to the doors of the embassy and wait. My mother recalls hordes of folks on standby—the elderly, people in wheelchairs, everyone that was granted an interview. That night the embassy told us that our status or "stamp" would be "refugee." The following day we returned for full medical examinations, a required step for clearance. We then came back to Riga to anticipate some more. You had to wait for years (it was three for us) for the official decision letter to arrive. Mail was unreliable, usually controlled and sifted through by the authorities. The Soviet authorities clearly had concerns about defection. After all, you could give away some state secrets or something ridiculous like that. Everything was done hush-hush because there could be economic or physical retaliation. But then the yellow envelope came. We were granted official permission to immigrate to the U.S., the land of opportunity and freedom. My dad had to make a trip to Moscow again to pick up the official documents, some of which we weren't allowed to open until you reached the Customs and Border Patrol counter in the U.S. My grandmother wanted to mark this special occasion with a treat, so she took me to the local market where she spent an arm and a leg on two bananas—one for me and one for my brother. Can you imagine? Bananas were considered a wildly expensive delicacy. To this day, I cannot let a banana go to waste in remembrance.

I have to say, just writing this brings tears to my eyes. I owe my sheltered, peaceful, privileged life to my parents. They gave up everything and everyone they knew to give me and my brother the world. What a stark difference between their world and that of my ancestors. The United States of America, even with its imperfections, is leaps and bounds greater than anything we could have imagined. This is the greatest country in the world, and my God, I'm proud to be an American citizen. The day we officially became citizens, in 1999, many tears were shed. We guard our Certificates of Naturalization as if they were the holy grail. They are quite literally our stamps of freedom. I keep my certificate next to my renounced Soviet identification papers to remind myself about that "Jew" stamp and never take what I have here for granted.

Back to the memories of my journey. Our flight left from Riga, Latvia, and flew to Helsinki, Finland; New York City; and on to Denver, Colorado. We packed a couple of suitcases, each to hold us over for the coming summer months. The U.S.S.R. government allowed each refugee to bring two suitcases with them. The rest of our possessions were taped up and mailed to a relative in the U.S. or given away. (We never received those boxes, so my parents went to work in the Colorado winter in their thin jackets. My dad would bike in the Colorado blizzards wearing his summer raincoat. He didn't want to waste any money on bus fare. He would rather it go to food. I swear my parents are saints.) Our savings for the trip was a whopping $500 for the five of us. We didn't know where we were going to stay. The immigration process was arranged by HIAS, a Jewish nonprofit organization that provides humanitarian aid and assistance to refugees, so they guided the whole ordeal. It was a giant leap of faith, and I'm in awe of the calm my parents exuded during this adventure. At this point in my adult life, I can only imagine the internal turmoil and anxiety they must have felt. We missed our connection in NYC to Denver, so we had to stay a night in a very cockroachey motel near the airport. I shared the bed with my grandmother and brother, had pizza for dinner, and watched as my parents looked at each other nervously, anticipating what lay ahead. The next morning, we hopped on the airplane to Denver and were greeted by the most wonderful family upon our arrival. They were volunteers for Jewish Family Service in Colorado and took us under their wing. They invited us for dinners and holidays and helped take a bit of the shock and awe out of being fresh off the boat. They helped soften the blow, and their kindness is something we'll always cherish. Twenty-nine years later, we still have the poster they created for us to welcome us to this country.

There are many notable memories from the time of our arrival. My dad remembers his first time at the supermarket. It was the King Soopers in Denver on Colorado Boulevard, where the mustard stood out. The amount of condiment options at our disposal in this country is outrageous once you think about it. We came from a place where food shortage was the norm. It wasn't just food that was a problem.

You wanted access to something? A type of food, perhaps a medicine, a duvet, heck, even an incubator for a preemie, you had to know someone or pay someone. I was that preemie who needed an incubator, and only because my parents' friend worked for a company that made them was my life spared. Shelves were empty and lines were long. That's where we came from. The norm was to get things "under the table." So anything from bananas to clothing without patches was a luxurious treat. The initial shock in the U.S. came from the abundance of stuff. Until the pandemic of 2020 hit, the concept of shortages for food, toilet paper, etc., was unheard of here. My parents were eerily reminded of their daily Soviet life when we started to experience the panic buying in the U.S. and the wild lines in the stores. It didn't faze them because that's the world in which they grew up, but of course, it shocked me.

My first school experience in the U.S. was at Hillel Academy—a religious school closely situated to the apartments we first settled in. I cried every morning before school. I didn't understand English, I didn't understand Hebrew, I didn't understand the new culture, and I didn't understand why the Hebrew teacher was so mean. (He was so strict. How could I be expected to learn Hebrew when I didn't even know what he was instructing in English.) It was a bit traumatic, but I suspect that's a common shock for any immigrant kid. Kids adapt, learn quickly, and so I did.

Moyn family (l-r) Yakov, Elina, Sofia, and Sam on a day trip to Vail, Colorado, 1992

It was a tough adjustment in the early years. We all had to learn English from scratch. My brother took on the role of my caretaker while my parents worked ridiculous hours. My mom had 70-hour workweeks, and my dad worked 96. My university-educated, career-driven parents took any job opportunity they could. It didn't matter whether my mom was an engineer or my dad was a programmer in Latvia; they would take any job here. It was hard to find work. But if it fed the kids and kept the apartment warm, the job was worth it. My dad stocked shelves, worked as a janitor, even worked at a nursing home wiping folks' behinds. My mom worked what seemed like endless retail hours. Eventually, my mom found a stable job as a librarian with normal work hours. It was a blessing, as this library had a massive number of Russian patrons. There, a small Russian community thrived. Immigrant kids took dance classes, math, Russian language, etc. It was a nice bridge between my old identity and the new American one. My dad won a contracted gig as a computer programmer, proved himself shortly thereafter, and ended up as a loyal 22-year employee for the Colorado State Government. At his retirement, the flag that flew over our state capitol was gifted by the governor to my dad and is framed in my parents' office.

My parents never spent money frivolously. With their stable jobs, incredible work ethic (my parents worked like dogs), and determination, they were able to buy our first home a few years after the big move. They came here with nothing in their early 40s, worked insanely hard, put their kids through college in this great country, all in the blink of an eye. My brother, Sam, worked the entire time he was in school, helping our parents as well. He guided me with his work ethic and commitment and helped me with the assimilation speedbumps he experienced himself. He protected me and was my biggest advocate. I remember when he convinced my parents to let me study abroad. He desperately wanted to do it himself when he was younger, but financially, this was a wish that was simply impossible for my parents to grant. So, he fought for those opportunities for me. Sam is still someone I look up to. He works so damn hard, puts family above all else, and with that, I know his kids will grow up wanting for nothing. We are truly living the American dream. This is the land of opportunity. Seeing my parents

Sam and Elina in Denver, Colorado, 1992.

struggle and give up everything for their children's future motivated me to push myself to succeed. That has been, and still is, the shining beacon in my life. My trajectory is success. If not for myself, then for the sake of my parents' sacrifices. What they did for us will not be in vain.

There were some tough moments as a little immigrant kid. The last thing you want to do is stand out. Are you the weirdo that has herring for lunch or doesn't get back-to-school clothes? It was always awkward when a friend came over. I desperately wanted my mom to make meatloaf or order pizza. But instead, my friends would stare in horror at the fish on the table—head intact. Wildly delicious, but my friends were appalled, and I was embarrassed. My brother wanted to play football in high school. What could be more American? Since participating in football included a hefty fee (new shoes, uniforms, etc.), my parents couldn't grant him this wish. So he joined the water polo team. Those swim trunks were affordable in comparison. I was luckier than my brother. I was younger, so when I entered high school and was ready to fully assimilate, my parents had more time to build a financial cushion. I wanted to play lacrosse. Okay. Join the dance team? Done. They were very careful with expenses but understood the value of experiences, teamwork, socializing, and got behind those things. Back-to-school clothes shopping was still scoffed at. "Why do you need new shorts and shirts? You have plenty in the closet." It was an argument I couldn't win. They come from a world where clothing was not discarded or rotated out like it is here. You have a hole in the shirt? Patch it up, because in the USSR, there was no other way. It's something I still argue about with my folks to this day. They will have nice new clothes, many times it's something my brother and I gifted them, but my goodness, they will wear down what they have until it falls apart. Then they'll wear it some more. It's heartbreaking and yet understandable. It does make you think about how much we waste here as a culture in comparison.

There was always a blend in my family between the old and new. We love American holidays, especially Thanksgiving. We make the turkey, butcher the stuffing, and serve herring with potatoes and sour cream in conjunction. If you go to an American event, you dress one way, but you dress completely differently if it's a Russian event. Sprinkle in the granola during my years at the University of Colorado at Boulder, and there's your third look. I spoke Russian to my grandmothers and a mix of languages to my parents. The Russian background meant excelling at school. At one point, my extracurriculars were accelerated math classes. Only when I capped out at being enrolled in honors classes did I put my American hat back on and participate in sports, varsity pom poms, and earn as much money as possible at my first job as a pizza maker to buy those ridiculous Abercrombie & Fitch outfits. I wanted to fit in, be cool. I roll my eyes thinking about what I valued then, but I think we all gain perspective about what's really important with age. I simply didn't want to stand out. I didn't know many kids who had my type of background. When I first came to this country, I stood out, and I was adamant about fitting in and not standing out any longer.

Moyn family (l-r) Yakov, Sofia, Elina, and Sam on a road trip in the Rocky Mountains, Colorado, 1995.

My family was always my guiding light throughout all of this. Without a doubt, there is something traumatic about being plucked from what you know (language, culture, country) and being dropped into a wildly new place. My only stability was my family. And because of our shared trauma, we've stayed incredibly close, and we are each other's rocks. We've grown together through the journey of initial shock, assimilation, and pride for our roots.

Aside from identifying as an immigrant, I also identify strongly as a Jew. Growing up, I knew and respected my Judaism. My family history was painful, but we survived and were proud of it. My dad spent 13 years baking matzah in the basement of a synagogue in Riga. He worked evenings and Sundays to supplement the family income after his full-time job. My parents got married under a chuppah. My brother had a bris, and even though it was dangerous and not exactly legal to practice our religion this way, the tradition and culture is something that they would never shy away from. As I got older, I learned about the dangers of this, so I'm terribly proud of my parents for defying Soviet religious oppression at great risk. I grew up fiercely proud, knowing that my grandfather stood up to his antisemitic Red Army commander. The man called my grandfather a "zhid" (a derogatory term similar to "kike"), to which my grandfather retaliated by punching him in the face. Naturally, for that he was penalized and forced to serve on the front lines during the war with the rest of the "criminals." He survived WWII and came home with a medal. In the U.S., my family and I celebrated the Jewish holidays the way we knew, and under the guidance of the local Russian immigrant-filled Chabad Center. Back in the Mother Land, your Judaism was kept private and behind closed doors, so it was a big change to encounter a public display of holiday celebration here. The local Jewish community we encountered here was primarily through former immigrants, so it was an "in-between-worlds" experience. The holiday services were in Hebrew and Russian.

University was my first experience out of the nest. I loved the diversity and freedom of it all, but it was also a time when I started to seek depth and meaning to life. I encountered the most incredible young rabbi and rebbetzin with whom I've built a lifelong relationship. They let me ask questions about our religious teachings, dip my toe into the very base understanding of Judaism, and then the depths of it. It was there, in the Chabad at C.U., that I started to further build confidence not only in my Judaism, but in my past, in my roots, and my immigration story. I became student president of the University of Colorado Chabad and was proud to publicly and heavily engage in Judaism. The Jewish story is thousands of years old, encompasses unthinkable traumas, stories of survival, and triumphs. And with this, my mindset started to evolve. I was proud of what we went through, my weird name, that my parents have accents, that I was born somewhere so far away and unique, that I can eat pizza or fish head without batting an eye, that I speak multiple languages, and that the world as I see it (while nuanced) gives me the ability to connect and understand the traumas of others so much more. I furthered my education by studying abroad in Israel.

I remember being almost bewildered at how I felt there—so comfortable in my Jewish skin, safe, protected, and not being a minority for once. I continued to travel to Israel, many times donating my time and money. I spent two weeks there in early 2007 rebuilding and painting bomb shelters battered during the last conflict with Lebanon. It was a way for me to help my fellow Jews. At least they're not being persecuted out of their homes in Israel, but they were still being shot at. I continue my involvement back home in the U.S., supporting organizations that fight for the Jewish people.

As an adult, I couldn't be prouder of my family's story. From rags to riches. From oppression to freedom. All cliché sounding buzzwords, but their reality in my life is undeniable. I understood why I wanted to assimilate as a child. I learned, I grew, and now I want to share my story. I swell with pride when I have the opportunity to tell my tale, and I wear my identity of being a Russian-speaking, Latvian-born, fiercely proud Jewish woman that loves America proudly and loudly.

Elina Moyn, Denver, Colorado, 2020.

I owe everything that I have—my education, freedoms, luxuries—to my parents. The risk they took to leave the U.S.S.R. completely changed the trajectory of my life. We left with nothing but gained everything.

I put this blip in my life on paper to memorialize the struggle and to send much love to all the immigrants that took the biggest leap of faith possible and left all they knew for a better life. ■

Moyn family (l-r) Yakov, Sofia, Elina, and Sam at a simcha in Denver, Colorado, 2018.

IGOR FUKS

NOW

I am 40 years old and live in New York City. After moving to the United States almost 30 years ago, I have lived in the New York metro area full-time outside of a four-year hiatus in New Hampshire for college. I am happily married with a soon-to-be four-year-old daughter and an adorable English Springer Spaniel named Attila. After a brief run as a lawyer, I have worked as an investor for the past 13 years.

I was born in Moscow, the only child of Jewish parents. I spent most of my first 11 years there. My parents and I lived near the iconic TV tower in the Ostankino neighborhood. At the time, it was one of the tallest man-made structures in the world, or at least in Europe. It was easy to orient myself to where we were in our neighborhood by staring at it. Our tiny one-bedroom apartment was located in a "khrushchevka," blocks of cheaply built five-story apartment buildings erected around Moscow after WWII to house an expanding population. Five stories were the standard because that was as tall as one could build without needing elevators. I have never returned to Moscow, and when I tried to apply for a visa as an adult and a U.S. citizen to show the sights to my wife, I was denied entry. But thanks to the magic of Google Maps, I can find the little courtyard where I used to run around as a child. The stores and cars look different on street view. The apartment buildings look depressingly the same.

We were one of the more fortunate families because we had our own apartment that was not communal. Although the apartment was less than 600 square feet, we had our own bathroom and a separate entrance. We did have to share a phone line with another neighbor, so if you picked up and they were on the phone, you could listen to their conversations and vice versa. I was taught very, very early on to never go near the phone without an adult and certainly not say anything even remotely substantive on the phone. The working assumption was that between the neighbors, a bored operator at the phone station, and potentially the authorities, someone was always listening.

We lived near the VDNKh (the Soviet Union loved long and cryptic acronyms) park, where I remember playing a lot as a kid. It had a pond with ducks, bumper cars, and various street-fair-type food. It was a treat to go with my parents, run around, and get some ice cream. There was a movie theater nearby in the basement of the Cosmos Hotel, which had a very cool space statue that you could try to climb and slide around as a kid. I remember going there to see the first *Terminator* with my dad. In retrospect, I was way too young to see the movie. The future flash-forward scenes gave me nightmares, and I couldn't sleep and would bother my parents at night for a while. They probably regretted taking me, but it was something I still remember decades later.

Igor near the VdKH Pavilion, Moscow, late 1980s.

Elementary school was very strict in a lot of ways. We had mandatory uniforms and red scarves as "Pioneers." Like all children, I had a decal with Lenin's visage on it. There were a lot of rules, and although I don't remember corporal punishment, goofing off was not tolerated even for young kids. There was definitely an implicit threat that something bad

Igor and his cousin Marianna, Moscow late 1980s early 1990s. Marianna is wearing a highly coveted Minnie Mouse shirt, which was nearly impossible to get in the old U.S.S.R. She has since left the U.S.S.R./ Russia to live in Spain, Kosovo, and Uruguay.

would happen if you were not obedient. On the other hand, the Soviet Union was amazing at teaching math and science. I coasted on my elementary school basic math education for years and years after arriving in the U.S. Subjects like history were primarily communist propaganda. As a seven-year-old, I could probably give a half-hour discourse on the life and times of Vladimir Lenin and the great battles of WWII, and so could everyone else around me.

In the '80s, people didn't really get killed for political views in the Soviet Union anymore. At the same time, you could still get a jail term for possession of subversive literature or movies or speeches. The school system strongly encouraged reporting one's own parents to the authorities for unpatriotic content. Thankfully I was never dumb enough to do that. I did, however, buy into the propaganda enough to want to see Lenin's tomb. It was like my Disneyland at age seven. I asked my parents every week, and every week they demurred. They were far from true communism believers by any measure and were worried about me being brainwashed. I never got to see it and now kind of wish I had. But I understand why they never took me.

I remember when a Soviet military propaganda specialist came to speak to us. I think I was in the first or second grade. He was a colonel or something like that. The Soviet army was heroized and fetishized by the propaganda. Heroes of WWII, saviors of the free world, etc. So it was a big deal to have a cool adult with military medals in class. He proceeded to tell us that the United States would one day launch a nuclear attack and try to kill us all. It was inevitable. One of my classmates innocently asked him what we could do to survive, and his response was along the lines that nothing would help, and if we were in the hit zone, we would all melt from the heat and die. I remember being very shaken up. Half of the students were crying right in class. Looking back on it, there was a good chance he was probably drunk, but I had nuclear war nightmares for years after that.

(l-r) Igor's uncle, father, younger cousin, and Igor at a family gathering in Brooklyn, New York, in the early 1990s. The mishmash of early 1990s teen fashion is from a combination of highly discounted and donated items.

My grandparents on both sides were Jewish as far back as there were records. My father's family traced their roots to a village near Vitebsk (now in Belarus). Vitebsk is probably best known as the hometown of the Soviet-French painter Marc Chagall. Maybe it's the colors or family history, but I have had a huge interest in Chagall's work ever since I learned about him in my teen years. My dad's stepfather was a taxi driver in Moscow. Because taxi drivers sometimes handled foreign currency, he was pretty well off under the Soviet system. Proximity to foreigners and the ability to use hard currency in the black market were at a huge premium. My father was an electrical engineer running a team of other engineers and had eleven patents to his name. Yet, we were not as well off as an enterprising taxi driver willing to bend the rules of the system because cash (specifically foreign cash) could make black market goods appear.

My mother's side of the family hails from a *shtetl* called Shargorod in Ukraine on its southern border close to Moldova. Shargorod claims one of the oldest synagogues in Europe. During the Soviet times, the synagogue was turned into a juice bottling plant and then basically left to rot. Even though I spent a lot of time in the town, I don't remember seeing the temple. These days there are organized trips by Israeli and American Jewish groups to see the area. My maternal grandparents lived in a garden apartment in town where there was a little main street. They kept chickens in a little coop. Although the town had been almost completely Jewish pre-World War II, the demographics had changed dramatically by the time I was born. Jews were a very small minority, and most moved out to the bigger cities.

I remember Ukraine very fondly. I used to spend the summers there to get out of Moscow. It was an overnight train ride from Moscow to Zhmerinka, Ukraine, and then a multi-hour car ride on a dusty unpaved road. When the train stopped in Kiev, especially at night, the city looked stunning from the window of the sleeper car. Sadly, I have not actually seen any of it otherwise. There were not many free travel opportunities in the old country since the regime greatly limited internal travel. Unless one had a relative to stay with, getting a "putevka" (i.e. travel ticket, completely foreign concept to Americans) was like winning a lottery prize.

I was very close with my maternal grandparents. My grandmother was home caring for my great-grandmother, who was well into her 80s at the time and lived into her mid-90s. My grandfather worked at the meat processing plant. Despite being 100 percent Jewish on both sides of his family going back as far as anyone kept records, he worked with—and ate—a lot of pork. Except for my great-grandmother, who was born under the czars in 1902 (we think), no one in my immediate or extended family kept kosher. My grandfather rode around on a black motorcycle with a sidecar. As a young boy, I thought it was the coolest thing ever. I can't even imagine the hardships my grandparents and my great-grandmother endured in their youth. They lived through almost four years of Nazi and allied occupation as young Jews during the Holocaust. My paternal great-grandfather died in the war, and my grandmother was one of five siblings of a household where the oldest male was her teenage brother. My daughter's first name is an homage to my grandfather to honor his memory and maintain some cultural tradition even though I don't practice religious Judaism.

I was almost 11 years old when I immigrated to the United States. My parents had wanted to leave when I was born but did not want to leave extended family behind. A few of my mom's cousins left in the '80s via Austria and Italy and ultimately settled in northern New Jersey. Then more extended family left for Israel. I was vaguely aware I had relatives abroad because high-value goods (VCRs, Sony televisions, boomboxes) would arrive at our Moscow apartment. Then the activity picked up, and I was informed we were moving to Israel. I had a workbook to learn Hebrew. I think it had a lion on it. The letters were confusing, and I was not making great progress. I did not know much about Israel other

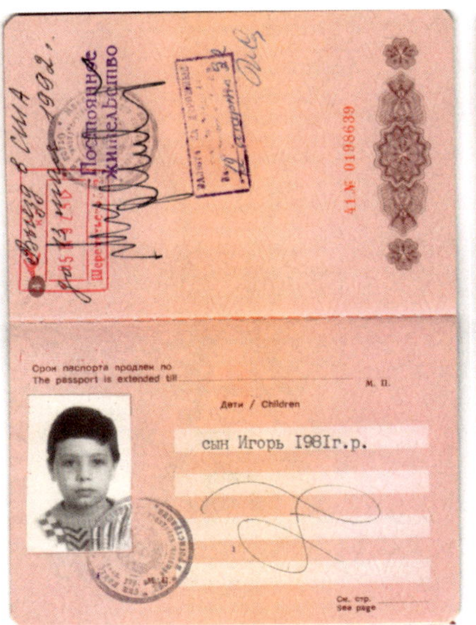

Igor and his mother Faina, Soviet passport photos.

than it was hot and I had family there. Then, one day I got even more exciting news: We were moving to New Jersey instead!

We were able to pivot from Israel to the U.S. by the grace of the Lautenberg Bill. Frank Lautenberg, a long-time senator from New Jersey, sponsored and pushed through legislation that added to the refugee quota for Soviet Jews. Thanks to him, I became a refugee of a failed state, and we got legal permission to enter the U.S. as permanent residents.

Until I touched down in JFK in April 1992, I had only seen America in the movies. I imagined the entire country would look like Hollywood—sun, palm trees, and ten-lane highways. My only other direct experience with American culture was fast food. Baskin Robbins, Pizza Hut, and McDonald's all opened in Moscow in the late '80s. The Moscow McDonald's was, at the time, the biggest in the world. It was a huge deal to go. I begged and begged my parents until they finally took me. We stood in a line that snaked multiple times around the building for many hours in blizzard conditions. By the time we got inside, I was quite sick. I don't even remember eating anything, and I broke out in a fever when I got home. Then we had to call a doctor. Probably the best thing I can say about the Soviet Union was that the doctors made house calls. If you had a medical issue, someone would actually show up. They were probably going to demand a bribe, but at least you didn't have to go anywhere. I eventually made it back to McDonald's, and it blew my mind. There was not a lot of processed food, so everything tasted different and amazing, and there were toys! Pizza Hut was a nice sit-down restaurant with a wine list and waiters. It was a big deal to go, but I was more of a burger guy.

My parents and I left Moscow on April 5, 1992. I had never been on a plane before, and I didn't know what to expect. I sat in the middle seat of a Delta (always had a sweet spot for them after that trip) flight from Sheremetyevo Airport to JFK. It was a very long flight, and I threw up the entire flight and felt half-dead by the time we landed. My mom's cousins and some family friends picked us up. We went to stay with family in Bogota, New Jersey, and soon after that got an apartment in neighboring Ridgefield Park.

The first hours and days in my new country are printed in my memory. As soon as we got off the plane, I couldn't believe the cars. In the Soviet Union, a foreign car, no matter how old and beaten up, was a status symbol equivalent to a Ferrari. Someone had a '70s Ford Granada in Ukraine, and he drove it with the swagger of James Bond. To have a car at all was a big deal. My immediate family certainly never came close to being car owners. So when my mom's cousin pulled up in a blue 1984 Buick Century with automatic windows, I naturally assumed my relatives were all very, very rich. One of my other relatives had a 1986 Mitsubishi Galant with a console that looked like an F-16 fighter. There were more buttons with lights than I had seen in my life. It was like being in a spaceship.

The supermarket also completely blew my mind. I remember stepping into the Grand Union in Bogota, New Jersey, and I thought I had passed the gates of heaven. There was beautiful-looking produce out in the open. There was ice cream and candy, all brightly labeled and attractively placed. There didn't seem to be a need to go to the back to ask your uncle's friend's cousin for the "good" food and barter for alcohol or who knows what else. We never were hungry or anything of the like in the Soviet Union, but meeting every basic need, including getting food, required a lot of effort. You couldn't just waltz into a store and hand over rubles to get whatever you wanted. You needed to know someone, have some illegally gotten dollars lying around, or you had to make do with the least common denominator of what was left around for the general population on the shelves. Walking into a bright, attractive space designed to get you to buy things that were more than the money you had was a completely foreign concept. Capitalism at work!

School in the United States was a colossal challenge initially. I was placed in the middle of the fifth grade in Grant Elementary in Ridgefield Park. I could not speak nor read a word of English. I was only vaguely familiar with the letters of the alphabet. I struggled to understand what was happening, and my English as a Second Language class proved to be a disaster. My mom complained to the school to get me out of it because I appeared to be learning more Spanish than English.

Given the town's diverse immigrant population, I soon found a group of friends from Egypt, Cuba, Pakistan, and Jamaica. Collectively, we resembled an oddball United Nations. My best friend was a fellow Russian speaker who had a few years in the country on me and could help me translate the basics. The Ridgefield Park school system at the time did not particularly police physical violence or bullying, and my new friends and I encountered a lot of aggression. At the same time, I recall those days very fondly because I was able to navigate a strange new country and make connections despite speaking almost no English whatsoever. I do remember sitting and struggling with the basic non-math homework for hours and hours to the point of tears because reading and writing were just so, so hard.

With the help of looking at comic books and watching cartoons, I was able to pick up enough language to meet the absolute minimums to start sixth grade, albeit with a horrible Russian accent. One of my less kind U.S.-born classmates would make fun of me and loudly repeat my biggest accent misfires. I had a hard time with the word "book" and would often confuse "v" and "w." He was also much bigger than me, and sometimes that would result in violent outbursts my way. Almost 30 years later, the cruelty of it all still stings. I certainly hope his children, if he has any, never experience anything of the sort.

In 2012, I threw myself a party to celebrate 20 years in the U.S. I invited a few of those Ridgefield Park friends whom I had not seen in many years. We had a few drinks at the Russian Vodka Room and reminisced about "those days" and how much collective bullying and nonsense we endured. At the same time, we were happy to have been foreign misfits who had each other. We were all struggling with the language, national identity, and some real poverty issues, but we held it together. I think about my friends from those days fondly.

At home we were quite poor but happy. My parents managed to somehow transfer our Moscow property, with keys exchanged there and a little bit of cash delivered in Brooklyn, but that was the extent of our assets. My parents spoke even less English than I did and were both doing menial manual labor. My mother, who had been a teacher in Moscow, cleaned houses for cash. My dad, who had a master's degree in engineering, was doing electrical work on new home construction. He then got a job doing keyboard repair in Secaucus, New Jersey, and he hated it. In the early 1990s, computers were expensive, so paying someone to fiddle with computer parts still made sense. He worked very, very hard to get his technical English up and running. On weekends he would go to the library at Fairleigh Dickinson University to keep up with his professional journals. I would go with him and run around the library and read old books of political cartoons that often made no sense to me, but I did enjoy the pictures. My dad worked harder and with more focus on the job of finding a job than I had ever seen anyone before or since. Simply put, there was no safety net for us and nowhere to go if my parents failed to get us financially situated. I had a very healthy fear that we would somehow run out of money. My parents, however, kept at it, and within two years of our arrival in the U.S., my dad managed to get a job that used his skills as an electrical engineer. As an aside, he has worked his way up within the same professional place now for more than 27 years. It was an amazing feat, and he still works weekends and still has that same drive that he had in the '90s.

Once we had some level of lower-middle-class income, it felt like we had won the lottery. We drove around in a 1981 Chrysler New Yorker Fifth Avenue Edition, purchased for $2,500 with an odometer that only went to five digits and I am pretty sure was at 150,000 and not 50,000 miles as the seller had claimed. The car did about eight miles a gallon (premium gas only!) but was so luxurious inside that I felt like the child of an ambassador. One day the fancy, aged Chrysler just died in the middle of the street, and my dad and I had to push it into a parking spot while my mom steered.

Around this time, we also decided to move. My parents went to the library and found the list of the best public schools in New Jersey. We visited a few towns and settled on Millburn. We found a garden apartment in a complex, the U.S. equivalent of where my grandparents lived in Ukraine. No chickens here, though. Instead, it was across the street from the highly-rated high school. My parents and I jammed into a very small one-bedroom unit. My parents were kind enough to give me the bedroom, where I slept on a futon, while they slept on a pull-out couch that doubled as the centerpiece of our living room.

My parents did an amazing job helping shape me into a functional teenager, especially considering the limited resources they had at hand. They invested so much time and whatever money we had into making sure I could go to school, had everything I needed and did not feel disadvantaged among my peers. They also demanded I get a job when I was in high school. At first, I hated the idea since most of my friends in our relatively affluent suburb did not work and, in fact, went to cool-sounding camps and on foreign trips during the summer. My first job was as a cashier in CVS, and it was horrific. I had a turquoise vest and got yelled at a lot by the customers who would get mad that their soda was supposed to be $0.99 per the circular but was $1.99 at checkout. As if it was my fault the system was set up to lure people in for cheap sundries and then hope they didn't notice when the pricing was off. I lasted maybe six weeks of complete misery and quit when I found a gig much more my speed working at a book shop. Encore Books was a struggling local chain getting its lunch eaten by Barnes & Noble and was in Chapter 11 restructuring, soon about to go completely belly up by the time I was leaving for college. Compared to slinging band-aids and condoms at CVS, selling books was heaven. I read a ton when it was slow in the store and learned how to gift wrap with the best of them. Sometimes my friends would come by and hang out and get books for themselves or as gifts. I still have not read a Harry Potter book, but I did sell a lot of them during the waning days of the 1990s.

In Millburn, I had a very overt outsider status. Foreign name, funny last name, still a heavy accent—I was very, very busy fighting. I lived very much on the "wrong side" of the tracks since the school district was divided between luxurious Short Hills and the relatively more hardscrabble Millburn. At the same time, I was able to connect with some incredibly friendly and kind boys and girls, who remain some of my closest friends in the world to this day. The best man at my wedding (and vice versa) is someone I met sitting at the end of the bench on the freshman soccer team. I am very fortunate to have found kids who befriended me, who were willing to look past my very tight clothing budget, lack of ski trips, and inability to hang out at my house because there was simply no room.

As I was making my way through high school, my mom dedicated a lot of time to make sure I maximized my educational potential. She read books and college rankings and understood the opaque college admissions process in a truly stunning way, given how foreign these things must have been to her. She was incredibly nurturing and supportive, but at the same time, I knew nothing less than full excellence would suffice. Failure was simply not an option. Between my mom pushing the right buttons and me lucking out with the right friend cohort and an absolutely amazing guidance counselor, I evolved from an off-the-plane immigrant with no English to a viable college applicant in under seven years. I found out that Dartmouth College accepted me for admission when I was having lunch in the back of the failing bookstore where I worked part-time. I was eating a turkey sandwich when the backroom burst open, and my parents ran in. My dad picked me up and was completely incoherent in his jubilation. It took me a few minutes to figure out what was going on. My parents had opened the big envelope (college decisions were still sent via snail mail in those days) and were ecstatic that I would have a great school choice. Since need-based financial aid was a lot tighter in those days, it meant years more of financial pain and sacrifice for them and years of nine percent interest rate student loans for me. My parents running into the bookstore to tell me about my college admissions was and remains one of the happiest moments of my life.

I have a complicated relationship with my Jewish identity. In the old country, being Jewish was akin to a nationality or something one was born into and passed on to one's children. My passport said "Jew" under the line for ethnicity. We were, however, forbidden from practicing Judaism and persecuted under the Soviet atheist totalitarian state. Even after moving to the United States and being free to participate in the Jewish religion, my parents did not opt in. Perhaps the U.S.S.R. beat it out of us. But they—and I—never connected with the ritual of organized religious worship of Judaism (or anything else). Nevertheless, I am 100 percent Jewish on both sides of my family and identify culturally as Jewish.

Even though I have never been back to my birthplace, I never forget where I came from. At the same time, I love my adopted country and appreciate being a naturalized United States citizen very deeply and intensely. The opportunities this nation has presented and the freedom it has given me to grow have been beyond my wildest childhood dreams since I learned I would be moving here permanently. Most of all, however, I am beyond grateful to my parents for taking a giant leap into the unknown. They were both settled into a comfortable middle-class professional life in Moscow. They had friends and careers, and economic opportunities were available to them as the U.S.S.R. was collapsing. With all of that, they chose to pick up whatever they could and move us halfway across the world to somewhere they did not speak the language, would not have the same resources, and sacrifice everything material they had worked for. They took a huge leap into the unknown to start over so their only child could have a chance at a better life. I am forever grateful for them for both doing that and the example they set for me once we were here. They both had the work ethic, perseverance, and mental toughness beyond anything I could capture on the page. To me, their journey of sacrifice, labor, and building a better life out of next to nothing in the face of hardship is the embodiment of the American dream.

LINA TETELBAUM

An American Tale, Lina Goes West

NOW

Lina Tetelbaum, 36, is a corporate partner at the law firm Wachtell, Lipton, Rosen & Katz. She lives in New York City with her wonderful husband, Matt, and toddler, Alex, and only a few blocks away from her parents, Anna and Yakov.

I remember once being asked to move office floors in my corporate law firm, from the sanctity and comfort of floor 25, where I had my "work-husband" nearby and had a very practiced path to the bathroom, to the unknown wilderness of floor 27. Let's disregard the fact that I would be moving into a virtually identical office, with all the identical amenities, in a change that would only marginally disrupt any patterns or connections in my life. I was devastated. I did not like change. I called my mother up to complain, citing the many ways I would be inconvenienced—nay, tormented—by this upheaval, this uprooting. My mother replied, "Well, change is hard. But change can also be good. Like that time I brought you to America."

Of course, any feelings of self-pity quickly dissipated. If the biggest challenge of my life was having to climb a few more flights of stairs, things were going well. This stark contrast between the comforts of my life compared to what my mother and father knew back in the Soviet

Union resurfaced many times and in many ways over the course of my life. At unexpected times. One night, I was reading the last few pages of the Harry Potter series, which I had voraciously devoured and stood on lines to buy. Can you imagine an American willingly standing on a line at midnight for something as unessential as a Harry Potter novel (and not even to use for toilet paper!)? When I got to the (spoiler alert) sad few pages about the passing of a major character, I wept like I hadn't wept in years. I wept like my puppy had just died. My father, seeing this, started laughing, which at first, I found rather insensitive. I demanded to know why he found my pain so funny. He explained, "Well, my grandfather cried about Hitler, and my father cried about Stalin. My daughter is crying about Harry Potter." Touché, Dad. Touché.

But let's start at the beginning. I was born Elina Tetelbaum on August 7, 1985, in Moscow, U.S.S.R. My parents thought about naming me Luba after my mom's mother who passed away before I was born, but they settled on Lina. I had no middle name because as Soviets, we used the patronymic Yakovlevna (daughter of Yakov). As an aside, this at some point led to much kerfuffle when my first social security card in the United States had me identified as Elina Jakouvlevna Tetelbaum, with initials E.J.T., an unrecognizable person to me, but who nevertheless had to go on until I could become a citizen and change my name back to the middle name-less identity I was actually born with. Jakouvlevna haunts me to this day, and I do wonder what social security agent thought it should start with a J.

Lina and Anna with Yakov's parents (Ilya and Pera) in their Moscow apartment.

Back to the beginning. We had a comfortable life compared to many Soviet citizens. We lived in a well-located apartment near Gorky Street ("The 5th Avenue of Moscow!" my mom still proudly declares). My father, Yakov, earned a PhD in electrical engineering and had a good job as a researcher in the oil and gas industry. His father, Ilya, was a prominent computer science professor at a well-regarded Moscow university. He and my father co-authored a book together that had more numbers than letters, and both are equally incomprehensible to me today.

Lina's paternal grandfather - Wikipedia entry.

My parents really thought I was something from a very young age. As my mother said in her speech at my wedding: "Every parent thinks their child is a genius. But in my case, it was the truth!" She was convinced that I could go to a place like "Garvard" (in Russian, your Hs are pronounced like Gs, like Gamburger). And looking back, it's hard to say she was crazy since, well, that is ultimately where I went for college. She could not accept that

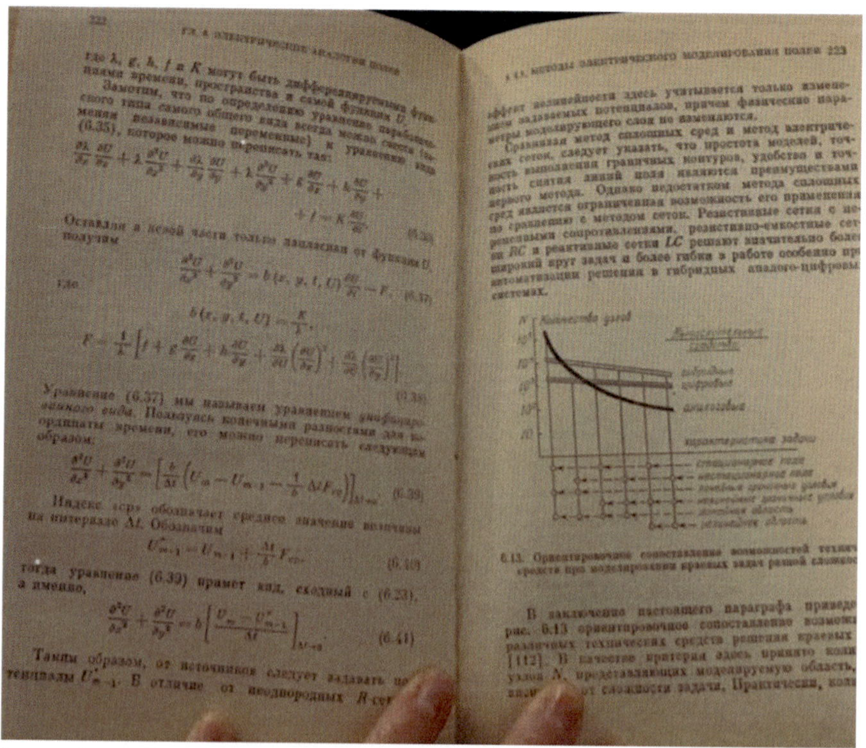

Excerpts from a book co-authored by Lina's father and grandfather.

someone with my perceived talents would be so limited in the U.S.S.R. on account of us being Jewish. The best schools and many professions were all but closed to Jews. Even my birth certificate listed my family's nationality not as "Soviet," but rather "Jewish."

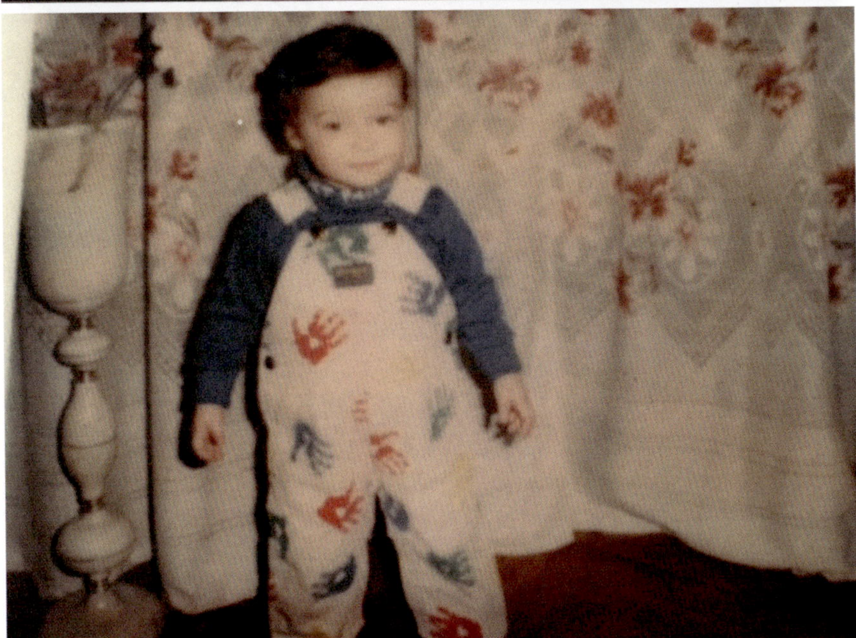

Soviet baby photos and wardrobe.

The decision about whether to try and leave Moscow for the United States was not an easy one for my parents, but ultimately, their belief that my life could be so much more outside of the U.S.S.R. tipped the scales in favor of leaving. My grandfather was ill, and for a host of other reasons, my father had to stay behind in the Soviet Union. So on September 17, 1991, I immigrated to New York City at the age of six with only my mom.

Lina and Anna, shortly before leaving the Soviet Union for the United States.

My mom surely had many things on her mind: "How will I learn the language? Where will we live? What will I do for work?"

I had only one thing on my mind, and I asked it on the plane heading to the United States. "Mommachka, are there bananas in America?" I had tasted a piece of a banana that my mother brought back from a trip she took to the U.S. in the 80s. I was hooked. I was a banana fiend. I needed bananas even though often we could not afford them.

This need was so deeply ingrained that 12 years later, when given the opportunity for a senior yearbook quote where I could memorialize absolutely anything about myself, I had only one thing to say: "May you forever afford bananas." What else was there to say? There was no bigger blessing I could wish upon my fellow classmates.

Those first few years in America were very tough on my mom, but she did the best she could to shield me from the stresses she must have been feeling. Our first stop was (the obligatory pilgrimage to) Brighton Beach. After that, a basement apartment in Flushing, Queens. Finally, we moved into a one-bedroom in Forest Hills, Queens, the place of my childhood. I made the living room my own and slept on the couch until I went to college. It's not something people can tell about me readily, that the first time I had my own bed was freshman year of college and my own room senior year of college. But it's a fact that I cherish because it has kept me from taking for granted the many beds and many rooms I have today.

Lina's Stuyvesant High School yearbook picture and quote.

No matter how much my mother protected and shielded me, I knew the stakes were very high for us. As a child, I kept a detailed diary filled with passages documenting even the smallest of expenses and the anxiety I felt about how that might impose on my mother. One day while walking to school, I fell flat on my face and had to be rushed to the emergency room. My diary entry for that date spoke of nothing other than my concern about how my mother would pay for the cab she had to take to the hospital. Of course, my mother always found a way, and countless people exhibited enormous generosity in big and small ways in those early days. It's these kinds of entries that

Entry from Lina's childhood diary.

remind me just how fearful I was that every good thing in my life could be undone.

Today was one of the most important days of my life. We applied for our Green card and went to an interview. I found out so many thing[s] on why we left Russia. It was because we were Jewish. I honestly think the judge denied our proposal (since we didn't do that well being interviewed) which means we'd have to go to court & if worst comes to worst be SENT BACK TO RUSSIA!!! My life here has been so great and I pray to God that the judge granted our approval. If ever I think not having enough cool clothes is a prob[lem], I'll think back to today, when there's a chance I won't have any clothes in Russia. After this my Mom and I had dinner ... and went to the [Synagogue] to pray since it was a Jewish holiday ... It was a good day, but it'd be even better if our Green card is granted. –Lina

But no matter how difficult my situation was, I always knew how much worse it could have been had we stayed.

Notwithstanding my preoccupation with cool clothing (which doesn't take Freud to tell me was at the root of a lot of my childhood insecurity), even at a young age, I knew that I had nothing to complain about. I knew that I had the opportunity of a lifetime, and it was up to me not to let my parents' sacrifices be for nothing.

It was a long road to citizenship. There were also moments so absurd they would be hilarious if the stakes were not existential for me. For example, I recall during one immigration proceeding being forced to use a Russian-English translator in immigration court, even though at that point my mother was a Russian-English translator herself for family court a few doors over from the immigrant court, and I had received a 1600 SAT score and could barely put together a Russian sentence.

One time I made a grave mistake. I was being interviewed by a judge asking the usual litany of questions they ask prospective citizens. Was I, and did I plan to become a prostitute? A war criminal? A Nazi? The usual. I did well. I knew I was not any of those things, nor was I planning to become them. But then he caught me. He asked me whether I was a member of any groups? Well, as a high school student, I certainly participated in many extracurricular groups. Was that what he had in mind? I didn't want to lie to the judge. "Yes, Judge, I am an active member of the Model United Nations." You could see my mother wanting to kill me from across the room.

"What is this, Model United Nations," asked the judge, with suspicion in his voice. Oh no. Was I to tell him that I simulated being other countries like China, Iran, Israel with other high school students where we professed loyalty to foreign powers as part of simulated conferences? Nothing could have sounded more sinister at the time. I don't know how I made it through that interrogation without getting my whole family deported.

Then came the day when I was finally eligible to take the citizenship exam. I had to study the answers to 100 questions, although only six or so would be asked to me on the actual exam. The trouble was, by then, I was a 3L at Yale Law School. So while the prompt, for example, could be "What is the rule of law?" the answer to which is recommended to be, "Nobody is above the law. Everyone must follow the law." You try asking a Yale law student what they think the rule of law means? Or what rights are protected by the First Amendment? I had to train myself to say only the recommended answers and not a word more. I had to train myself to forget Constitutional Law 101.

Lina accepting #1 citizen trophy at her citizenship party.

But I had done it. I had passed. So came the happiest day of my life, November 4, 2009. (I suppose my wedding day and birth of my son have come to rival it!) I got sworn in as an American citizen in the Brooklyn Federal Court Building at 225 Cadman Plaza. The magistrate Judge Drew Carter swore me in. He was a former colleague of mine at the Federal Defenders of the Eastern District of New York who had just been promoted. That moment felt truly full circle, being sworn in by someone I could work alongside.

My two favorite professors in law school, Professors Amy Chua and Jed Rubenfeld, threw me a citizenship party for the ages, replete with "communism vs. capitalism" jello shots, as well as a red, white, and blue cake (which actually was green, white, and blue because the baker was color blind). My friend Kendall, who shared an office with me during our summer at Wachtell, Lipton, Rosen & Katz, sent me the best present a newly minted citizen could dream of: a bouquet of banana-shaped cookies. I finally had paved the way to unlimited bananas. Years later, my mother would say in her wedding speech, "And now I have to beg her to eat bananas."

Yakov, Lina, and Anna at their citizenship party in New Haven, Connecticut.

I got married in the Finger Lakes of New York State to the love of my life, Matthew Charles Anderson (Hebrew name: Mordechai Yitzach Anderson), father of my son, Alexander Isaac Anderson (Hebrew name: Eliyahu Isaac Anderson). I think about all that had to happen to bring Matt and me together, from such different corners of the universe, and create this amazing boy: 3/8 Russian, 1/8 Georgian, 1/8 English, 1/8 Italian, 1/8 Swedish, 1/8 Irish, 100 percent Jewish. My mother and I both gave birth to our firstborns at the age of 34. I marvel at this given how different her first 34 years of life were compared to mine, and yet, how we both found our way to motherhood at virtually the same moment in life. The closer I come to the age she was when she boarded a plane from the Soviet Union to New York City, at 41, with me, her six-year-old daughter, in tow, leaving behind her friends, family, and husband, the harder it becomes to fathom how big of a sacrifice it really was. There is no single decision that has shaped the course of my life more, and nothing in this world I am more grateful for.

When my husband converted to Judaism a few years ago, he decided to write his final paper about my journey to the United States. He titled it, "An American Tale, Lina Goes West: My (New) Soviet Jewish Family's Journey to the United States." He wrote:

As Lina and her parents spoke to me about their experience and the resolve they exhibited in the face of persecution, I began to consider formally converting so that we could create a Jewish household together (something that they were denied the ability to do in the Soviet Union). Given the principle of matrilineal descent, our children would be considered Jews by most religious authorities regardless of what I decided to do. But that did not feel like enough to me. To create a truly Jewish household, I thought I should intensely study the religion and convert. My heart was already there, but I believed it was a very important signal to our future children to have their father stand before his family and friends and declare himself a Jew. That is the type of family Lina, Anna, Yakov, and I hope to create. It may seem a bit odd to some that a Presbyterian from Upstate New York and a little girl from Moscow found love and hope to build a Jewish household together. But, then again, that's America and its promise.

The last few years brought me a number of blessings in quick succession. I got married in May 2018, made partner at my law firm in November 2018, got pregnant in March 2019, and gave birth to Alex in November 2019. Each one of those moments could fill its own chapter. But one of the sweetest, proudest moments came in August 2019, when after over a quarter century living in that one-bedroom apartment in Queens, Matt and I purchased an apartment in Lincoln Square, a center of all culture, for my parents to retire and grow old in. We moved them in right before

Lina, Matt, and Alex in their New York apartment.

Alex was born and, incidentally, right before the 2020 COVID-19 pandemic. My parents went from Muscovites to Manhattanites. I went from a little banana-loving Soviet immigrant to a lawyer, a wife, a mother. An American. ■

ALEX ROSIN

NOW

I am a 50-year-old short, stocky white male. In 1997, I met my wife in South Korea as she was planning to leave for Switzerland to study. Fortunately, I was able to convince her that the United States had just as much potential, and we now have two daughters, one aged eight and another fourteen. We currently live in Bethesda, Maryland, where I work as a medical director for an insurance company and practice emergency medicine locally.

I was born on November 18, 1970, in Gomel, Belarus. Memories are often contextual, and much of the detail is probably reproduced by our brain simply filling in detail via association and context. I do remember several vivid moments that are on the spectrum, from horrific to nostalgic. There was a play date with several friends, in which we all claimed to be some important member of the politburo. I confidently claimed the position of defense minister, to be quickly reminded with a definitive matter-of-fact comment from my friend that "kikes" cannot hold such positions. I don't remember being upset or even fighting this, but it clearly stuck in my mind because I remember this caustic event approximately 42 years later.

Not all my memories are on that side of this spectrum. There is also the crisp white snow on a bright mid-winter day when we would take out our rugs and dust them by flipping them over and over. There were neighborhood hockey games in which I played goalie, full of energy, yelling. I spent my summers at our family "dacha," a Russian version of a summer home in the countryside, where I would spend all summer with immediate family and relatives and still have vivid images of swimming and playing in the lake with my cousin Gena. My parents would take us into the woods to collect mushrooms. I had no idea which were edible or poisonous, but this was apparently a learned skill for my parents. In our garden, we grew cucumbers, radishes, potatoes, and scallions. We used these ingredients in our daily meals, and one of my favorite dishes was *zharenaya kartoshka*, a combination of sautéed onions, mushrooms, and potatoes. I was taught that Belarus was known for its potatoes, like Ukraine was known for its bread.

September 18, 1972, Gomel, Belarus.

My family was probably considered middle class. My father was a foreman at a construction company, and my mother was a school teacher. My grandfather drove a truck, delivering mostly construction supplies. In those days, this was apparently a lucrative position that allowed him to participate in the pseudo underground free market, since they did not have Home Depot there.

VIENNA AND ITALY

In August 1979, there was excitement in our household, as everyone passed around a thick letter with a foreign address and large colorful stamps that would allow our family—my parents, sister, and maternal grandparents—to emigrate to Israel, something that my parents had planned for over one year. Around the same time, my father received another letter, this one from the Red Army, which was looking for a few good men in Afghanistan. During his pre-deployment medical

September 18, 1972, Gomel, Belarus.

clearance, he developed severe leg pain and was told he would still need to serve unless he opted for a vein stripping surgery in the affected leg. After general anesthesia and one unattractive scar, we began our journey by train to Moscow. There, the adults were strip-searched for state assets and our documents reviewed. The next destination was Poland. There my memory is of rushing with suitcases bigger than me to board yet another train, shoving these massive suitcases with everything we owned through the windows and doors, rushing to not miss the departure. This time we were headed to Vienna. To my parents and grandparents, this boarding process must have been incredibly stressful. For me, it brought back memories of excitement. My sister was only two and probably did not remember much. Vienna was like another world. The buildings were beautiful, European, and it appeared as someone turned the dimmer up one notch. It seemed brighter than the homeland that we left behind. We spent approximately two weeks there, mostly selling the black caviar that we brought with us, to have money for the rest of our journey ahead.

We arrived in Italy, our final transitional destination. There we went through customs and immigration and were brought to a suburb in Rome, where we planned to make a temporary home while we waited for our asylum application to the United States to be processed. We spent the first few weeks in the markets and streets, among other immigrants and gypsies, emptying those large overstuffed suitcases, selling matryoshka dolls and other Russian souvenirs we had brought with us. These seemed popular with the locals and tourists. We either had good fortune, or my parents were skilled because we quickly sold everything we had brought with us. This luck would run a short course, though. My father had a man purse, an item which my maternal grandfather loved to criticize. For whatever reason, he did not like my father, something I still don't understand, and had warned him against placing the family documents and our money in it. While my father was walking on a busy street, a moped zoomed by and took everything of value our family had at the time, including our travel documents and money. I can't imagine how my parents must have felt, losing everything they owned, particularly the opportunity for a better future for their children. Fortunately for them, and ultimately me, the immigration authorities had a copy of our travel documents. The ability to survive in Rome for potentially another several months proved a little bit more challenging, but again luck played a major role. It turned out that my parents had childhood friends from Gomel, who were ... well, it's still not clear to me what they were doing in Italy. To this day, I still suspect they were part of the Russian mob. These friends helped my family with a place to live and the food we found on our dinner table each night.

FIRST DAYS IN AMERICA

We finally received the long-awaited notice from America. We were accepted and would be traveling to Miami Beach, Florida. I have two memories of those first days that are still vivid and palatable in my mind. The first was the movie *Godzilla* playing in the hotel lobby, where we would spend our first few days. It was memorable for me because the movie would flip from this huge animal destroying things to toothpaste commercials and back and forth periodically. We did not have commercials in Belarus, so this seemed somewhat schizophrenic to me and something that I still laugh about now. The other memory was from a fruit market across the street from our hotel. I can still see and smell those beautiful, exotic bright yellow bananas. To this day, when I peel a banana, the sweet fragrant aroma cascades memories from October 1979.

Our first week in America was spent bouncing between several hotels, with my family (including grandparents) essentially living in a single studio apartment. Once we found permanent housing, my grandparents settled in a one-bedroom apartment above the fruit market and my parents in a two-bedroom corner apartment on the other side of Miami Beach, where I would spend the next several years of my life. These first days were not easy for any of us, and we each faced different challenges. We did have meaningful and significant support from the local Jewish community and welfare programs, like food stamps and health care.

My parents' days were long and exhausting. My mother would clean apartments for the local Jewish families that were part of the network that helped us settle and would often take me with her. There was no place for me to go or anyone to watch over me, so she knew I would be safe with her, and I could help her with vacuuming. This was the job, the chore that I remember. In the evening, she would attend classes to learn English and later to obtain a certification as a medical assistant. My father would work all day remodeling apartments and then as a cook at a deli, most days coming home after midnight, bringing home cuts of bread and smoked salmon that the restaurant did not want. He would repeat this routine six days a week. There was not much time for sleep or any time for socializing. Occasionally he would take me with him to side jobs, where I would act as his surgical assistant, having the screwdriver or Allen wrench ready at just the right time. I would also clean things up, and for this, the customers often gave me a dollar or two, which he matched. On his one day off per week, he would take me to the recycling facility, where I would drop off plastic bottles I had collected during the week to collect the deposits. My maternal grandmother would match the money I earned each month and took me to the bank to open my first bank account. In those days, the banks would offer gifts like alarm clocks with a new account and, more importantly, interest rates on certificates of deposit were 15 to 18 percent. My grandmother, like my mother, cleaned apartments and my grandfather drove a bus for the Jewish Federation during the week and a taxi on weekends. They would save every penny and send a portion to their other daughter, who was still in Belarus. Both my sister and I spent a lot of time with our grandparents while our parents worked. Unlike my parents, my grandparents continued to prepare and eat foods from their past. I can still taste the freshly made gefilte fish she made from carp and the fish head soup my grandfather would make. My sister was only two when we came to America, and as a result, her early memories of those first days are probably less vivid than mine. However, what's interesting is that she has maintained more of a connection to our Russian past than I have. She and her family were stationed in Ukraine, where her husband of Russian and Ukrainian descent was the U.S. Assistant Air Attaché at the U.S. Embassy. They have three beautiful children with Russian names, and they celebrate the Russian Orthodox Christmas and Hanukkah. She is fluent in Russian and still enjoys some dishes like selyodka, borscht, and shashlik.

SCHOOL/JUDAISM

I was enrolled in the local Leroy D. Feinberg elementary school, where the new Russian immigrants were grouped and placed in ESL classes. This is where I met one of my closest friends, German Lebedin, with whom I still have a very close, family-like relation today. There was a sense of community among the Russian kids, and learning English came easily to most. As children, we could assimilate quickly and easily, absorbing the new language and culture without much effort. Miami Beach in those days was very different than it is now. The art deco vibe and preservation of the old architecture started prior to our arrival but did not get into full swing until years later. At the same time, in 1980, the Mariel boatlift added approximately 125,000 new immigrants from Cuba. There was some strain between the two groups, and I remember several rumbles. As a result of this tension and encouragement from the Jewish community, I was enrolled in a yeshiva. I felt accepted and special there and was absorbed by the sense of community, all of us belonging to the same tribe. But beyond the surface, I was a world apart from the rest of the students there, both socioeconomically and in our connection to Judaism.

While we were Jewish and proud of this heritage, only my grandparents celebrated the holidays and followed any Jewish tradition. For my parents, the practice of Judaism was not part of their everyday life. Soon after arriving in the United States, both my father and I were circumcised. I was nine, but my dad was 32! We never spoke about it, but I think he was grateful for being able to leave the U.S.S.R., and this was his sincere way of having a closer connection to the people and heritage that allowed him to bring his family closer to a better future.

It was not until I visited Israel as a third-year medical student on a military psychiatry rotation that I truly understood both my own and my parents' connection to our heritage. We were all proud Zionists, who did not practice Judaism, and Israel seemed full of people like that. In the yeshiva, I stuck out like a sore thumb. I wanted to desperately belong and did my best to study Hebrew and the Talmud, but I think even at that age, the other kids could not get beyond the reality that I was different. I wore t-shirts with the name Eric on the back that were donated to us by wealthier families. When confronted by other kids about whether my name was Alex or Eric, I had to hastily claim that Eric was my middle name. Incidents like this highlighted the socioeconomic difference that was impossible to ignore. It was challenging to practice and incorporate my new yeshiva knowledge at home, where my parents ate pork and looked in dismay when I would reprimand them for turning on the light on Sabbath. But, interestingly, I have only happy memories of my yeshiva days. Playing dreidel, rhythmically singing the beautiful prayers, and being able to read Hebrew.

My moment of fame came with a competition to bring the most food item labels with the kosher symbol. Since my family ate non-kosher foods as well, I was at a distinct disadvantage. To my surprise, on the final day of this contest, a man named Sal showed up at my house with his wife with several boxes of labels, ultimately helping me win and claim the prize. I felt special that day, an outsider who prevailed and was admired by every other kid in my class. Sal was a generous man who had two sons, was very kind to me, and acted like a pseudo godfather to me. He bought me a suit, new shoes, and shirt and had funded my bar mitzvah. A picture of me dancing in my new suit with a rabbi still hangs at my mother's house in Miami Beach.

After one year at the yeshiva, my parents used the expiration on my free tuition and our move to North Miami Beach as reasons to enroll me in Greynolds Park Elementary. It was there that I met my other best friend, another Russian immigrant, Alex Khutorsky, with whom I have also maintained a very close relationship to this day. At this point in our transition to life in America, things were progressing very nicely. I spoke fluently in English and adjusted culturally, making non-immigrant friends and eating burgers with fries. My parents bought their first house and took us on our first vacation to Orlando Disneyworld. We drove there in our bright yellow Datsun and stayed in a Motel 8. We were moving up in the world. The highlights for me were the bumper cars, which I rode incessantly, probably driving my parents and sister crazy, and the train ride with the song "It's a Small World" that still plays in my head to this day.

We settled in North Miami Beach comfortably, moving forward in every way. My parents, at that point, had more stable, well-paying jobs, and my sister and I worked hard in school. I attended North Miami Beach High School, a local high school where I was a proud member of the math club. While I never won any of the competitions, I genuinely loved math and had a great time traveling to the competitions and being with other kids who shared my passion. I took a number of advanced placement classes and was able to skip almost one year when I transitioned to the University of Florida in 1988.

In 1991, I had decided to apply to medical school, and my father suggested that I look at the military. His rationale was twofold—affordable education and an opportunity to give back to a country that gave so much to us, a country we now called home without any reservations or regrets. Our new motherland. I took his advice and joined the military. I went to a local army recruiting office and inquired about options for attending medical. They informed me that there were two options: apply for the Health Professions Scholarship Program with one of the military branches, or apply to Uniformed Services University of the Health Sciences. I did the latter and was accepted to join the army class of 1996. The school's main mission was to prepare medical officers for the three military branches and the public health service. My father passed away from Lou Gehrig's disease five years ago, but while he was alive, he carried my business card, laminated, proud of my service to this country, both while I was stationed in South Korea and then during one of my longest deployments to Iraq.

FINAL REFLECTION

Without a doubt, our history shapes who we are at present and who we will become in the future. I am certainly no exception. My initial years in Belarus, followed by the early days in Florida, clearly molded my personality and guided me on the path I have taken over the last 40 years. I am grateful to my parents and grandparents for having had the courage and strength to uproot from everything familiar to them—language, food, family, work, and daily life. To move across the globe with two small children, not truly knowing what was waiting for them. Not knowing the language or having the funds to be able to afford to make mistakes. But what they did have was an unparalleled desire to provide a better future for their children and themselves, armed only with education, good health, and remarkable work ethic.

Through seeing their struggle as a child, I learned to work hard and be grateful for the opportunity to work hard, be frugal, look for and engage opportunity, and not be overwhelmed by adversity. It was from the Jewish community and the people in America that the idea of being kind and helpful to your fellow man, which our parents taught us well, was reinforced. As a result, in every challenge or stressful situation I have found myself in, I have tried to bring to the surface the lessons that my family and early life in America had taught me.

While I now think of myself as American and legally I am, the voice inside my head still speaks both Russian and English. My favorite foods are still red caviar on blini and *zharenaya kartoshka*. I have never been back to Gomel but have thought about visiting one day, simply to see where I was born and lived the first few years of my life. I have tried, although without much persistence, to teach my kids Russian and have gotten the expected result. Neither one of my daughters has a huge interest in Russia and finds stories of my childhood depressing, by their standard. To this, my advice to them and all the children of immigrants is to tap into the heroic experience of their families and use their determination and strengths in their daily challenges. ■

KARINA KLEVER

NOW

I finally reached the fifth decade. I've been so proud and honored to have been the primary breadwinner for my family my whole adult life. My son is now 25 and has a debt-free bachelor's degree. My dad made me promise to take care of his wife of 44 years, and his artwork, right before he passed. I've done this by being financially independent (I'm happily divorced and get no financial support from anyone). After working in corporate America for many decades in executive-level positions, I now own my own company. I gleefully live in Thousand Oaks, California. However, I travel all over the U.S. in my van-sized RV to visit my clients.

Q: HOW OLD WERE YOU WHEN YOU CAME TO THE UNITED STATES?

I was nine when we left Russia in 1979, but because we went to Vienna first, I was 10 when we arrived in the U.S. in 1981.

Q: WHERE DID YOU LIVE WHEN YOU WERE IN RUSSIA?

St. Petersburg, which was then known as Leningrad. My dad was an artist. We had a government-assigned apartment, and we also had a government-assigned art studio. The artist's studio was downtown, which was where some of the difficulty came in. Since the government was providing housing, they called the shots on what they wanted to be painted. But my dad was an abstract artist, so he didn't do too well staying in the lines, so he painted what he wanted to paint, which was often in opposition to what was allowed. That's where a lot of his difficulty started, and we got kicked out of Russia. He never stole or raped or hurt or robbed, or did anything bad. All he ever did was paint art and was in constant trouble because of it. He tried hiding his capabilities by hiding art behind makeshift walls. I slept in drawers when I was five and six years old and hid him, as well as his paintings, from the KGB before we left.

Q: AS A YOUNG KID, HOW MUCH DID YOU KNOW ABOUT WHAT YOUR DAD WAS DOING? DID YOU KNOW THAT THE GOVERNMENT DIDN'T LIKE IT?

I knew my dad painted. Before we had currency as we know it in the world, there was a barter system, and my dad would sell paintings for chicken and cans of peas and things that were at a deficit over there. I distinctly remember that a bunch of people would come to our house all the time, and they'd always be bringing stuff—food, clothes, you name it. And we lived really well. I mean, we always had the basics like food and clothes. I didn't have a lot of toys, but it didn't seem to matter because I was always busy with the importance of what my dad was doing. I learned how to use a paintbrush before I learned how to use a pencil.

I'm also an artist, but I never gave myself the luxury to paint because I had a family to help sustain. I made a choice to get a job in computers and pay the bills so that everybody else could be creative, including my dad and brother and my son. That was my role in this world, and I'm blessed to have had the opportunities here in the U.S. But over there, I knew that my dad was an artist because I painted with him, and I knew that that was a rarity, and I knew his talent was extraordinarily special.

Q: HOW MUCH PRESSURE DID THE GOVERNMENT PUT ON YOUR FAMILY TO LEAVE? WAS IT A DECISION, OR DID THEY FORCE YOUR HAND?

It wasn't at all a decision. It was, "You're going to get jailed forever in Siberia, or you leave." By the middle and late 1970s, art had a sort of following—not what we know today as social media, but more of a fan base of people who appreciated and enjoyed artwork. I was aware of the following in Moscow and St. Petersburg, but there were probably other cities as well. When it got out that the artists were blacklisted because they couldn't conform to what the government wanted them to paint, there was an uproar. This fan base uproar was really the only reason we were given the opportunity to leave. If the artists didn't have a fan base, we might not have been that lucky to have been given that option. There were other artists out of the artist group to which my dad belonged, who were also offered the opportunity to leave, and everyone took it from what I know.

The artists who were given this opportunity were participants in exhibits across the cities. My dad had participated in an exhibit informally called "the bulldozer exhibit." The artists were told they could freely put up easels in the park during the summer. Then the government arrived with bulldozers and demolished everything, killed two people in the process, and destroyed tons of artwork. The government started putting the artists in jail. My dad was shaved, starved, jailed, and tortured. All because he painted.

Q: WHAT WAS THE NEXT STEP FROM THERE? HOW DID YOU GET TICKETS? DID YOU HIDE THE ARTWORK IN YOUR FRIENDS' HOUSES?

The government bought us tickets, and we quickly liquidated the studios and hid artwork. We had rolled up canvases all over St. Petersburg, many places in Moscow, and also Ukraine. This was before Ukraine was a separate country.

A few of the artists in this group intentionally burned their studios down. Their logic was—if I have to leave to save my life, I'm not going to let anybody else enjoy my artwork or use my paints, easels, or canvases. And so they basically set the entire studio on fire. But we scattered my dad's collection in different places.

We hid some artwork in the apartment of one of my dad's friends, where we rolled up a few canvases, and we put them up in this little narrow spot in the attic in the kitchen. The KGB came to her house and interrogated and pressured her. She got so upset that she died from the pressure right in front of her son. The son later called us to say that the paintings were secure, but his mom was dead.

Q: TELL ME ABOUT YOUR LIVING SITUATION IN THE U.S. I UNDERSTAND YOU MOVED AROUND TO DIFFERENT CITIES. WHERE DID YOUR FAMILY LIVE AND FOR HOW LONG?

When we arrived in the U.S., we lived in New York. From there, it was a bit of a blur. We lived in Upstate New York, Vermont, and Los Angeles. We'd gone back to Vienna a few times and lived in Paris. After arriving in Los Angeles in 1987, my parents never left. I continued to move around until I permanently returned to Los Angeles in 1998.

I believe much of our moving around was my parents finding a place where they felt they belonged—a sense of community and trustworthy friends. We tried to connect with people everywhere we went. In the end, we all realized that home is where the heart is.

Q: DID LIFE IN AMERICA LIVE UP TO WHAT YOU THOUGHT IT WOULD BE? OR WAS IT TOTALLY DIFFERENT?

I didn't know what it would be like, so I didn't really have any preconceived notions. I was excited that my dad was not getting chased down anymore. So for me, that was the excitement. I didn't care where I went, as long as I didn't have to keep hiding my dad from the KGB.

On the flip side, the perpetual moving wasn't very stable. I didn't make any long-term friends and never really knew where we would live next. The silver lining to this is that I became a minimalist, am resilient, and can make friends with pretty much anyone and not judge them.

The life-long difficulty for me has been picking and choosing influences from two very different societies. I'm lucky that I get to select the best of either world, depending on the situation. Sometimes, the American in me makes decisions, and other times, the Russian in me makes decisions. It's taken me decades to select what part of which culture works for me. The journey to get to this point was sometimes tough.

Q: WHAT WAS SCHOOL LIKE FOR YOU IN AMERICA? WAS IT DIFFICULT TO FIT IN SINCE YOU WERE MOVING AROUND SO MUCH?

School was really, really tough. English was hard because, by that point, I was already fluent in German from Vienna and Russian, of course. Russian and German both have genders. English has no genders, and it also has letters that make no sense to me. In English, there's an S and a K, and then there's also a C that makes both sounds. The second hardest thing was the vanity, the materialism, the keeping up with the Joneses. I also was conscious of being too tall. I'm six feet tall, so I was always taller than everybody else. Plus, my parents were so socially inept, so they couldn't give me any coping mechanisms because they came from a place that had a completely different culture, in which none of these things prevalent in the U.S. apply. Sometimes it was hard to make friends.

We also had anti-Soviet animated videos we would watch in school. I remember one, which showed a kid diving under his desk. And then you see a huge rocket coming in and blowing up right at the top of the table where this little kid is hiding, and everything around is just blackened. The problem is the people who threw the bomb in the video were Russians. So every single time they played this stupid video, I was pummeled at the playground. There were groups of 12, maybe 15 kids, just beating up on me, pulling out my hair because I was the bad guy. We just sat in class where the whole class was told that I was the bad guy because I must have a bomb somewhere in my armpit or something. Because the bomb is the thing that's going to kill everybody, and the bomb comes from the Russians, and I'm the only Russian in their lives. So, of course, their fear and anger and anxiety and all of these horrible things got taken out on me because of this association.

I remember they would all tell me that their parents said that Russians were bad as well. The Russians are the bad guys in this society across the board, and this is culturally reinforced. By default, I was instantly the bad guy and would often hide my identity since the Russians have been hated since the Cold War. When you look at mainstream movies, radio shows, or even cartoons, the bad guy has a Russian accent. I had to learn to surround myself with people who didn't have these preconceived opinions and would see me beyond being just a Russian.

Q: MY PARENTS TOLD ME STORIES LIKE THAT. DID YOU EVER BEFRIEND ANY OTHER RUSSIAN-BORN STUDENTS?

It was hard because we kept moving around. At church, I was friends with the priest's daughter, who was from Brazil but spoke Russian, and another girl from Bulgaria. They called us the Three Musketeers. My safe zone as a youth was more church than school because school was brutal since no one would be friends with me either due to my lack of English, or being tall, or being Russian.

Q: HOW DID YOU MAKE ENDS MEET?

I started working when I was 14. For my dad, this idea of having to pay rent every month was kind of weird because he came from a place that gave him a place to live. So when we moved into the apartment in Brooklyn, there was a grocery store called Speedway Met on Ocean Avenue. And the day I turned 14, I went to work there. I also worked at the library. So I was contributing to the family and helping with rent. I was horrified by the prospect of being homeless. This set the stage for the rest of my life. I have been the primary breadwinner for my family my entire life and never relied on anyone to support me.

Q: HOW DID YOUR PARENTS ADJUST WORKWISE? WAS YOUR MOM WORKING?

I think our number one charter was to make Papa successful. I don't think he knew how to do anything other than paint. It just wasn't in his blood to have any business sense. When we first got here, he got a job at a shoe store in Glendale, and it took about six weeks for the owner to realize that his financial books weren't matching the inventory. It turned out that every time Papa would come to open up the store in the morning, he would see homeless people lying there at the door, and he would give a bunch of homeless people shoes. So that was the only job my dad ever had in America, which meant that Mom and I needed to work. My mom had jobs at Woolworth, a retail discount store that you may be too young to remember. She and I had a few different jobs, and somehow, we managed to survive.

When we got back to the U.S. in 1987, she and I both went to computer school, and once both of us graduated, she got a job, and she's been in that career until recently. And that's how my IT (information technology) career started. I became a computer programmer in April 1989. So it took a while for my mom to figure out that she needed a skill set here in the U.S., and up until then, it was pretty tight. We were pretty broke because my dad's artwork did not always sell, and he never mastered English. He came here in his 40s. In Russian, he could speak with the most beautiful poetry. He was a master of the Russian language. But he could never master his English.

Q: YOU RETURNED TO THE U.S.S.R. IN 1986. THAT'S VERY UNUSUAL FOR IMMIGRANTS.

Yeah. This is where the story connects to 1986, when I was 16, so jumping ahead a little. A few different things happened that were a catalyst. When we left the U.S.S.R. in 1979, the offer from the government was—we will spare your life, but you won't ever come back here. We bounced around, trying to find a sense of home. For my parents, who were in their 30s and 40s at this point, that was tough since they had already established a strong life pattern and culture and habits and a sense of familiarity in Russia. There was good and bad where they came from, just like anywhere, so that wasn't the point. It was just what they were familiar with. Imagine picking up in your 30s and trying to make the rest of your life in Japan or somewhere like that.

Several years after we arrived in the U.S., in 1982, we learned that my mother's mother got sick with cancer. And my mom, who left her mother's home in Ukraine at age 16 and had a lot of guilt, kept trying to go back to Russia, which is why we kept going to Vienna, to get closer to the border. We also kept going back to New York because the consulate was there. And my mom kept trying to see her dying mom and promised to do so before the end of 1982. My mom never made it to see her mom, who died 10 minutes after the new year arrived in 1983.

My dad had an easier time selling artwork in Europe than in America, but we were unable to live there full-time. The only people interested in buying his artwork here in the U.S. were unusual in that they appreciated abstract or politically charged art. Overall, this is a fractional minority because most people gravitate toward well-defined art.

Q: WAS IT EASY TO RETURN?

My parents started petitioning to go back in 1982 when my mom's mom was dying. My parents were trying to get a visa to see my grandma before she died, but it wasn't permitted since we had relinquished our Soviet citizenship when we left in 1979. Between 1982 and 1986, we lived in Vienna and Paris and spent lots of time in New York and Washington D.C. Our angst to return was steadily growing. We really wanted to get back and kept going to cities where we could petition to go back since there were embassies or consulates there.

Finally, in 1986, the Soviet government gave us paperwork, but they gave us a very small window to use it. They said that if we wanted to go back, we had pretty much a week to get there by the end of the year. So there we were on December 28, 1986. We flew out of New York's JFK Airport, with lots of press in attendance who covered the group of Soviet immigrants who had decided to return to the U.S.S.R.

Our intent in going back was to try to reestablish our lives. At that point, I had a baby brother, and I was 16. Although we lived in America, I never had a sense of belonging or friendship or longevity or security or community because we moved around so much. I was always living out of my suitcase. So I was hoping to find "home" over there.

Q: SO YOU WERE IN THE U.S.S.R., AND WHAT WAS YOUR DAD DOING? WAS HE CREATING NEW ART OR SMUGGLING IN HIS OLD HIDDEN ART?

When we went back to Russia in 1986, we contacted everyone we knew and started gathering all of our artwork at the house of one of my dad's students in St. Petersburg. We brought canvases and rolled up artwork on trains from Ukraine and Moscow, all back into her apartment, middle-of-the-night stuff.

We were also visiting a lot of other people. My dad used to be married before, so I have sisters and cousins that I keep in touch with. Plus, it was nice to see Mom's family as well. I have a very large extended family overseas.

We made it a mission to get the artwork out of Russia. This involved trucks and barters and stamps and all kinds of sneaky stuff to get the artwork in Paris. We had to make quite a few trips. It was winter and cold, and it took months. Many packages were put on a plane and arrived in Los Angeles.

Q: BUT YOU WENT BACK TO THE U.S. IN 1987? WHY?

Yes. Why did we leave Russia? We left because they gave us an ultimatum. The Soviets said, "If you decide to stay here now because your family is here, your friends are here, then you have to give up your U.S. citizenship." And we had gotten our U.S. citizenship in 1982. So that wasn't going to happen. In the end, it looked like America was more home than Russia.

Q: HAD THE U.S.S.R. CHANGED BY THE TIME YOU CAME BACK IN 1986?

Things changed dramatically. I'm going to get a little political here, which I rarely do by design. Several generations of Soviet people who had lived in a place where their basic needs were taken care of were being asked to navigate a new world and fend for themselves in many ways when the Iron Curtain came down. Up to that point, unfortunately, generations had instilled an attitude of "I don't have to work too hard because it's going to be okay because I'm going to get stuff for free," which resulted in a broad mental state of entitlement.

When we returned, we caught the country in a different game. The majority was sure that someone from somewhere would magically take care of them, and they didn't really have to do anything. They thought that everything necessary for life would just "poof" arrive. The other, significantly smaller, group of people wanted to create their own future and be their individual selves, and now they were allowed to do so. These two opposing demeanors caused rifts in the general populace in many ways.

In 1986, Gorbachev met with other world leaders and declared that he would be bringing down the Iron Curtain. He stated his support for artwork, culture, religion, all things that were previously repressed. Just like artwork was outlawed, so was all religion. Lenin put his mugshot where all the icons used to be in churches. People who had walked around cities with boarded-up churches and synagogues, all of a sudden, were able to see synagogues and churches in their city for the first time in their life. It was really raw.

Against that new backdrop, as we were catching up with family and friends and taking care of the artwork, we were told that we had to surrender our U.S. citizenship. With that ultimatum, we decided to go back to Los Angeles instead.

Q: SO ONLY AFTER YOU ARRIVED, THEY TOLD YOU THAT YOU NEEDED TO GIVE UP YOUR U.S. CITIZENSHIP IN ORDER TO STAY. DID YOU HAVE TO TALK IT OVER FOR A WHILE, OR WAS IT AN IMMEDIATE DECISION THAT YOU WANTED TO LEAVE?

It was immediate. It was like, "How much longer can we stay before we have to give this up?" We decided to maximize the time that we would be in Russia because we had friends and family there. Still, we knew we were going back to the U.S. instantly because the country (U.S.S.R.) was in a state of total disarray, and it was no longer the right place to be. For the many difficulties we had in America, it was all of a sudden more home than Russia.

Q: YOU WERE ALMOST 17 AND BACK IN THE UNITED STATES. WAS THERE ANY CHANGE IN THE UNITED STATES WHEN YOU CAME BACK? OR WAS IT MORE YOUR PERCEPTION OF IT THAT HAD CHANGED?

Nothing in the U.S. had changed, but our perceptions changed.

Before, we had a "grass is greener" concept at play due to familiarity, and now that was shattered.

Q: DID YOU LAND IN LOS ANGELES WHEN YOU CAME BACK? WHAT GRADE DID YOU START AT?

We landed in Los Angeles, which is where the artwork went. I had a year and a half of high school left according to my age. We showed up at the local high school and showed them my transcripts from Vienna and Russia. I was studying Latin and higher math and science than in the U.S. Still, they basically refused to acknowledge my overseas credits and told me that I would be graduating high school when I was 22, though they were only "accountable" for me until I was 18 (this was accompanied by some shoulder shrugs). I offered to take the hardest test they could find to let me test out of the class/subject, but they refused and sent me to a special school, which taught the toughest crowds—kids dealing with drug problems, pregnancy, illiteracy, and so on. I took a bus at 6:30 every morning.

The school was a mess. It had metal detectors, but the thing I most remember is how dirty and smelly it was. The instruction was just a bunch of reading, followed by test taking. It was a half-day at that school, and then I took a bus back to the regular high school where I had electives and extracurriculars. I painted and did makeup for the drama class and sewed costumes.

I was assigned a book at the morning school, which represented one subject in regular class. I would take the quizzes and tests at the appropriate page breaks, passing one subject every two or so weeks. This subject would take one whole academic school year. I was fired up because when I calculated it, I would finish all the necessary credits in time with my peers. There was a catch. I guess it was pretty unusual for people to get through one subject every two weeks, so the principal who would write me the little pieces of paper that signified the completion of a subject called me to her office. When I got there, it was clear she was angry. She said that nobody passed these classes in two weeks. But I was determined to get it done because the high school had told me that when I hit 18, I would no longer be their responsibility, that I could get a GED. But I wanted a regular high school diploma. The principal suspected me of cheating and, at one point, assigned chaperones to watch over me, even as I went to the bathroom. But I ended up finishing two years' worth of academic curriculum in that half a year.

I continued with my drama and all of that stuff and graduated half a year early. Everybody my age graduated in June, but I graduated in February. I was also going to computer programming school at this time. It made for a long day. I'd be at the bus stop by six in the morning. I'd be downtown until noon. I'd be in school until three. I'd walk and get my baby brother from elementary school. I would feed him, walk to the city bus stop, go to computer programming school, come home, do homework for school and computer programming school, and repeat. I graduated from the computer programming school in April, and this company called Litton in Woodland Hills came in and asked to see the students with the 10 highest test scores. That's how I got hired, but I worked the graveyard shift. I was a computer operator for two and a half years after that.

Q: WHY DID YOU CHOOSE TO GO INTO COMPUTER PROGRAMMING AS OPPOSED TO A DIFFERENT PROFESSION?

I read an article about careers for the next 20 years. I remember one line in the article that said that computing was a man's profession because women were less than four percent of the computer workforce. And as soon as I read that, I knew that's the career I wanted to go into because it was hard for me to work with many women, mostly because I didn't care about fashion as much as they did and didn't have a goal of being a dependent when I grew up and be supported by someone. I wanted to be independent more than I wanted my belt to match my shoes to match my purse. In Russia, everyone had a higher education. There was no concept that a woman would go to college to find a husband. There was no "Mrs." degree.

Knowing full well that I wasn't interested in being saved by the prince depicted in many movies, I wanted a career that would help sustain my family, challenge me, and allow my growth. I didn't want a handout, and I didn't want to be homeless. I did want my own profession, and I wanted to be financially independent, and the thought of working with men was fantastic. All of these things contributed to my decision to move into the computing profession. But it was that one article that helped me decide on IT as my life-long career. I've worked with mostly men now for over 30 years and have to admit I have really enjoyed it. Yes, there are some mean outliers out there, but for the most part, it's been wonderful. There are more women in this profession these days, and I'm rooting for more women to join the field! The wonderful women in my profession are great multi-taskers, problem solvers, and creative solutionists who bring so many amazing things to the industry. I just wish they advocated better for themselves without becoming mean, without dismissing their femininity, without doubting themselves so much.

Q: HOW DID RELIGION PLAY A ROLE IN YOUR LIFE IN RUSSIA AND HERE IN THE UNITED STATES?

Before we left Russia, you couldn't go to church. It was not allowed. After we came to America, we went to church for a few different reasons. First, we didn't know anyone, so it was a social outlet. Second, it was kind of nice to go to church because we hadn't been able to go to church for so long. Freedom of religion was one of our freedoms. And that's where I had my friends, Tanya and Lucy. I had a circle of friends, and unlike in school, they didn't belittle me and beat me up. They were also weird like me, so it made it okay.

Over the decades, we'd occasionally go see churches across the world to appreciate the architecture and listen to a great sermon, but regular attendance fizzled for a myriad of reasons.

I don't go to church now, but I do believe in a higher being. I didn't even christen my son. I raised him with the freedom of letting him decide what works for him because I have close friends who are Jewish, Christian, Hindu, Muslim, atheists, and everything in between. The good people around me have wonderful souls, and their religion is a supplement. My son needs to own being a good person and picking a religion if that's what he wants to do.

Q: AFTER GOING THROUGH SO MUCH—THE CONSTANT MOVING, SWITCHING SCHOOLS, BEING BULLIED, HAVING TO LEARN ENGLISH—HOW DID YOU OVERCOME ALL THAT AND BECOME SUCH A FRIENDLY, OUTGOING PERSON?

You take yourself everywhere you go. As an example, I hate the alarm that tells you to get out of bed in the morning. To this day, I love to sleep. I hated the alarm when I lived in Vienna, and I hated the alarm waking me up when I lived in New York, and I hated the alarm when I lived in Russia. I hated the alarm when I lived in Wisconsin and Ohio and back here in LA. I say it that way because I take myself everywhere I go.

Happiness is already inside every one of us. It doesn't wait for you to be in a certain city or particular continent; it's always there. Just because I'm in a new city doesn't mean that something new or magical is going to happen in my life, or something is going to magically change, or I'm going to have a different outlook. Everywhere I go, there I am—all of the good and bad about me is always with me. This means I still hate the alarm clock in the morning, but I've learned that only I can control how I react to the world. It's very empowering not to look to other people, other cities, other companies, and friends to be happy.

I've heard bad words associated with describing Russians many times in my life. At some point, you build resilience and wish whoever is saying this to you would have a nice day anyway. I have always told my hires over the years, "Be a duck. A duck lives in the water, eats in the water, swims in the water, sleeps in the water. But somehow, the duck is never wet. The duck has feathers with oil, and water just rolls off the feathers. Be a duck. You're going to be around people who are mean, resentful, bitter, and angry. You know what? It's okay. Be a duck. If you want to be angry and resentful and horrible, and just a mean person, have fun with that. Just please don't be in my space."

On the topic of mean people, enter my two failed marriages. I think that a lot of my childhood had to do with two failed marriages because my parents set some high expectations for me. Two weeks after my parents met, they were married. And then I was born. They had a wonderful relationship, living together all around the world for 44 years until my dad died. They were so enamored and in love with each other. I thought that when I got together with somebody, I would just automatically have a wonderful relationship with them. Meanwhile, I paid alimony and child support to my first ex-husband and alimony to the second. They just saw me as a workhorse, and they took me for a nice ride.

Q: DO YOU HAVE ANY ADVICE FOR KIDS OR PEOPLE IN GENERAL WHO MAY BE GOING THROUGH THE SAME EXPERIENCES THAT YOU WENT THROUGH WITH IMMIGRATION?

Put your head down, get busy, stop feeling sorry for yourself, and feel a sense of productivity and importance. Find people who have kindness in their hearts so that you only surround yourself with goodness. Go become independent. When you haven't taken money from anyone, no one can tell you what to do, what you should think, or how you should behave. Being financially independent is one of the most important things in this world, in any country. I'm not talking gluttony or showing off bling or extremes. Find a profession that provides for you for the rest of your life. Have your own money, and this is especially critical for women. Build your own life and never have anyone's blood on your hands. There's no quick trick to this. Start where you start and build from there being accountable for yourself.

The next important thing is to get out of your own head. We all have our insecurities, and the more bad thoughts we give them, the more they win. Then we start believing the negativity, and then that consumes our lives. Get busy. This country has the most opportunities of any country in the world, hands down. Go make yourself an opportunity. I'm going to give you my favorite quote. There's a letter, and the letter reads: "Dear Pessimist and Dear Optimist. While the two of you were busy arguing about whether the glass was half full or half empty, I drank all the contents. Sincerely, Opportunist." Go get it done. Stop feeling sorry for yourself. Stop feeding the monsters in your head. Go own your world with pride. ■

ALBERT EPSHTEYN

NOW

I grew up in the Baltimore area, attended the Krieger Schechter Day School for grades 5–8, then Pikesville High School, and then earned a BS in biochemistry followed by a PhD in chemistry from the University of Maryland College Park. Now I am 42, married to a wonderful wife and mother, and we have two super cute (but quite mischievous) boys who are seven and two years old and a cute Chinese Crested dog named Thumbelina. We live in the Washington, D.C., area, and I currently work as a research scientist for the U.S. Navy.

THE EPSHTEYN EXODUS AND METAMORPHOSIS OF 1989

When offered the chance to share the memories of my family's move from the former U.S.S.R. to the U.S. for this book, I jumped at the opportunity. These stories and anecdotes have been passed back and forth within our family countless times, so now it is not exactly clear which bit came from whose recollection as they live on in our collective conscience. The events outlined herein span from the early summer of 1989 until the spring of 1990—about 32 years ago. I am recording my memories here to the best of my ability. In advance, I ask for forgiveness if my story, my recollection, is not fully congruent with those of others who experienced the same events.

Imagine that you are 10 years old and enjoying your summer vacation, hanging out with your friends and loving life. I mean, life is really good when you are 10, right? You are clothed, fed, have a roof over your head, and the only worry on your mind might be about where you might get your next ice cream or what trouble you can get yourself into while playing with the kids in the neighborhood. Not many 10-year-olds experience a conversation with their parents that goes something like this:

"Alik, you know Mom and I have been thinking about this for a long time, and we have decided to move to America."

"Papa, America? But when?"

"We are making the arrangements right now. We will probably leave sometime in the next few months. You may not go to school in September. We need to figure some things out. We will be selling all our belongings. We can only take a few suitcases with us."

It was the summer of 1989 in Minsk, the capital of the Belorussian Soviet Socialist Republic (B.S.S.R.), which was one of the 15 republics that made up the Union of Soviet Socialist Republics (U.S.S.R.). This city of roughly 1.6 million inhabitants was my home. In school, we were taught that the U.S.S.R. was our Motherland, which we were obligated to love and defend with our very lives! To this day, I remember the pride I felt in this nationalistic ardor. It was all-consuming. It made one feel like you were a part of something important. Something big! It had been about four decades since the end of World War II, but we were still constantly and continuously preparing to defend the Motherland once again. Certainly, the threat of a war with the United States of America was omnipresent in the back of everyone's mind. And yet, here we were—about to join the enemy. We were leaving for America, and the prospects were positively exhilarating!

Up to that point, I had had what I perceived as a pretty good childhood. I remember always being happy. No, I do not mean content. I was really happy. I always felt like the world was mine to explore and make my own. There were no limits to what I could accomplish. In retrospect, this feeling was certainly misguided. Being a Jew in the U.S.S.R. meant the very opposite.

Although I was a good student and quite a patriotic young citizen of the U.S.S.R., there was an internal duality to my identity. Although outwardly I was an ideal young Soviet citizen, inside I never truly felt at home. Only about three or four short years before this, my dad revealed to me that we were not exactly like all the other people around us. Apparently, we were different. He said, "Alik, you know we are Jews. We are not Russian. We are not Belorussian. Alik, you are Jewish. You know, many very important people in history were Jewish." (*Note: Being Jewish is an ethnicity. We are Ashkenazi, so ethnically we are not Russian. It's the same if you are Polish and live in France or Japanese and live in Belgium. This idea is usually lost on Americans for whom nationality and national identity are more important. The U.S. is a melting pot, so after a few generations, tracking one's ethnicity becomes rather cumbersome.*) He proceeded to tell me about Moses and the Ten Commandments, about the Magen David, and that many scientists, composers, and revolutionaries, including Karl Marx and Albert Einstein, were Jewish.

This really impressed me. At the time, I attended the "zeroth grade," which I guess is the equivalent of kindergarten here in the U.S. So the next day, after the regular classes were over, we were in extended care, and it was supposed to be free playtime before our parents picked us up. I gathered all my friends around in a circle and began proselytizing. I gave them the whole megillah about Moses, King David and his shield, how Karl Marx was Jewish, how there were so many Jews who helped the Soviet revolution, about all the great composers, scientists, and especially Albert Einstein—my namesake!

My dad loves telling this particular story. By the way, he is a pretty darn good storyteller. Anyway, he loves telling of how he arrived to pick me up that evening. He makes this amazing grimace and describes the pale, or even ashen, face on my poor teacher (who happened to be Jewish). She apparently pleaded with him. "What are you telling your child? Please stop! I will lose my job! They will think I have poisoned his mind!" He later had to explain that I did not need to reveal everything that I learned at home and that being Jewish was a difficult thing. And from that, I learned that I should not go around telling people that I am Jewish, and it would likely make my life much more difficult.

So, by the summer of 1989, when my parents revealed to me that we were leaving to make a new life across the ocean, I understood, with my whole being, that our move to America was connected with our Jewish identity. At 10 years old, I had already directly experienced anti-Semitism. I never did feel quite at home in my homeland, and now my family and I would have the chance to find a new home where we could be ourselves.

In the following months, my parents efficiently sold off all our stuff. They got rid of nearly everything. Almost all of our clothes, furniture, and any other trappings of home they had amassed over a decade of domestic life together had to go. This had to be done because we were allowed two suitcases per adult and one suitcase per child when we were leaving. Also, we were not allowed to take anything deemed valuable out of the U.S.S.R., including money. We were only allowed $100 per adult and $50 per child.

The caveat was that these were limits imposed on the refugee travelers during their journey, but my father found out that it was possible to ship some crates ahead to New York, and the plan was to try to ship at least some things of value. My parents decided to pour much of the money they made from the sales into paintings, specifically ones they wanted to keep in their future home in America. I don't know whether this was a fully coherent idea. Did they want reminders of their past life around them, or was this a guttural urge to retain something?

Through an old friend who was part of the Minsk art circles, they met a refusenik Jewish artist by the name of Iosif Greenberg. Iosif was an interesting character, and my parents hit it off with him. My dad still keeps in touch with him to this day. As an artist, Iosif was consumed with the Jews' injustices under the Soviet regime, and paintings exuded this motif. Coincidentally, this was a perfect connection in theme with my parents' life experience, and they immediately fell in love with his art. They purchased multiple large pieces from Iosif and a few smaller ones with views of Minsk by the Belorussian national painter Chaim Livshitz (the father of their friend who was in the Minsk art circles). Most of these pieces reside in my parents' home to this day. They are a constant reminder of what we left behind and, in turn, an important reminder of how far we have come since then and how truly thankful we are to now be American.

❧

It was October 31, 1989, just nine days until the fall of the Berlin Wall (which, of course, no one knew of at the time). During our travels, we would be traversing through the heart of Europe, but since this was before the days of the Internet, and we would be living in countries where we did not speak the local tongue, we were going into a nearly complete information blackout. By the time we would land in New York, a lifetime of events would pass just a short three months later. Coincidentally, the world, and we through our experience, would be completely transformed.

At last, the day came when we would have to leave. My sister, Dina, who was six at the time, and I had spent the last few weeks living with my maternal grandparents in another part of town as my parents made the final preparations. On the day of our departure, my grandfather's brother, who came from Riga to say goodbye and had a car, drove all of us to the site where we were to board a bus that would take us to another life. I remember the atmosphere at the departure site, all the serious faces of those leaving, not knowing what to expect. Everyone was making a leap of faith into the unknown. The occasion did provide an escape in that everyone was scurrying about trying to keep busy, maybe trying to not "think" and instead just "do." Everyone was in a hurry, not wanting to miss their chance at a new life—not wanting to "miss the bus."

There were five of us leaving, including my parents, my sister, and my father's mother, who, being a widow, had nothing tying her down and cast her lot with us. My mother's parents had the option to come with but opted to stay. My maternal grandmother had been crying her eyes out ever since she had found out we were leaving several months before, and certainly, that day was particularly difficult for her. *(Note: After the political and economic situation in the U.S.S.R. deteriorated over the following year, my mother's family, including her parents and her brother with his wife and my young cousin Anna, as well as my aunt's parents and her brother, joined us two short years later.)*

Somehow, I do not remember the exact details of how, despite my grandmother clutching at us and wailing, we loaded our luggage and boarded the Soviet (Hungarian-made) Ikarus model bus bound for the western border town of Brest—"Gorod Geroy" (Hero City—a WWII moniker). The ride was a two-day affair with Vienna as our final destination, but first a stopover in Krakow. We made our way westward on the main highway toward the border with Poland, and almost like in a fairy tale, suddenly the sun came out, and the mood on the bus got animated and chatty. I would describe it as almost celebratory. It was a real-life but slow-motion getaway!

To this day, I remember us crossing the border. The mood on the bus got quiet and tense, perhaps because we were all somehow incredulous that "they" would actually let us out. But anticlimactically, the process was rather uneventful, as I do not remember the customs or the passport control. What I remember most vividly is the actual crossing when the bus rolled over onto the Polish side of the border. As a 10-year-old child, I remember this sense of amazement—wow! Everything was so neat! And clean! And bright and colorful! The roads were nice. The grass was nice. There was no litter. All the small houses were neat and kept up so well. I never knew this was possible. This was to be the theme of our entire journey westward toward America. With every step, we were gradually more and more amazed at humanity's progress and, by contrast, how retrograde our Soviet existence had actually been. To this day, that was my main reference point in life. Everything from that point got brighter and better.

I clearly remember how quaint and neat the little hotel where we stayed in Krakow was. It was our first night of freedom. The next day we kept driving through the Polish countryside and then into Czechoslovakia. Toward evening we stopped in Bratislava, right on the border with Austria. We had to change buses at that point, as the Soviet bus could not cross into Austria.

I distinctly remember when we crossed into Austria and drove into Vienna. Even in the dark, it was such an impressive sight. We were unloaded next to some small hotel with all our belongings. I remember helping my father carry our luggage and stack it in a specific spot designated for us. This was when my dad took me aside and looked into my eyes, and for some reason, what he said next changed my life. He said that we needed to guard our things to make sure they were not taken. We spent the night in the hotel lobby, waiting to be sorted into some type of temporary housing arrangement. All this while my dad and I took turns in the cold Vienna night, standing next to the pile of our belongings. I'm pretty sure at some point, I just fell over next to my mom and sister and woke up the next morning. This was the moment when I gained the necessary awareness and began to process and understand exactly what my parents had done. They had left everything—all that they had built back in Minsk—and they were moving to the U.S. in search of a better life for themselves, but more importantly, a better life for their children. And this realization transformed me. That was when I realized that I had certain responsibilities to my parents and my grandparents and to all my patriarchs and matriarchs—everyone who survived and sacrificed so I could have a chance at life in America. L'chaim! To life! I now realize that this was the moment that forced me to live up to the meaning of my name, Albert, the responsible one. To this day, I never revealed to anyone that this was my real bar-mitzvah, when I became a man.

Our stay in Vienna was relatively short, only 28 days, but packed chock-full of adventures. The charity, the American Jewish Joint Distribution Committee (JDC, or the Joint) that sponsored this mass exodus of Soviet Jewry, placed us in a communal apartment. I now realize that this was quite an accommodation. It was a grand flat in the middle of Vienna, in an old building. The apartment had three large and one smaller bedroom, a bathroom, and a kitchen. Each bedroom was given to a different family, so we had neighbors, and it was quite a full house. All five of us slept on cots in one room until my mom got sick and was in the hospital almost the entire time we were in Vienna. That was certainly an adventure, but she received great care there. My 75-year-old grandmother also had medical issues. She had already had three heart attacks, and although she was a trooper, she wasn't in great shape by that point in her life.

Two specific episodes in Vienna were particularly emblematic of our immigration process. One episode started that first night when the bus dropped us off at that small hotel, and my dad and I were guarding our belongings. Vienna welcomed us with one of our bags going missing by the end of that night. We had been warned that the local thieves got wind of when refugees were being dropped off to wait to be sorted and were pilfering luggage. Hence, my dad instituted the night watch. To this day, we don't know what happened to that bag. The irony is that the bag contained very little of anything of real monetary value—just a few of my mom's perfumes, cosmetics, and most importantly, our flatware. So, the loss technically was not great, and we didn't really fret about it until we got to our apartment and it was time to eat. Imagine being in a strange city where you do not know the language or customs, and you have to go out and try to find some kitchen implements.

To this day, my parents love to tell the story of them walking in the middle of Vienna and walking into a silversmith store with only a couple of dollars to their name. They were looking at the fancy silverware that cost hundreds of shillings, and, in their own words, their eyes were popping out of their orbits. Apparently, this is when my mother first attempted to remember some of the German that she had learned in school and the Yiddish she'd learned at home to communicate with the store proprietor (she still swears that Austrian German pronunciation is very similar to Yiddish). Somehow, she managed to explain to the woman what they needed, and the lady went into the back of the store and brought out a few plain, steel spoons, which only cost a few shillings (still a small fortune in my parents' eyes). That evening we dined in style using these beautiful new spoons that we now appreciated so much more. I believe my parents still have them.

The other episode happened the first night my mother was in the hospital. Afterward, my dad went food shopping and came back portraying a good mood, perhaps trying to keep up our morale in the face of this setback. He asked us to sit at the table and said that he had a surprise for us. He demonstratively slowly removed a carton from his bag and said, "I got you guys some apple juice!" Dina and I were super excited! He immediately opened the carton and poured us two cups. I greedily took the first gulp and quickly spit it out.

"Dad! I think it's gone bad!"

"What do you mean?" He tried it and laughed. Apparently, wine and hard cider were sold in regular supermarkets. The carton had a nice apple drawn on it, and without the benefit of a smartphone at one's disposal, it was pretty tough to tell the difference between apple juice and hard cider.

Somehow we made it through our stay in Vienna. Dina and I spent our days playing with the kids from the other families in our apartment. Eventually, my mother came back from the hospital, and she was feeling much better. Now it was time for us to move on to the next phase of our trip.

From my parents' stories, it was only later that I understood that our stay in Vienna was necessitated by an obligatory negotiation with the Israeli Embassy. At this point, if we had opted, we could go directly to Israel. However, like many other Soviet refugees from our immigration "wave," my parents had other ideas. This meant our next adventures would occur on Italian soil, near Rome, where the Americans had a staging area for the onslaught of Soviet Jews.

If I had to assess what the entirety of the immigration process was like for me as a 10-year-old kid who, up to that point in time, had made few trips outside of Minsk, it was quite an exhilarating ride to be suddenly thrust into the heart of Europe, to see Vienna and Rome. Suddenly the world was much larger with so much to offer. Even being poor refugees, my parents found ways to get us to the Vienna Kunsthistorisches Museum and the Museum of Natural History in Vienna, the Colosseum, ancient ruins of Rome and the Vatican, and quite a few other historic places and landmarks. It was clearly important for them that this was still an educational experience for us, and they portrayed (quite successfully) that this trip was an adventure we were all having together.

Upon our arrival in Rome, we were placed in a little roach motel called Sporting. I call it a roach motel because that is most appropriate. When one got up in the middle of the night to get a drink of water, switching the lights on in the kitchenette caused the table to undergo a sudden transformation from a cognac brown to pure white. This would be our base for two weeks, while my parents got us registered to receive a stipend from “the Joint” (Joint Distribution Committee) of 1,000 mille lire (the equivalent of U.S. $700 at the time). They then had until the end of the two weeks to find a rental for us using these funds. The stay in Rome went by quite rapidly, and one day my dad arrived home sporting a huge smile. “I found us housing! We’re moving to Ladispoli!”

Ladispoli was a beach town about 45 minutes outside Rome and was one of the most common destinations for Soviet Jews to rent temporary quarters for their layover in Italy. In the off-season (we got there in December), the rentals were cheap, and who doesn’t want to live in Italy next to the warm Mediterranean? My dad had found a one-room hut next to the commuter train tracks running toward Rome owned by a farmer and his wife who grew arugula and green beans. The rent was 700 mille lire per month, leaving us 300 mille lire (U.S. $200) for food and other necessities. Due to this meager food budget for a family of five, our staple foods were potatoes and kiwi fruit that my parents purchased at the central town market. They were the cheapest, nutritious, locally grown produce. The potatoes were a familiar staple for us, as that was one of the main agricultural products of Belarus. On the other hand, the kiwis were a completely new experience, and quite honestly, the novelty still has not worn off to this day. As an exception to the potato and kiwi diet, for our New Years’ celebration that year, my parents got three portions of honest-to-goodness Italian ice cream to split among the five of us. That was some of the best ice cream I have ever tasted to this day.

At that point, we had no idea exactly how long we would be staying in Ladispoli. We knew that some refugees were stuck there for many months, and some even well over a year, waiting for their “guarantor” paperwork from the U.S. to come through. Those who had left the U.S.S.R. without relatives in the U.S. were throwing themselves at the mercy of securing general guarantorship from the large Jewish communities in U.S. cities such as New York, Chicago, and Los Angeles, or perhaps hoping to go to Canada or Australia. We did not realize how lucky we were that we had a relative, my dad’s cousin, who had taken care of everything for us behind the scenes. But at the time, we did not know what to expect, and my parents were settling in for the long haul.

My sister and I were placed in a Jewish school run by the Joint, and this was our first exposure to Jewish culture, Hebrew, and Judaica. We started school at the beginning of December, with Hanukkah just around the corner, and my first brush with Judaism and Jewish history was the story of the Maccabees, the Jewish partisans who expelled the invaders and restored the Jewish temple in Jerusalem with just one small vessel of holy oil left to power the temple menorah and the eternal light. We learned that although there was only enough oil in that vessel to last a day, miraculously, it lasted an entire eight days—the time necessary to press and purify new holy oil.

We celebrated the miracle of Hanukkah for the first time at home. At school, we were shown how to carve out a Hanukkah menorah (Hanukkiah) from potatoes and to roll cotton balls into small fuses that could be used to burn cooking oil. We were told that during the Holocaust, Jews in camps and ghettos made Hanukkiot in this manner, which also made this process meaningful for our family. I brought a photocopy of the Hanukkah blessings home from school. The whole family gathered around the kitchen table, and for the first time in my life, we lit Hanukkah lights in our family circle. I lit the shammash (the "servant" candle, which is ritually lit first), and reading from the words written in the Cyrillic script (I did not yet know how to read Hebrew), for the first time in my life, I intoned the blessing "Baruch atah Adonai, eloheynu Melech ha'olam, asher kid'shanu, b'mitzvotav v'tzivanu l'hadlik ner shel Hanukkah" and lit the first light of our potato Hanukkiah. It was magical. Our Jewish identity was out in full view, and we were so very proud and so very free. We had the oil and the potatoes that were useful not just for making the makeshift Hanukkiah, but my grandmother whipped up a batch of latkes that would be the envy of any wealthy Jewish family.

Ladispoli was the center of Soviet Jewish refugee life, and therefore the site of a very lively open-air market where anyone could try their luck at selling their wares. This was another way for refugees to recoup some of the money they could not bring with them directly. Instead, they bought up wares, or trinkets, in the U.S.S.R. to try to transform them into currency at the market. My parents came prepared. They had brought an entire giant duffel bag full of matryoshka nested dolls, Soviet optics (cameras, binoculars, etc.), wind-up toys, etc. While we were at school, my parents would go to the market and try to sell their trinkets. In fact, they did relatively well at the market. By the end of our stay in Italy, our family savings, the beginnings of the Epshteyns' generational wealth amounted to just over $800!

Indeed, their time at the market was not spent for naught. Not only did they make a bit of pocket change to get them started in their new life in the U.S., but they also gained quite a few interesting anecdotes. They love to tell the story that next to them at the market there was another Soviet family, who, as a novelty item, had brought a giant bag with rolls of Soviet condoms (imagine hundreds of condom packets stitched together). These weren't your average condoms. These were true Soviet tools designed to rapidly bring communism to the masses. That is to say that they were designed not necessarily to prevent pregnancy. Still, during the act of love-making, you were ensured to have thoughts only of the Communist Party leaders who constantly had a steely hold on your manhood. These entrepreneurial folks had quite an ingenious marketing campaign. On the one side of their improvised stall, they were selling children's trinkets, and one of them would be yelling "Gioco Russo por bambino!" (Russian toy for kids).

On the other side, the other would be holding the giant bag of Soviet rubber technology and screaming, "Anti-bambinos rusos!" This worked quite well. All the Italians walking by were laughing their heads off and gladly handing over their American dollars.

The time in Ladispoli passed quickly, and one night in mid-January 1990, we were all sleeping peacefully in our hut next to the train tracks when we heard a knock on the door. I think my dad thought it was Paolo (the farmer landlord) and that perhaps something was amiss. He jumped out of bed, disoriented, half asleep, and opened the door half-panicked in his tighty-whities. What we heard next was the word TRANSPORT. We had been granted entry to the U.S. We had a booked flight to Baltimore, Maryland, with a layover at JFK Airport in New York City! We were now only a few short flights away from our new life. It's difficult to imagine how we got any sleep that night.

Twenty-three years later, in April 2013, my wife and I honeymooned in Italy. With our first stop in Rome, we had a rental car, and I convinced her that we should take a day and drive to Ladispoli. It was a most interesting exercise. It was certainly the same place, but it also wasn't. The town had grown quite a bit, roughly doubling in area, but the transients were now seasonal workers, mostly from Poland (EU migrant workers), instead of Soviet Jewish refugees. We trudged around town, walking through the town square where the big fountain is, and I reminisced about the large crowds of refugees gathered here to listen for their names to be called for an appointment at the American Embassy in Rome. We strolled through the small adjacent part that used to be the site of the small market and now was standing quite desolate. And we walked to Via Pisa by the train tracks. I half hoped that we would see Paolo with his wife sitting there, sifting through arugula or green beans, but alas, that was not to be. Instead, we saw an abandoned house, and my wife snapped a touristy photo of me in front of the old gates. Our final stop was at the main restaurant in the middle of town where I made a point of ordering the most expensive bottle of wine and the best food off the menu while I retold my wife stories about how the last time I was here, in Ladispoli, I scoured the streets for change to buy myself an ice cream. Metamorphosis.

Twenty-three years later, in April 2013, I called my parents in Baltimore from Via Pisa 3 in Ladispoli.

So, just like that, on January 25, 1990, we boarded an Alitalia charter flight from Rome to New York. Our mood was celebratory. We were finally en route to our "forever home"! The most memorable bit from that flight was the in-flight food packaging with a cute pink piggy with a big red X. Finally, we landed at JFK Airport, initiating the process of turning into our American selves. At JFK, we were greeted by nearly the entire wing of the Karasic side of the family (my dad's mother's first cousins from her mother's side, who had kept in touch with us for two generations since leaving Russia in the early 1920s), as well as my grandmother's brother-in-law (the father of cousin Irina, more on her below). It was truly a memorable family reunion. They spent the next many hours with us at JFK until we finally were able to board our connecting flight to the Baltimore Washington International Airport, which was supposed to leave that evening but kept getting delayed. To this day, we remember that truly happy day and the time we got to spend at JFK Airport.

Upon landing at JFK on January 25, 1990, we were incredibly tired (as can be seen in the photo). Our extended family greeted us for a lovely family reunion (left to right) Uncle Boris in the fedora (Irina's father); Morris Karasic; my grandmother Faina with flowers; my father with my little sister, Ann "Honey" Karasic; me; my mom; and Mina Karasic.

One more thought on that evening at JFK. This was, in a way, the final culmination of the visual transformation I observed throughout the trip. It began when our bus rolled across the Soviet border with Poland, with a continuous and stark contrast of improving everything—sights, air, technology, life. The transformation was tremendous from Poland to Czechoslovakia, Austria, Italy, and now, finally, the U.S. Here I was, standing inside the JFK terminal on the evening of January 25, 1990, looking out the window over Jamaica Bay onto the New York skyline. I remember this as though it was yesterday. The most impressive thing was seeing the lights of the cars crossing over a bridge. I could immediately judge that these were no tiny little Soviet or European models. These were the giant American land-yachts designed to traverse oceans of land. I would liken this sight against the New York night skyline, that it was for me what perhaps others before me experienced coming to New York through Ellis Island and seeing the Statue of Liberty (which I would visit much later).

In Baltimore, at roughly 4 a.m., after more delays, my dad's cousin Irina (the very one who helped organize this entire transition and sponsored us in the U.S.) and her boyfriend met us. At the airport, we also met Ronnie Karasic, another of my dad's cousins and the son of one of my grandmother's cousins who greeted us at JFK, representing the Baltimore branch of the Karasic clan. Together, they greeted us and took us to our new home, an apartment that Irina arranged and fully furnished for us in Baltimore. January 26 is an important anniversary in our family. It is the birthday of Epshteyns in America.

We made America our home and took to it like fish to water. Finally, we had found a place where we could fully embrace our Jewish identity while pursuing happiness with life and liberty intact. By all accounts, the coup that my parents pulled off, with the amazing help from cousin Irina, was a complete success. My dad's mother received a life-saving heart surgery soon after our arrival, which gave her a new lease on life, and after which she has trotted around the globe, and she is still with us at the ripe old age of 106 (baruch hashem). As I already mentioned, my mother's side of the family joined us a couple of short years later. My sister and I were welcomed by the Solomon Schechter Day School (later renamed the Krieger Schechter Day School) and received so much love and care and an amazing Jewish education, as well as becoming fervent practitioners of "Tikkun Olam."

I think the last memory that may be an appropriate episode to end this tale of exodus is us piling into Ronnie's new car for a ride up to New Jersey for Passover. Honey and Larry Karasic and family welcomed us into their home in Asbury Park, and that Passover was quite an experience! We celebrated the exodus of the Jews from Egypt, an escape from the rule of a foreign tyrant. One could not ask for a more direct parallel to our own experience of the prior six months, and to this day, Passover is the most important Jewish holiday for our family.

So, in retrospect, this immigration thing was one of the most formative events in my life. I must admit that writing about it made my eyes slightly well up with tears more than once, but it also often made me smile and laugh. If I had to summarize how this experience has shaped me, the thought is quite concise: I am blessed to have the perspective to be eternally grateful. That is not a bad way to go through life. And from my perspective, this experience may be what drives all first-generation immigrants who come to America. They have such a contrasting perspective in that other reference point that the other place where they lived in no way could ever compare to our new homeland—our America. The bottom line is that maybe that is missing for those who have never experienced it. I truly believe that we all need that kind of point of reference to help us find meaning. Our own relativity, if you will. So, perhaps, for me, writing all this down is, in a way, a prayer and a way for me to pass this gift of perspective, of another reference point, on to my children and anyone else who cares to read it.

YULIA TAJONERA

NOW

I'm 51 years old, live with my handsome husband and our cat Sunshine in Queens, Forest Hills. After graduating from FIT in Fine Arts major I became an artist and a muralist. I have had numerous art exhibits and was reviewed by NY Times, Daily News and Newsday newspapers. I also appeared on a Japanese TV show. We travel extensively throughout the world.

Q: WHERE DID YOU GROW UP, AND WHAT WAS YOUR CHILDHOOD THERE LIKE?

I grew up in Minsk, Belarus, and left when I was 10 years old. My parents were very young when they met. My mom was 18, and my dad was 28 at the time. I was born when my mom was 20. My parents divorced when I was about five. My dad is Jewish, and my mom is Russian Orthodox. My dad always wanted to leave, so they ended up separating because of that reason. My dad wasn't sure if he was going to take me with him or not. When I was 10, it was up to me to decide whether to leave or to stay.

My dad was a jeweler, and my mom was a waitress in a high-end place where government officials would go. So we always had a lot of food because of her job. My mom grew up in a family that had a rough time after the war. There was a lot of poverty and never enough food

Mall where Yulia's dad worked as a jeweler.

to eat. She had five siblings. I think she chose to work in the food business so that she could feed her family. And during the Stalin years, my dad's father was sent to a gulag in Siberia for opening a letter. There was this letter about monetary reforms in the country, and it was supposed to be opened at a later date, but his coworkers conned him into opening it earlier. Then the same coworkers told on him, and he ended up being sentenced to hard labor for eight years in a gulag in Siberia. His wife—my dad's mother—wanted to be near the prison to support and feed her husband, so my dad grew up in Siberia for part of his life. My grandmother was from the outskirts of Belarus, where there were a lot of Jewish villages. Their family had some kind of clothing business, which was doing well before the war, so they were well off. But during the war, their whole family was killed by the Nazis when the Germans invaded. When she met my grandfather, they moved to Minsk, where my dad was born and where I was born.

Yulia's neighborhood in Minsk.

We were living with my maternal grandparents when I was born because there was a housing shortage. We ended up living in a two-bedroom apartment with about 10 people, including my grandparents, my aunt, and her child. Shortly after, when I was about two, we were able to get our own house, which looked like a barracks house. These houses were built by German prisoners. We had no running water, so we had to walk a few blocks to get it from the well. There was no central heat, but we did have a fireplace. If we needed to use the phone, we had to walk to a phone booth a few blocks away. But at least we had electricity. We shared a big yard with a lot of neighbors, and that's where we hung our clothes to dry after laundry. My mom would bathe me in this metal bathtub in the backyard. I was so embarrassed.

We had buildings in the city, many of which had been destroyed in the war and rebuilt by the time I was born in 1970. Right in the middle of the city, there were neighborhoods that looked like rural villages. Chickens and roosters were running around. People had pigs. I could pick berries off the street and would feed myself outside in the garden.

My mom remarried. My sister was born when I was six years old, so I took care of her while my mom was working. Every other day she worked late. I probably shouldn't have been home alone with my sister, but I was basically a babysitter at a very early age.

Q: DO YOU REMEMBER SCHOOL?

I do remember my school. I would walk to school because there was no school bus or anything. I remember it was very cold in the winter, and I would walk bundled up. One day was about minus 30 degrees Celsius, and they closed school because it was so cold. I didn't know the schools were closed, so I still walked to school that day, but of course, when I got there, it was closed, and I had to walk back in that freezing temperature. I remember thinking, "Oh, this is really cold."

I had a lot of good friends in school. Everybody was kind of poor. I remember one boy with whom I was doing homework. They lived behind the barracks in an abandoned train. One friend lived in a communal apartment with many families sharing one kitchen and one bathroom.

Q: TELL ME ABOUT THE DECISION TO LEAVE.

When I was 10, my dad got permission to leave. He had already married again, with another child, my sister, who was six or seven years younger than me. My two sisters— the one my mom had after she remarried and the one my dad had after he remarried—were born around the same time. So on weekends, I would see my dad, and during the week, I stayed at my mom's. My dad lived in a very tight studio apartment with his wife, her son from a previous marriage, and my baby sister—five of us in that one studio.

I remember that my dad got a visa, and he said that they would be leaving. The visa was for Israel, but he mentioned that we could switch in Italy and go to America. So my parents sat down, and they told me, "This is the situation. Your dad is leaving, and he wants to take you with him. But if you leave, you might not ever see your mom because you can't go back. Once you leave, you can't go back."

My grandmother, my friends, and all my relatives also told me, "But if you stay, you won't see your dad." And I really love my dad. So the decision was up to me.

I stayed up late at night, thinking and thinking, asking myself, "What am I going to do with my life? I have to make a decision, to choose my mom or my dad." The life I saw in Belarus was pretty harsh. It was the only thing I knew.

I loved my family and my friends, but I saw a lot of drinking. A lot of men drank. I remember walking by beer halls with lots of drunk men sitting or lying outside. And I thought to myself, "Well, if I stay here, I don't want to get married to one of these men who is going to be drunk." I didn't see a great future because I was Jewish and looked it. I think 99 percent of people had very white skin, blue eyes, and blonde hair. I stood out because I always had really dark hair and looked more like I was Armenian or from the Middle East. So people knew I was not from Belarus. There were incidents when I was attacked in school. People started calling me names, and they threw rocks in my direction. Like all Soviet passports, mine said my nationality was Jewish because whatever your father is, that's what they went by. Even though my mother was not Jewish, and I was half-and-half, it didn't matter. I would hear things on a bus like, "Oh, look at those Jews." They would write things like, "Jews, go back to Israel," and things like that. There was anti-Semitism, and my mom knew it. So my mom told me it was really up to me. She didn't want me to live in an anti-Semitic place. She knew I would probably have a hard time getting into universities or getting a job, basically that I would have a hard life.

We were part of the second wave of immigrants at that time. I think there was a seven-year gap between them because my dad's best friend was already living in New York. He was sending *Architectural Digest* and other magazines so we could see how beautiful America was. And it did look so beautiful. He would send me gifts, like clothing and bubble gum. I remember those gum wrappers, which had cartoons in them. I was looking at those magazines and fantasizing that I would be living in one of those beautiful houses. I thought America looked like *Architectural Digest* houses for everyone.

Q: TELL ME ABOUT THE ACTUAL DEPARTURE. IT MUST HAVE BEEN TOUGH TO SEPARATE FROM PART OF YOUR FAMILY.

I made the decision to leave in 1980. We were not allowed to take a lot of stuff with us. I had a change of clothing, a few dresses and skirts, a pair of shoes, and some other items I no longer remember. My mom cut my long hair really short to resemble a boy's cut because she was afraid I would get lice when traveling.

My dad's friend told us that we should take a lot of stuff to sell in Italy in the outdoor markets. We ended up taking a lot of sheets and matryoshkas (wooden nesting dolls) and playing cards and perfume called Red Moscow. We were only allowed to take $500 with us, and I remember my dad had all his jeweler's tools. My mom was able to travel with us by train to Brest, on the border between Poland and Belarus. After that, at the immigration checkpoint, we would have to separate basically forever. I remember at that checkpoint the customs officer rifling through our suitcases and throwing things to the side, sorting our life's belongings into piles of things we could take and things we couldn't. They took all my dad's tools away. Then I remember seeing that the train was almost leaving, but we still had all our stuff strewn across the table. So we quickly shoved it all into the suitcases and rushed to a metal door to wait. I remember the door opening and closing, and my mom was already on the other side of it. And I remember thinking that this was the last time I would ever see my mom. So I kept crying. I just remember standing there and crying and crying, and the door kept opening and closing. I kept seeing her face and then not seeing it as the doors opened and closed. It was tormenting me, and I wished the door would close so that I would stop crying. I remember how our relatives and my friends came to the train, and they were waving goodbye and crying. That was a really sad day.

I was 10 years old and had my four-year-old sister with me, and I was wheeling her around. At the last minute, my stepmom threw a fur coat on me that she had with her. We barely made the train, but I remember being happy to be inside and leaving.

Soon, we were approaching the Polish border. The Soviet Union was very strict, and no one was allowed out, so it was a big deal to pass a Soviet border, even to another Warsaw Pact nation. Before we left, they took our passports and cut them right in front of us. They said, "Now you are stateless." They told us we were traitors.

Q: AT THAT POINT, WHO WAS ON THE TRAIN WITH YOU?

My dad, my stepmom, and my baby sister were on the train with me. My brother, Serge, the son of my mom with her new husband, was left behind because he had the same situation as me, but in the opposite direction. His dad, who was staying behind, did not want him to leave. So Serge ended up not seeing his mom for about eight years, just like me.

We were traveling together with other immigrants, and I remember the smell of valerian, a home remedy root used by some for heart palpitations and anxiety. Everyone was taking those drops, and I still remember that smell. But I remember being excited too. Armed guards came in and kicked us out so that they could search the compartments. That was scary since that was the first time I had seen armed soldiers.

Q: SO YOUR FIRST STOP WAS VIENNA?

Yes. It was pouring rain when we got there. I think my dad was trying to speak German because he had studied it, but it wasn't working. And the taxi driver took us to the wrong location and dropped us off. Now we were in the middle of Vienna somewhere, and rain was falling. Eventually, we found a phone booth, and my dad got the correct address.

I remember Austria being so beautiful but very gray. Somehow I felt excited because I was 10, and for me, it was an adventure. I hadn't realized then how much I would miss my mom and the rest of the family who stayed behind. I was just focused on the next new thing. Our hotel room had one room with four beds and a big round table in the middle. I was so excited because it felt like a completely different world. I remember going to the store for the first time and thinking, "Wow, they have so many sausages." The sausages were everywhere, just hanging from the ceiling. In Belarus, we had to stay in line for hours, and here there were sausages just hanging from the ceilings. I also remember these chocolate rabbits wrapped in beautiful wrapping paper. I remember wishing that my mom could see all this food. I remember the long lines in Minsk, and often people didn't even know what the lines were for, but you got on the line, thinking it must be worthwhile since there is a line. We even waited in line for toilet paper. So I was amazed at how beautiful everything was and just how much abundance there was.

Q: WAS ITALY NEXT?

Yes, we took a train to Rome. I found Rome to be a little dirtier by comparison to Vienna. It was more crowded, and it seemed very old. It is, of course, an ancient city. It was very hot, and there was no air conditioning. We slept with the windows open and wet the sheets to cool off. We would go downstairs to eat, and I would see all these immigrants sitting at a long table, and I was just so happy to be inside a huge cafeteria since they were giving us so much food. I remember these long baguettes with butter and jam. I had never seen a baguette before.

I remember also trying to sell items inside our hotel room. We were trying to sell sheets, and the Italian buyers didn't quite understand the triangle holes, which were a deliberate Soviet design to allow you to tuck a blanket inside. We didn't speak Italian, so we had a hard time demonstrating that one. I think we stayed in Rome for only a couple of weeks. By this time, I had started writing letters, mostly to my mom, and I started drawing. I had been drawing since I was five, and Rome, with its history and beauty, provided the perfect backdrop. As we went to different sites, I would sketch them and send them to my mom. I remember being in a church and seeing Jesus everywhere and on the cross, and I ran out. I had never seen a church before. I think those images of Jesus suffering on a cross scared me.

I also remember my first love. I fell for a 14-year-old immigrant boy when I was 10. His name was Igor, and he was my first love. But I ended up getting my heart broken because he fell in love with another older girl—my first love and first heartbreak all in Rome.

Then we moved to Ladispoli, a suburb of Rome where we—together with many other Russian immigrants—would wait for our asylum to be approved. Our visa was for Israel, but my dad wanted to go to New York, where he had a friend. He also had friends in Chicago and San Francisco, so we weren't sure where we would end up. We rented a one-bedroom cottage in Ladispoli. The cottage was about four blocks from the beach, and the beach had black volcanic sand. At that point, we were running low on money, and food was an issue. So we were kind of living off Nutella.

I remember finding these pine nuts inside pine cones and munching on them. My dad and my stepmom were fighting. They were yelling and screaming, which was the first time I heard that.

My dad and I would go to the outdoor market to sell things to make money. At 6 a.m., we would put out a little table with the stuff we had brought. My dad said that I had to shout, in Italian, to get people to come over. We sold playing cards, perfume, and matryoshkas. I was happy to stand there and sell stuff. It was a great experience. And with that money, we were able to buy some clothes. My dad had instructions from his friend who had preceded us in the immigration journey, who told us to buy winter coats, jeans, shoes, and boots, among other things. I was so excited because we were able to buy such beautiful things. I remember a sweater and a sundress. I had never had clothes so beautiful, and I thought I would wear them every day.

Then we had to go to HIAS, a Jewish agency that helps refugees make the journey. They were trying to ask us why we were going to America instead of Israel. They really wanted us to go to Israel because Israel needed people. My dad and stepmom were fighting over what to do. My stepmom wondered whether we should go to Israel, but my dad was pretty resolute about going to America. Eventually, we ended up going to New York.

Q: TELL ME ABOUT ARRIVING IN NEW YORK. WHAT WAS THAT LIKE?

I remember the plane we were on, a big TWA jet that I don't think they use anymore. I remember the flight attendant serving me Coca-Cola. That really brought it home that I was going to America. I was so excited. I told myself that America would be the most beautiful place I had seen, more so than Austria and Italy. We arrived at JFK, and my dad's friend picked us up and drove us to his place not too far from the airport in Flushing, Queens. As he was driving, I recall thinking, "Wow, this doesn't look pretty at all." I remember seeing one brown brick building after another and thinking it looked horrible. I didn't like it at first. But then my dad's friend took us to Baskin-Robbins, and I couldn't believe how many flavors they had. The friend also made us a great dinner. He cooked us lobsters, which I had never had before.

My dad's friend let us stay with him for a few weeks. We had $2,000, mostly from the sales in Italy. We soon found a two-bedroom apartment in Brooklyn for $300 a month. The prior renters were moving to Florida and offered to leave all their furniture and silverware for $150. My sister and I shared a room. The walls were plain. We had no pictures, so I drew and covered all four walls with pictures from top to bottom—ladies with hats, Pepsi-Cola, palm trees with monkeys. I just kept drawing.

Q: WHAT ABOUT GOING TO SCHOOL? HOW WAS THAT?

I remember that I did not like my first school. I didn't speak any English, and I sat in the back. I was in fifth grade but had no idea what was going on. There was so much diversity—Italians, Hispanics, Blacks, Asians, and a few Russians. I sat next to another Russian girl named Irina. She was a character—a bit chubby with very wiry hair—and kids picked on her. So I expected to be bullied too. They took us to a boring ESL class. The teacher was telling us what a dog and a cat were. I wasn't learning much. I remember, though, that when it came to math in the regular class, I always knew the answer, and people were amazed. To me, it was easy because the U.S.S.R. had more advanced math education in earlier years. So I started becoming more popular. But I was still mostly an outcast. At lunchtime, we would sit separately from the other kids because we didn't speak English.

Q: HOW DID YOU LEARN ENGLISH?

A lot came from commercials and cartoons on TV. I would watch about six hours of TV per day with my sister. So in one year, I was already fluent in English. It wasn't from ESL classes, but from watching TV and playing with kids outside.

Q: WHAT ABOUT YOUR PARENTS?

My parents got jobs. They both got a job at the Hyatt hotel. They took courses. My stepmom was doing secretarial typing work, and my dad got a job making jewelry, but it was very low pay, so we struggled with money. Then the Grand Hyatt (on 42nd in New York) opened in 1980, and my parents stayed in a long line to get job applications, and they both got hired. They worked at that hotel for a long time, and I ended up working there for 26 years. Eventually, my parents left there. My stepmom became a dental assistant and then a phlebotomy technician, but she later regretted it and said the Hyatt was the best job ever because of the generous benefits. My dad also ended up leaving, but then he came back again and got a pension. He's retired now.

Q: WHERE DID YOU LIVE DURING THIS TIME?

We left New York City after a year and a half to go to Rochester because my parents thought New York was very rough. New York was pretty bad back in the eighties. There were a lot of drugs. You couldn't even go to Union Square Park because there were drugs and homeless people everywhere. We stayed in Rochester for a year, where it was quite cold. We then moved back to Brooklyn because the job and pay prospects in Rochester were quite low.

We always lived near the Russian immigrants in Brooklyn, basically Brighton Beach.

I was switching schools all the time, and I was frustrated because just as I would make friends, it was time to leave. I was 16 and was getting depressed and rebellious. I was going through a lot of turmoil in my life, and I missed my mom, who I hadn't seen for six years.

I was quite Americanized by that time. I think I even stopped speaking Russian. Gorbachev then took over as general secretary in the U.S.S.R., and he opened the borders to allow people to travel back to Russia. I was able to see my mom, my grandparents, and cousins in 1986 or 1987. I was a different person, and my mom didn't recognize me at the airport.

I had a punk haircut, so many different colors in my hair. It was heart-wrenching seeing my mom and sister. My sister was about 10, the age I was when I left. I had been sending them gifts over the years, which they treasured. My sister worshiped me.

Q: YOU ENDED UP GOING BACK TO LIVE IN THE U.S.S.R. FOR A WHILE, RIGHT? WHAT WAS THE CONTRAST LIKE?

Yes, after that visit to see my mom and sister, I decided that I would go back to spend some time there after I graduated high school. I went back and lived with my mom for a year in Belarus. I decided to take a gap year before college. The country had really transformed during my absence, but the contrast between the U.S. and my life there was also very stark. I remember there were no shopping malls, and they had only three channels on TV. I had become an MTV junkie in America, watching Madonna and Michael Jackson, so that was different. My life was so different from the life I was observing in Belarus. People had so little, but they treasured all these little things that were precious to them. I started to change my attitude completely. I grew my real hair out, and I stopped wearing makeup. I started reading my mom's Russian books—the classics like Tolstoy and Dostoevsky—and relearning Russian. I even started a stamp collection! My life completely transformed.

Q: WHAT DID YOU DO WHEN YOU RETURNED TO THE U.S. AFTER A YEAR IN BELARUS?

When I returned, I got a scholarship to an art college. My parents wanted me to be a lawyer or a doctor or something that makes a lot of money. But I wanted to be happy. I wanted to do what I wanted to do. My parents didn't have a lot of money, but I got a scholarship because my grades were high. My grades had not always been high, but it really transformed me after returning from that first trip to Belarus. I woke up and realized that I had to work hard, so I started to study and do art shows again (I was in the newspaper a few times).

I really enjoyed college. And then I ended up working in a restoration company because I had a degree in antique restoration. But I got sick from being exposed to chemicals, so I decided I didn't want to work in that field. I took a part-time job at the Grand Hyatt, where my parents were working, and still did art on the side.

Q: HAS YOUR MOM EVER COME TO THE U.S.?

Yes. In 1990, my mom and sister came as visitors, and I sponsored them, and they stayed. Now they both live here and are American citizens. My grandmother was able to come here, but she passed away shortly after arriving in the U.S. My brother, Serge, came too. But the journey was different for them. They just had to take one flight. We had to go through months and months of the immigration journey. They missed out on the fun part!

Yulia and her mom near the Palace of Culture in Minsk.

Their transition was also hard because they had to leave their family behind. Life was hard because they didn't speak English, but they adjusted. They love America and are such patriots. On the Fourth of July, my mom starts crying.

Q: DID YOUR JEWISH IDENTITY CHANGE AS A RESULT OF COMING TO THE U.S.? DID YOU GO TO SYNAGOGUE OR JEWISH SCHOOL OR CAMP?

In the beginning, I did go to Jewish camp. My sister, Yelena, went to a yeshiva (Jewish day school) for a year or so. I learned how to do shabbos (Jewish sabbath), but we were not religious. Of course, my parents would celebrate the Jewish holidays because of the tradition, but we did not go to synagogue much. We ended up going once or twice. My dad is not religious at all. I'm not sure he even believes in God. His view is, "When you die, you die. That's it." But my stepmom is more religious.

Q: DO YOU SPEAK RUSSIAN NOW?

Yes. Since I went back to Russia when I was 16, I relearned the language and made Russian friends. So when I came back here, I made it a point to speak Russian again and make Russian friends. So I always speak Russian with my dad, mom, and stepmom.

Q: WHAT ABOUT OTHER PARTS OF RUSSIAN CULTURE–FOOD, LITERATURE, ETC.?

Yes, absolutely. I have a lot of Russian book classics. When I came back from Belarus, I packed my bags with all the old classics and still have them. So I read the Russian classics. My husband is Filipino, but he knows how important Russian food is to me. I always have Russian food, like salmon caviar.

Q: DO YOU THINK THERE WAS ONE PARTICULAR MOMENT WHEN YOU THOUGHT YOU HAD BECOME AN AMERICAN AS OPPOSED TO BEING RUSSIAN OR EVEN RUSSIAN-AMERICAN?

Yes, when I went back to Belarus, I really felt American. I was very conscious of the lack of freedom there, this feeling that you can just become anything. I can be anything. I can say anything. Wherever I go, whenever I'm on a plane flying back to America, I feel so happy to be an American.

Q: I KNOW IMMIGRATION WAS A HARD JOURNEY. IF YOU HAD THE OPTION TO, WOULD YOU MAKE THE SAME CHOICE TO COME TO THE U.S.?

Yes, absolutely.

Q: DO YOU HAVE ANY ADVICE FOR CHILDREN WHO MIGHT BE GOING THROUGH IMMIGRATION RIGHT NOW?

Be strong and fight hard because things will get better and better. Always have hope and never give up hope, even though the situation may seem hopeless. Take it one day at a time. ■

REUVEN KIGEL

NOW

My name is Reuven Kigel, and I'm 48 years old. I live in Passaic, New Jersey, with my wife, Devorah, and four children, aged 20, 18, 16, and 14. I am a religiously observant Jew but was not born that way. I started my career trading stocks on Wall Street, and after a few other stops along the way, I attended yeshiva in my mid-30s and now work as a college campus rabbi.

Q: HOW OLD WERE YOU WHEN YOU IMMIGRATED TO THE UNITED STATES?

I was five and a half.

Q: CAN YOU TELL ME A BIT ABOUT YOUR FAMILY BACK IN THE U.S.S.R.? WHERE DID YOU LIVE? WHAT DID YOUR PARENTS DO?

We lived in Kiev, Ukraine, and both my parents were engineers, perhaps typical for Jewish Russians. We lived in a two-bedroom—actually, it was two rooms, not two bedrooms—plus a kitchen, with my parents and my maternal grandparents, so five of us. It was very small quarters. No one had any money, so we also had no money. We didn't have a car. My father was the worst communist ever. So the first chance we had to get out was in 1978, and that's when we left. I was five and a half years old at the time, so I was definitely going along for the ride.

Q: I KNOW FIVE YEARS OLD IS PRETTY YOUNG, BUT DO YOU HAVE ANY VIVID MEMORIES OF WHAT THE OLD COUNTRY WAS LIKE? WERE YOU AWARE OF ANY PROBLEMS, OR DID YOUR PARENTS SHIELD YOU FROM THEM?

I was completely aware of everything that a five-and-a-half-year-old should be aware of, which is not everything. I had not started school yet because first grade started at six, and then they didn't have kindergarten or anything like that. So I hung out with the kids in the neighborhood. I was a kid, and I made good friends, and that was it. There are still pictures that we have of me with them. I was not aware of any problems whatsoever. It just didn't come up. And my parents definitely didn't want me to tell everyone that we were going to America. But it was clear that we were going somewhere, so they told me we were going to Yalta, which is a vacation area inside the Soviet Union. Later, I believed we were moving somewhere, but I had no real understanding of America.

Q: DID YOUR GRANDPARENTS COME WITH YOU OR WAS IT JUST YOUR PARENTS?

My grandparents on my mother's side, with whom we lived, were about a month behind us in the immigration process. So by the time we were leaving, we had a pretty good idea that they were also leaving because they already had their papers.

Q: DO YOU REMEMBER ANY ISSUES WITH ANTI-SEMITISM?

No. I was completely aware of everything that was going on, but I was five years old. I'm just saying it was so I was aware of what a five-year-old is supposed to be aware of. But I didn't go to school, so I didn't see much. So I had zero awareness of any anti-Semitism.

Q: WHAT WAS YOUR IMMIGRATION JOURNEY LIKE? DID YOU STOP IN VIENNA OR ITALY?

Yes, we started off with Vienna for nine days, and I vividly remember eating hot dogs and drinking Sunkist. In Russia, I did not want to eat anything. I was forced to eat food that tasted like *mannaya kasha,* which is like bland cream of wheat or cottage cheese. Then we got to Vienna, and in the park, I had some hot dogs and Sunkist, and I said, "Oh, I like this." The three of us stayed in a tiny little hotel apartment for nine days. I remember my father was trying to speak Yiddish to everybody during that time because it's similar to the German language.

Q: WHAT HAPPENED AFTER VIENNA?

After Vienna, we went to Italy. We started in Rome, in a hotel packed with lots of other Russian immigrants. Shortly after, we moved to a little town called Ladispoli, a suburb of Rome, and we shared an apartment with another family. We had one room in this apartment, and I was in the same room as my parents. The other family was a very nice family, and we are still friendly with them today. I remember there was a park across the street that I used to go to and play in. I think I picked up a few words of Italian, but we knew we weren't staying, so I didn't take the time to learn it. I was hanging out mostly with other Russian kids who were immigrating.

Q: ARE THERE ANY SPECIFIC MEMORIES THAT REALLY STAND OUT TO YOU FROM THAT TIME?

I remember the whole family getting together for my father's 30th birthday party, which we celebrated in June 1978. It's amazing for me to think about how young and mature he was to take this immigration step at that age. I have distinct memories of the people we lived with. There was a 16-year-old that would take me around. I remember almost getting hit by a bus, and I remember getting lost in a flea market. My memories are regular memories of a five-year-old.

Q: HOW LONG WERE YOU IN ITALY?

Three months.

Q: AND AFTER THOSE THREE MONTHS, DID YOU PACK UP AND MOVE TO THE U.S.?

Yes, we arrived in the U.S. on July 12, 1978. We were greeted by one of my parents' friends who had gotten here a few years before us, and he took us to New Jersey, where we had some relatives. Also, my mom didn't really want to do the whole "Brooklyn thing." We went through HIAS, the Hebrew Immigrant Aid Society, and we landed in a pretty bad neighborhood called East Orange. Our whole building was full of Russian immigrants. I just started playing with the kids there, including some of whom I had met in Italy during the journey. I also started learning English by watching television.

Q: WERE YOUR PARENTS ABLE TO PICK UP THEIR JOBS AS ENGINEERS, OR DID THEY HAVE TO WORK IN A DIFFERENT FIELD?

My mom actually spoke English because back in Kiev, she had gone to a school where they learned English, Russian, and Ukrainian. So she was pretty much fluent, certainly extremely proficient. She very quickly got a job as a chemical engineer, and my father pretty much right away started working as a mechanical engineer. He may have spent a couple of months working at a supermarket for a relative, but that was not the best fit for him.

So my parents got jobs in their field, and then we had to move out of the subsidized housing and moved to a place called Irvington, New Jersey.

Q: WAS THERE ANYTHING ABOUT THOSE FIRST FEW MONTHS THAT STANDS OUT?

Because we had spent three months in Europe, it wasn't a complete culture shock. Since Europe is Western, America felt much more familiar by the time we got there.

But I had my circumcision at age five years—not days—so that's something quite memorable.

Brooklyn, 1980. Reuven (then known as Steve) is in the upper right with fellow Russian immigrants.

Q: HOW WAS THE START OF SCHOOL FOR YOU?

So first, I was only hanging out with Russian speakers before I started school. We were all learning English at the time. At the time, we were living in Irvington, New Jersey, a tough neighborhood. I started at a Jewish school, a modern Orthodox day school. The biggest advantage I had compared to other immigrants that you are profiling is that I was young. I started school in kindergarten, so no one was "ahead of me." Nothing was going on. We were all learning the ABCs still. There was only one tier of Hebrew because even the American kids didn't know any Hebrew. There were two tiers of English, so I was in the lower tier, but my teacher moved me up after a month.

Q: DID YOU EVER FEEL LIKE SOMETHING WAS MARKING YOU AS DIFFERENT FROM ALL THE OTHER KIDS?

Well, this is sort of funny now. My father didn't like sneakers at that time. So he wanted me to wear shoes or sandals, which was not the first choice of footwear for American kindergarten boys. So there were a couple of rough days. I wasn't bullied, but they were giving me a hard time about wearing sandals. So I came home and announced that I could not wear them anymore. There were a couple of Russian immigrants in the school with me—a handful, but just enough.

Q: SINCE YOUR SCHOOL WAS A YESHIVA, WAS THERE A DISCONNECT BETWEEN WHAT YOU LEARNED AT SCHOOL AND YOUR HOME LIFE?

I remember the tour of the school, and I kept hearing the words kosher. I didn't know much about it, and it sounded like the Russian word "koshka" (meaning cat). So I was thinking that maybe they were going to feed us cat food because they kept saying kosher, and to me it sounded like "koshka." So when I got home, I told my parents, and they told me no, that "kosher just means fresh." The other thing was that my parents grew up in a society where they told them communist propaganda in school, and then they came home, and their parents tried to undo it. But it's one thing to do that when you're a teenager or even 10 years old, but when you're five or six, kids are excited to learn. So my mom made a commitment, about which I only found out later, that whatever I learned in school she would allow it to pass and say things like "Oh, that's wonderful!" or the like. So when I came home and talked about Shabbat or Jewish holidays or God, she didn't contradict it (as she might have done in the U.S.S.R.) but just said, "Oh, that's not what we do, but it's nice that you're learning it." It was very neutral and accepting.

After second grade, we moved out of Irvington, New Jersey, and into a neighborhood in Millburn, New Jersey, with a good public school system. Then, in third grade, I started going to public school.

Q: HOW RUSSIAN DID YOU FEEL DURING THIS TIME?

By the time I went to third grade, I felt completely acclimated as an American. And unless I would say it, no one would have any idea that I had come from Russia three years earlier.

Maybe the most Russian thing I did growing up was going to the "bungalow colonies" in the Catskills from fifth to ninth grade. A lot of Russian immigrant families would send their kids there with grandparents (with parents visiting on weekends). It was like camp, with sports, swimming, and grandmas chasing us to eat lunch. Besides that, my Russian influence was not significant. I didn't have any siblings, I didn't have any Russian friends, and there were barely any Russian kids around me (maybe two or three out of several hundred in high school).

Q: WERE YOUR EXPERIENCES IN SCHOOL EVER MOTIVATED BY HOW HARD YOU SAW YOUR PARENTS WORK?

I don't think I saw my parents work hard, particularly. I thought they had white-collar nine-to-five jobs.

Q: TELL ME ABOUT LIFE AFTER SCHOOL. WHAT DID YOU DO AFTER YOU GRADUATED HIGH SCHOOL? HOW DID YOU BECOME RELIGIOUS?

I went to the University of Michigan after high school. We had a language requirement, so I decided to take Russian. I had already studied Spanish in high school and decided I wanted to learn how to read and write in Russian. After college, I started to work on the New York Stock Exchange.

But something happened when I was in college that transformed me. I got into a very bad car accident during my college years, which caused my father to start becoming religious. At that point, besides going to synagogue twice a year, I was doing nothing Jewish. I wasn't against it. I knew God existed. I just didn't think he wanted us to do anything besides having a good time. So when my father became religious, I basically thought he had gone insane. But when he handed me a copy of the Torah shortly after I graduated college, and I started reading it for myself, that's when I realized that God wrote this, and not a bunch of guys, which I had previously thought because of some secular classes. In college, I had taken philosophy classes, which covered the "great books," including the Bible, but from a secular perspective. So when I started reading the ArtScroll edition of the Torah, with commentaries, I decided that it would behoove me to do what it says. I saw that God wanted me to do something and thought it would be pretty fun.

I was 23. I knew I wanted to do what it said in the Torah, but I knew it wouldn't be overnight. I knew it was going to be a bit of a process, so I just started on the journey. It was easier because my father had already become religious, and my mom was not so far behind.

Q: LOOKING AT IT TODAY, WOULD YOU SAY THAT YOU'RE RUSSIAN-AMERICAN OR JUST AMERICAN?

I would say I'm a Jew living in America and very grateful to be living in America.

Someone may ask me where I'm from, and I'll say I'm from the former Soviet Union. In my job as a rabbi in the CUNY schools, that's useful, and most of the students have parents from Russia or that part of the world.

Q: HAVE YOU EVER GONE BACK TO THE FORMER U.S.S.R. TO VISIT?

No. I'm not necessarily planning on it, but I don't know where things will bring me.

Q: TELL ME ABOUT YOUR NAME. I UNDERSTAND YOU HAVE USED SEVERAL NAMES. WHAT WAS THAT ABOUT?

My Russian name is actually Slava. So when I started kindergarten in 1978, during the height of the Cold War, people recommended that I not go to school with a name like Slava. So I was trying to figure out what to do and what kind of English name to pick. I was watching a lot of TV at that point. I was watching this absolutely ridiculous show called *The Six Million Dollar Man*, where the main character was called Steve Austin. So I picked that name for myself, and I really went by Steve I until I started working as a rabbi 13 years ago. So for 30 years, I went by Steve, and people that knew me by that name will probably still call me that. Now I go by Reuven, which is my Jewish name.

Q: HOW DID YOU MEET YOUR WIFE?

I met my wife at a synagogue on the Upper West Side of Manhattan, a place called Aish HaTorah, at 83rd Street and West End Avenue. We met one night after Shabbat services, and then we got married about five months later.

Q: DO YOU THINK YOU HAVE PASSED DOWN RUSSIAN VALUES TO YOUR KIDS? OR IS IT MORE OF AN AMERICANIZED EXPERIENCE THEY ARE GETTING?

Definitely some old-school Russian values. Not everything that kids do is OK. I have teenagers, and I know it's easier to say that whatever you want is OK. My wife is American, but she was very much on board with us giving the kids more of a Russian-style parenting experience. We are raising our kids in the religious Jewish way as well. Luckily I had no negative experiences that many other Russian immigrants had. Obviously, people have their normal ups and downs; that's part of life. I had those, but that was not because I was Russian or Jewish. And most importantly, coming to America enabled us to have religious freedom, and I was able to freely choose—as an adult—to be an Orthodox Jew. Only in America! ■

SVETLANA GITMAN

This Is Better Than Disneyworld

NOW

Svetlana Gitman, age 34, lives in Chicago with a long-term partner. She is an attorney and alternative dispute resolution professional.

My immigrant story could have been completely different. When my parents were married in 1977 in Kharkov, Ukraine, they were gifted a visa to the U.S. by one of their friends who had won it in a diversity lotto. My mother tells me that my grandfather (her father) told her it was out of the question—they could not go. My grandfather feared that he would be thrown in jail, or worse, if my mother left for the United States. My mother was 20 years old, risk averse, and she loved her father. And as a result, our journey to the United States would not start until 16 years later.

My father's younger brother immigrated to the United States in the early 1990s, and when my father came to visit him, he learned that all the propaganda he had been fed about America all his life was false and America was a land of opportunity. In 1993 my family was granted refugee status by the United States government and given an opportunity to relocate permanently with help from the Hebrew Immigrant Aid Society. My paternal grandparents, parents, sister, and

I boarded a plane in Moscow on November 16, 1993, with a couple of suitcases. The five of us had never been outside of Eastern Europe and had no idea what to expect. We landed in Chicago, Illinois, and my father (age 41) and mother (age 36) started rebuilding our lives.

Svetlana and her sister at a park in Kharkov, Ukraine, in 1990. One of the rare photographs where we are not wearing matching sweatsuits.

When I was a teenager, I lamented my parents' decision to wait almost 20 years to finally move to the United States. I've made endless lists of ways our lives could have been easier if they had just left in 1977. My parents could have been educated here and had wonderful job opportunities. My sister and I could have been born here. My parents could have formed a strong foundation and would not have had to work multiple jobs throughout most of our childhood to provide us with the basics. Those that know me well know that I truly believe that everything happens for a reason. I often tell myself and others that everything happens for a reason, even though you may not know the reason for years (or decades) down the road. I'm glad my parents included me in our immigration story. If I were born in the United States, I would never appreciate the opportunities this country has given me nor the sacrifices of my parents. I grew up being envious of others for having parents with job connections or wealth that would ensure their kids never had to understand what student debt felt like. However, now

Family photo from Ukraine, circa 1991.

I'm grateful for the path my parents carved for me because it's given me something invaluable. I am an independent, self-sufficient, self-made woman who can do anything I put my mind to. In other words, I am grateful for the hardships we experienced in our early immigration days because they've ultimately enriched our lives in ways I could not have predicted.

THE PROMISED LAND

My family spent hours in front of the television when I was young. Since I was the younger sibling, I was also the television remote control. Back then, our black and white television had a turn dial, and because I was the most gullible one, I was always expected to change the channel on command. Our computer was similarly pre-historic. I think the only capability it had was to play a Tetris-like game.

As a family, we loved (and still love) watching television. One of our favorite shows was about life in America. I remember seeing an episode about Halloween and thinking it was kind of creepy that there were skeletons everywhere, but also really cool that kids would get a lot of candy. My father joked that we could just hang me on the door as decoration because when I was six, I did not eat a lot (I wish I could say the same now) and looked almost skeletal. The other program that left a lasting impression was a special about Disneyworld. I was mesmerized by the teacup ride. I had to ride them. When our visa documents were ready, and we started packing for our move to the U.S., my parents told me that we were moving so that I could go to Disneyworld. Sold! I had no qualms about moving to America. I was going to get to ride the teacups!

When we landed in Chicago, Illinois, I realized I had been duped. This was definitely not Disneyworld. However, a place called Jewel-Osco (similar to Fred Meyer, Kroger, Marianos or any generic big grocery store) was just as magical. It was enormous, and there was food everywhere. The shelves were constantly full, and there were at least 10 different types of cookies and a whole aisle dedicated to candy. Best of all, you could go into these stores whenever you wanted. You never had to line up early in the morning and stand in line to get in. I can still remember (more than 30 years later) standing in long lines with my mother back in Ukraine to get bread on certain days of the week. I mostly remember this because I inevitably always had to go to the bathroom and remember my mother screaming at me to hold it in because there was no way we could leave the line if we wanted bread or milk that week. Forget Disneyworld. American grocery stores were totally worth the move.

It was strange to me how easily you could buy food in this new world. The way we paid for food was even stranger. I don't remember using currency in Ukraine. I can only remember using "coupons." I remember them looking very similar to paper tickets, and they were valued by their weight. Joking aside, and sarcasm de-emphasized, the store clerks would literally throw all the coupons you brought onto a scale and determine the total value based on the weight. It was just like going to Chuck E. Cheese or any arcade as a kid. You bring all the tickets you received to the person behind the counter, and they weigh them, and then you pick the polyester giant stuffed animal of your choice that matches the value of those tickets. I guess here in America, we would use green bills with faces of dead presidents instead. Luckily we did not have to cart them in plastic bags. Each green bill seemed to have a significant value, so you just used a few at a time.

I was also confused why everything we bought was purchased at indoor markets rather than outdoor markets. In America, not only did you have to buy food indoors, the food had pre-set, non-negotiable prices. In Kharkov, most of our food was purchased in outdoor markets, where we got to offer the seller an opportunity to get our business by telling the seller how much we were willing to pay, otherwise known as bartering. You had to do a special dance where you ask how much, the seller gives you a price, you act like it's outrageous and start to walk away. When you've taken about five steps, the seller yells another price at you. You stop and shake your head for a while, then roll your eyes, and then begrudgingly finally accept. Those who have a lot of time repeat this dance routine a few times to negotiate the most favorable agreement. I still don't fully understand why I can't go to Costco and suggest an alternative price to the $4.99 rotisserie chicken they have, but whatever. To this day, Abt appliance store in Glenview, Illinois, is my family's favorite because bartering is allowed. Abt—you get us!

I know I've left a huge unanswered question. Did my parents ever take me to Disneyworld? No—at least not right away. For my 26th birthday, I gave my parents the opportunity to clear their names. And so I finally went to Disneyworld and got to ride the teacups. I was the only adult in line unaccompanied by a child and also sat in a teacup by myself. My mother and sister were too embarrassed to accompany me. It might have been the Mickey Mouse shirt I was wearing, the giant birthday pin I proudly displayed on my chest, or the ice cream stains all over my clothes from the free ice cream sundae I got since it was my birthday. I really didn't care to be honest. My father wasn't able to make the trip because, like always, he was working. But my sister videotaped it and sent him the clip, and so I hope he felt the same joy I felt that things finally came full circle, and he was able to make good on his promise, even if it took 20 years.

MONKEY, ELEPHANT, TOILET: THE EARLY DAYS IN THE U.S.

A few days after we arrived in America and went through days of immunizations at the local Jewish Community Center, it was time for me to start school. I turned seven years old ten days after we arrived in America, which meant I would be in first grade. I had gone to school for a few months in Ukraine before we left. My memories of school in Ukraine were very intense. You were graded on a scale of one to five, but anything below five was the equivalent of failing and would bring shame on your family (or at least that is what your parents told you). Your whole life was determined by how successful you were in school. So my parents took the same approach to our education here in America.

Step one was for me to learn English. My sister had a private tutor in Ukraine who taught her English. My parents also took some lessons before we left. I knew zero English except for universal words like Barbie or Mickey Mouse. My parents prepared me for my first day of first grade by teaching me three essential (in their minds) words: toilet, monkey, and elephant. The first I understood because it was necessary for survival, and I did not want any accidents that brought shame on my family. The other two, monkey and elephant, were most likely misguided attempts to make me seem normal to the other kids. My parents didn't realize that the most common question kids asked me was for my name. So those three words were my only choices for a response. None of them were good options, but luckily my family moved the following school year, and by that time, I knew enough English that kids at my new school could call me by my real name.

Although I learned to speak English rather quickly through the help of *Full House* and *Married With Children* (clearly my parents' level of English comprehension was questionable because anyone who has seen *Married With Children* knows it is not kid-appropriate). I do remember some hiccups. For example, learning about the "silent h." I volunteered to read out loud during one reading lesson, and the whole class roared in laughter when I kept pronouncing the "h" in the word *honestly* and then mistakenly not pronouncing the "h" when I read "one hundred," which sounded like "one undred." So confusing. What is the purpose of using letters if you do not plan to pronounce them? Are they there just for show? That just seemed unnecessarily tricky and silly. Luckily as a seven-year-old, I quickly memorized the correct pronunciation of words and words with the infamous "silent h." But really, why is the English language so confusing? Even decades later, when my parents would regularly call me to ask how to spell something correctly, I would still feel for them and have flashbacks of that loud laughter from the day I read about the honest rabbit that ate one hundred carrots.

While I've forgiven my parents for the English words they chose to teach me, I have yet to forgive them for my wardrobe in those days. Even the teachers were speechless when they saw my huge animal fur hat the first day of winter when my parents made me wear it so I wouldn't catch pneumonia and die. *Side note*: I had pneumonia as a child, and I did not die. Those two do not have an absolute relationship like my parents told me, and their parents told them. The hat probably weighed more than I did at the time. But my parents didn't care. They were probably so traumatized from their own experiences with the Soviet healthcare system that they would rather have me go to school looking like the offspring of Smokey the Bear. My mother, to this day, still wants to buy me a norkavaya shuba (fur coat), with a hood, of course, every winter. The idea of riding the Chicago public transit system in one of those beauties makes me crack up every time I think about it and also brings back memories of the look of shock on those teachers' faces.

Making me look cool was not one of my mother's talents. Packing "kid-friendly" lunches was also a giant fail. It was a hard sell getting a seven-year-old to agree to trade their peanut butter and jelly sandwich for my caviar butter sandwich. Kids also did not care for *katleti* (Russian hamburgers made from ground chicken or beef), cold hard-boiled eggs, containers of sour cream (don't ask), or dill pickles. These foods that I hated as a child, I now crave all the time and feel a sense of comfort when my mother makes them. Also, to date, I still have never had a peanut butter and jelly sandwich. Now that I think about it, that combination sounds disgusting, and caviar butter sandwiches are amazing. I'm glad I never gave them away. It would have been a terrible trade from an economic perspective since caviar is way more expensive than peanut butter and jelly (that is the Jewish in me talking).

My parents also never explained to me why I don't have a middle name. I tried on my own to explain what a patronymic is, but that only made me stranger than my caviar butter sandwiches. What's so hard to understand about people calling you by the "feminine version of your father's first name"? Oh yeah, that's totally normal—or as Borat would say—NOT!

I'm not sure I cared that much back then that kids thought I was weird, mostly because I wasn't too impressed with my classmates. I still remember entering my first-grade classroom on that first day of school. I expected to find a group of well-behaved children sitting upright in their chairs with their hands folded in front of them and their mouths completely shut. You know, the Soviet way. I was horrified when I walked in and saw twenty or so seven-year-olds spread out around the room talking at the same time. I was mortified that some were actually sprawled out on the floor as if they were watching television at home. That would have never happened back home. What was this uncivilized place I was thrown into? I remember thinking for a brief moment that my parents had lied to me and taken me to an orphanage. That is a common Soviet parental threat (or at least I thought so). If you do not behave, we will give you away to an orphanage full of other misbehaved children. Well, here I was. They had finally made good on their promise. It must have been because I didn't again make my bed that morning.

My teacher, who I now thought was more of a warden, introduced me to the class, and all the kids waved their hands at me. I remember that calmed me down, but that didn't last long because soon thereafter, we all were told to sit at our desks and that we would have a math quiz. Oh no. I hate math. I seriously became an attorney so that I would never have to do math. The papers were passed out face down as this was going to be a timed quiz. We were supposed to answer as many questions as we could before the teacher said, "Time's up." Anxiety kicked in full speed. Oh no! I left my first-grade class in Ukraine right before we got to long division. Now all these Americans would see how stupid I am. And then the teacher screamed, "Ready, set, go," and I turned over the paper. What I saw mortified me more than my fear of not remembering how to do long division. What I saw was horizontal rows of simple addition and subtraction problems like 2+4 and 7-1.

Not only did my parents send me away to an orphanage, but the orphanage thought I needed special education. The kids even had calculators for simple addition and subtraction. I remember wondering if the teacher would give each of us an abacus. You know the rows of movable beads strung on a wire that represents digits. If you know how to use it, it really can be faster than a calculator. As an adult, I once went to an antique shop and found a beautiful dark brown wooden abacus. I got emotional seeing it and immediately asked the owner how much it costs. He told me $25, but I would first have to teach him how to use it. I remember trying to explain to him that this particular abacus was more of a pocket calculator rather than a TI-83 graphing calculator, but at that point, he lost me and told me just to give him $20, take the abacus, and leave. What is most humorous is that I proudly display it on my coffee table for all to see, and most of my friends think it's some kind of fancy coaster for hot dishes.

That first day of school was the only time in my life that I thought school (or math) would be easy. Regardless of how I felt toward the

American education system, I only had one choice when it came to education—do well or you will bring shame on the family. One quintessential characteristic of the Jewish culture is the value placed on education. To the Jewish people, you can be poor, but you cannot be uneducated. That was pretty much the standard my sister and I were held to throughout school. "Why did you get 99 percent and not 100 percent?" Or, "If you're not going to get an A in pre-calculus, you can go bag groceries. You don't need to go to college." When I used to hear my father say something like this, I would throw my hands in the air and leave the room mad. Now that I think about it as an adult, he was totally right. It's clear I knew the material, so why make a silly mistake and get 99 percent when I could have been more careful and received a perfect score. I might be saying this because I've turned into my father. I still have to remember not to hold others to this unreasonably high standard, mostly because I want to have friends and be liked. Spoiler alert: Although I haven't taken a math class since high school, I did not pursue a career in the grocery industry. I became a boring lawyer instead, and my sister is a medical doctor. My parents earned PhDs in reverse psychology and master's degrees in Jewish guilt.

My first-grade class photo (1993). I am front and center, directly in front of the teacher.

OUR AWKWARD IS MY NORMAL: MY TEENAGE YEARS

One would think that because I was so young when my family moved here, my teenage years must have been really normal because I was accustomed to American society by then. Sure, that sounds logical. But when your first name is Svetlana, it's kind of a dead giveaway that you are not the typical American. My peers certainly did not think that I was one of them. Anytime we talked about the Soviet Union or communism in my high school history classes, kids often made disparaging comments and then gave me a look of "I'm so sorry to say this. Please don't hurt me." I always looked back at them with the kind of stare that suggested that a man named Boris would soon come to their home, knock on their door, and they will never see their family again. I gave them this stare not because their comments were harsh but because they were ignorant to think that everyone from the former Soviet Union was a communist or secret spy.

It wasn't just the kids who said crazy things. One of my history teachers corrected my pronunciation of Mikhail Gorbachev. I get it. I was six when I left Ukraine, so maybe I speak with an accent, but my teacher was American and did not speak any Russian, so I was thoroughly confused about why or how he knew how to pronounce Gorbachev's name correctly. I think I also gave him the "You will never see your family again" look because he never corrected anything else I said that semester.

Luckily I did have some Russian friends in high school who similarly had their own immigration stories so they could relate. It was normal for me to come home and find one of my friend's cars in the driveway and my friend hanging out inside with my father. My father would say, "Oh, I ran into her in the store, so I invited her over for some selyodka (herring)."

My inner dialogue would always say, "Oh, sure, who could pass up an invite to eat some disgusting smelling fish with a crazy man."

I also used to get texts from friends that they ran into my parents at a Russian restaurant. I'd always respond with, "Well, did they at least say hi?" hoping that they weren't too intoxicated and somewhat polite.

"Oh yeah, of course," my friends would respond. "They even invited me to the table for some shots and herring."

"Okay," I thought to myself. "They acted somewhat civilized."

Speaking of uncivilized. The most uncivilized idea I ever suggested to my parents was (drumroll please) sleepovers. First, they didn't understand why I wanted to sleep on the floor of someone's basement in a large puffy pillowcase with a half dozen other teenagers. When put in perspective, their confusion makes sense. Why would I want to sleep on the floor when I had a comfortable bed? They had to sleep on the floor out of necessity. To this day, my mother still hates the idea of spending the night at my home or anywhere outside her bed. (Except five-star all-inclusive Caribbean resorts. She loves the idea of sleeping in those beds.)

I know every teenager thinks her parents are embarrassing. To some extent, that's true. But my parents were a different type of embarrassing because they actually weren't embarrassing at all. They were amazing and hilarious, but I was just too young to appreciate it. Random memories from my teenage years pop into my head, and I can't help but laugh out loud (usually in a public place, during inappropriate times). For example, I recall once having friends over after school for dinner. Fidel Castro was on the news that night, most likely not because of his humanitarian spirit and commitment to human rights. My father thought it was appropriate to tell my friends how excited he was when Fidel Castro came to the U.S.S.R. when he was young. He told my friends about how he gathered with his friends in front of the one television set in the apartment building his family lived in. He also proudly divulged the fact that he fanatically waved Cuban flags in excitement. Some of those friends never came over for dinner again. Their loss. My mother is a great cook. That alone was worth listening to any of my father's colorful stories.

Those of my friends who weren't scared off by my father's stories loved coming over because of my mother's cooking. My friends were not the only ones who loved my mother's cooking. In fact, anytime I traveled anywhere within a 25-mile radius of my parents' friends, I always had to bring something my mother made. When I decided to attend the University of Minnesota in Minneapolis, that meant I would be living very close to my father's good friend, Captain (or at least that's what I call him). When I came to campus for orientation, Captain requested I bring my mother's dill pickles. That wouldn't have been my first choice, but no problem. My mother prepared a two-liter glass jar of the most pungent-smelling fermented pickles and haphazardly wrapped the jar in saran wrap and put it in a Victoria's Secret bag for me. My father told me to just carry them onto the plane and not to worry because, you know, my mother sealed the pickle jar airtight. It's spillproof. I boarded the plane with the jar of pickles, soaked in pickle juice (TSA restrictions about liquids were much more relaxed in 2005), and put the jar in the overhead compartment above my seat. About 20 minutes into the flight, the passengers around me started to make a sour face, as if the smell of saltwater, dill, and garlic was suffocating them. I knew exactly what had happened but pretended like I was equally disgusted. I probably even commented on the awful smell and the insensitive person who brought smelly food onto the plane.

When we landed, I had decided that I would leave the jar in the overhead compartment and book it off the plane. I was way too embarrassed to claim them in front of all the passengers. I planned to tell Captain that airport security had taken the pickles away from me. But then I heard a passenger say, "Oh, there's a name on the bag—S. Gitman." Damn it. My mother labels everything, including my food! She clearly thought that by writing my name on my food, others would be too fearful to take it. That rationale might have worked with my bananas when I was eight years old, but I don't think this stops adults. And in my current situation, it actually incriminated me. I grabbed the bag quickly and sprinted off the plane. I never flew Northwest Airlines again. I will always wonder if the great pickle disaster of 2005 eventually led to NWA's demise and eventual absorption by Delta Airlines a few years later.

NORMAL IS RELATIVE: MY ADULT YEARS

Another aspect of my upbringing that I never understood was why my parents went out of their way to do EVERYTHING for my sister and me. They never wanted my sister or me to do something by ourselves or feel like we were alone. They insisted on always driving us to the airport before a trip, even when it was a work trip, and we were getting reimbursed for the taxi or when it was completely out of the way. It was not uncommon for my father to drive two hours in rush hour traffic to drive me somewhere instead of putting me on a train and letting me take public transport. That's just the way it was. So I wasn't surprised when my father insisted on taking me to Minnesota so he could personally drop me off at college. My dorm mates and roommate were surprised because my father also brought up a giant case of fine spirits and wines and left it with us. He said he didn't want us to drink "bad stuff" and get sick. He also gave me one piece of final advice for surviving in college (or maybe in life in general) that I will never forget. It's ingrained in my mind not because it was so sentimental or profound but because it was hilarious and amazing. He said, "Eat soup every day," hugged me, and left my dorm to go see Captain (and probably eat smelly pickles). He had either sampled all those fine spirits before dropping them off, or he was passing on some more of that Russian craziness like, "Don't open the window because the draft will make you catch pneumonia, and then you die." I ate soup almost every day. (It turns out to be a fantastic cure for hangovers.) I credit my father for my survival in college and life in general.

Photo from my graduation from the University of Minnesota-Twin Cities, 2008.

BACK TO THE U.S.S.R.

In 2013, my sister and I surprised my parents on our 20th anniversary in America. We decided we would take them on a trip back to where we came from. I called it our "Back to the U.S.S.R." tour. I crafted two very realistic-looking airplane tickets. When I presented them to my parents, it was a mix of excitement when they saw handmade airplane tickets, quickly followed by a look of fear and the following words: "You're taking us back? Why?! We spent so many years trying to get out. We don't want to go back!" Not exactly the reaction I expected, but we quickly pivoted and decided that a Northern European cruise was better. To keep with the spirit of a homecoming, we selected a route that stopped for two days in St. Petersburg, Russia, where a wonderful guide showed us around and made us fall in love with the city.

It didn't take long for me to pick up on the cultural differences and get a taste of real Russian customer service. We stopped at a bakery for lunch to get some *piroshki* (dough filled with meat/vegetables of your choice). We must have stopped after the lunch rush because the options behind the counter looked slim. In her polite and eloquent Russian, my sister asked the woman at the counter what flavors they had this afternoon.

The teller responded with, "Do you have eyes? Can you see? Those are your options." My sister was mortified at the response, as in how dare someone speak like this to a customer.

She turned to me to share her outrage, but I was hysterically laughing. Once I caught my breath, I turned to her and said, "We're in their country. Pick your *piroshok* while she's still willing to serve us." She looked disgusted and left me up there to order. I think back to my response now—we are in their country—and it reminds me of the constant dichotomy I feel in my identity. When I am traveling abroad, locals often ask me where I am from. I can understand the confusion. I'm usually traveling with my mother and speaking Russian with her but English to others. When those locals ask me about my origins, I always respond that I am American, from the United States. I usually don't say I am Russian unless asked by a Russian person since Russians can sense each other from miles away, pretty much like echolocation. My reasoning is that since I have spent most of my life in the U.S., it's more accurate to describe myself as American. However, when I meet someone new in my daily life in Chicago, and they ask me where I am from (as in what city or state in the U.S.), I always make it a point to tell them that I was not born in the U.S. I don't know why I do this. The only explanation I can think of is that I want to let people know right away that I'm not the typical American, in case my super-common first name doesn't give that away. I still don't know how to define myself. I'm American when it comes to the clothes I wear, the news I read, or my belief in free speech. But I'm definitely Russian when it comes to empathy (or lack thereof), my love of raw and pickled vegetables or my disgust at splitting bills. (I'll get it this time. You can pick up the tab next time.) I also swear in Russian. It just sounds much more serious. So overall, what does that make me?

HIDDEN LESSONS FOR THE ETERNAL STUDENT

When I was growing up, it was hard to watch other kids go to sleepaway camp, get new cars, and have their college educations paid for. It made me wish that my parents used that visa in 1977 and came to the U.S. then. Today, I'm extremely grateful that I got to experience this journey with my parents. If my parents moved here in the 1970s, I would have little appreciation for most things in my life. Most importantly, I would not know how to love my parents as much as I do now. A lot of my friends think it's bizarre that I would rather hang out with my parents (over my friends) any day of the week. But those friends that know my parents get it and often ask if they are free to come along when they invite me somewhere.

While it seems like the pickle incident of 2005 might have been the worst moment of my life, the worst moment of my life was when my father unexpectedly passed away in 2020. Soon after his death, one of my colleagues sent me a note sharing that she felt my pain and was going through the same thing. She told me that she had lost grandparents, best friends, and a soul mate, but losing a parent was the worst heartache she has ever felt. I think she is right. I always feared the day I'd lose a parent because I truly believe I have the best parents in the world. Somebody once asked me if I could know one thing about the future, what it would be. I responded that I would want to know how much time I had left with my parents. My parents taught me so much throughout our unique journey together, but what I've come to realize is that they never taught me how to be without them. I don't mean it in the sense that they never told me practically what to do when they passed away. What I mean is, they never told me how to fill the emptiness I would feel without them.

Even in my father's untimely death, he found a way to teach me one final lesson, almost as good as the soup lesson. My father taught me that nothing is forever. My father was victorious in everything he did. He got his family out of the Soviet Union and rebuilt a beautiful life for them, raised two successful daughters, bought a beautiful home, battled a very aggressive cancer like a champion, and became a friend and confidant to everyone he met. Even in the toughest times, my father always stressed that you always have to keep fighting no matter what. Those were the same words I said to him when allowed to see him at the hospital a few days before he passed away. I didn't and couldn't say goodbye, mostly because I couldn't comprehend the idea that he would leave me.

A piece of me died the moment my father died. My biggest fear was that I would forget all the amazing memories we shared. So I started keeping a journal where each day I write down a funny memory or quote. In this way, it feels as though he hasn't left because I picture him laughing just as hard as I do at the collection of hilarious stories and quotes I've compiled. My absolute favorite memory is from sometime around 2013 when my cousin (my father's cousin's daughter) came to visit us. My cousin is also my best friend (even though I did not meet her until I was 21 years old since her family left for Los Angeles via Italy when I was a baby). My father had friends over while my cousin was visiting. These were his childhood friends from Zhytomyr, Ukraine. They had also immigrated to the United States in the early 1990s. My father was telling my cousin that, at some point in history, my father's family and my cousin's family lived in the same two-bedroom apartment. My cousin was confused about how so many people could live in a two-bedroom apartment. She was specifically confused about how a dozen people could share one bathroom. The room erupted in laughter when she asked that question. When my cousin asked what was so funny, my father responded,

Photo from a family trip to Lake Geneva, Wisconsin, in 2016, taken at a restaurant where each guest was asked to wear a hat they could choose from a collection. My dad couldn't help himself.

"That you think we had indoor plumbing!" That's how I choose to remember my father, with a smirk on his face, lots of wit, and a great punch line.

My father could diffuse any tense situation with his humor. Although I am not as funny as my father, my father designated me as the defacto toastmaster at every gathering. That meant that I would be responsible for giving the first toast. In my family, you do not start eating until you raise a glass and toast. It doesn't matter what you are toasting to. It doesn't have to be anything monumental like a birthday or an anniversary. Getting a new pair of shoes is enough to drink and celebrate. To say it was a lot of pressure to always give toasts would be untrue. While it was slightly stressful to always come up with new content, it wasn't actually stressful because everyone would cheer and drink no matter what I said. In that sense, it probably didn't matter at all what I said. In any event, our guests would most likely drink enough to forget even the most ridiculous toast.

HIAS

THE HEBREW IMMIGRANT AID SOCIETY
333 Seventh Avenue
New York, N.Y. 10001-5004
(212) 613-1323

STATEMENT OF ACCOUNT

DATE 2/09/94

CLIENT [illegible] MOISEY
CASE NO. [illegible]
NAME AND ADDRESS MOISEY GITMAN

DEPARTURE DATE [illegible]
CONVEYANCE [illegible]
DESTINATION [illegible] CHICAGO

I. COSTS

TRANSPORTATION — OVERSEAS 3,820.[illegible]
LOCAL
BAGGAGE
OTHER
TOTAL COSTS $ [illegible]

II PAYMENTS

PREPAYMENT
EXCESS BAGGAGE
REPAYMENT
TOTAL PAYMENTS $

III. BALANCE

AMOUNT DUE HIAS $ [illegible]
OR
REFUND DUE DEPOSITOR $

IMPORTANT NOTE
Your loan is a legal obligation. It is your responsibility to send in a payment each month. Make your check or money order payable to HIAS, and write your case number on your payment.
Thank you.

The statement of account issued to my grandfather by the Hebrew Immigrant Aid Society in 1994 covered the cost for the six of us to relocate to the United States. I didn't find this document until 2021, and it blows my mind that $3,820 changed the lives of six people (and our descendants) forever.

One particular Saturday night gathering with my parents' closest friends specifically stands out in my mind. I was in high school and unprepared when my dad signaled to me to give the toast. Unfortunately, I had nothing. No new shoes, celebration-worthy test scores, or Soviet holidays to celebrate. However, that day in my Russian Studies class, we watched a clip of Lenin giving a speech. I hadn't paid attention to the footage (cell phones just came out, so I was busy texting), but I did hear him say, "Study, study, study," in a very stern, powerful tone. And since my father was all about excelling at school, I figured I could work with this. So when my father gave me that "give the toast already, we want to eat" look, I proudly stood up and in Russian recited, "Study, study, study ... like the great Lenin said." None of my toasts before that day, or since, have been as random or such a tremendous hit. Now, as I forge forward on my immigration journey without my trusted guide, I continue to study, study, study (and learn, learn, learn) like the great Lenin (or Leonid Gitman) said. ■

ALEX KHUTORSKY

NOW

I am 49 years old, married with four children, two of whom are in college and two still in secondary school. After spending my entire adult life in the New York City metropolitan area, where I went to college and graduate school and worked as a lawyer and investment banker, I recently moved to Philadelphia. I am now an executive at a Fortune 500 company based in Delaware. I have no passions.

I was born in Kiev, Ukraine, in April 1971. My memories of that place and time are mostly loose, random fragments, at times joined together by context, but mostly not. My family—parents, brother, and toward the very end of our time in Kiev, a baby sister—lived in a nondescript housing project, probably five or six stories high, which contained within its small orbit practically my entire world. My maternal aunts, cousins, grandmother, and father's parents lived a short walk away. The children spent most of our time outside, playing in a courtyard that was transformed into a hockey rink every winter. My older brother Igor (now Gary), his friends, and I would explore the woods behind our home. It was not uncommon then to find in those woods spent shells or a Nazi helmet or some other relic of the Great Patriotic War, which had concluded only three decades prior. Remnants of that war were everywhere. Indeed, it's impossible to overstate the long shadow it cast over the Soviet Union. There wasn't a family in our acquaintance that didn't endure some great tragedy during the Second World War. My mother's father, a commissar in the Red Army, disappeared in action during the war's first days. And great uncles and aunts were swallowed up, soon thereafter, by the Holocaust. The war's memory was an ever-constant presence, more so than even the revolution itself.

Alex in the Soviet Union, circa 1974.

The second theme pervading my memories of the Soviet Union is a distinct sense of otherness, specifically Jewishness. Although I knew nothing of religion then, I cannot recall a time when I was not aware of my Jewishness. Jewishness was imposed upon us by others, but we also hung on to it for protection. Most of the friends, neighbors, and acquaintances in my life were Jewish. I assume this was a world deliberately constructed by my parents and those like them to help keep antisemitism's reach from encroaching onto their children's daily lives for as long as possible. And for the first six years of my life, it mostly worked. Of course, my parents have lots of first-hand accounts of antisemitism from their own lives, and some even from mine, but my memories of such incidents from the Soviet Union are few.

VIENNA AND ITALY

We left the Soviet Union on August 12, 1977. I remember very little of the days surrounding our departure, although I know they were hectic. Our most prized possessions, including a Czech-made cabinet and matching assorted furniture, were crated and removed, leaving our apartment mostly bare. Jewelry was carefully sewn into our coats to evade legal limits (which permitted taking away only one wedding ring and one piece of jewelry valued at less than 250 rubles per person. Many goodbyes must have been said, and many tears undoubtedly shed, although I remember none of that. A small contingent of family and friends accompanied us to the airport. Some would not come for fear of professional and personal repercussions. As my aunt learned soon after, such fear was justified when she was demoted from a senior position at the telephone company. My last memory of the Soviet Union is of my harried mother, being reassured by a kindly airline attendant that the airplane that was to take us out from behind the Iron Curtain would not leave us behind.

A few short hours later, we arrived in Vienna, Austria, less than 1,000 miles away, but a wholly different planet in every way that mattered. I have but a single memory of Vienna, of exiting the airport and immediately seeing two policemen standing guard, armed with machine guns. For whatever reason, and despite all the militarism of the Soviet Union, that image has stayed with me my entire life.

After only two days in Vienna, during which we never left our hotel, my family and I boarded a train to Rome. We could choose to settle in Italy or stay as long as it took to get a refugee visa to a handful of countries then welcoming Soviet Jews. At that time, those countries were Australia, Canada, and the United States (in addition to Italy). Of course, we could also immigrate to Israel, which stood then, as it does now, an open haven for Jews from all over the world. My parents had quickly decided on the United States, which offered the quickest entry time at a four-month wait. Our ultimate destination in Miami Beach, Florida, would be finalized only weeks before our final departure and depended at least in part on where the Jewish Federation had the volunteers to support our arrival. Unbeknownst to us at the time, the Federation had a sophisticated infrastructure and network of volunteers who helped immigrants like us find housing, education, and jobs and otherwise supported our transition to the New World.

Our sojourn in Italy took place in Ostia, a seaside resort outside of Rome. We shared a small apartment with an enormous terrace with another Jewish family. During the day, my brother and I would attend a "school" set up by Jewish aid agencies to prepare immigrant children for their new lives in the West. I do not recall any teaching or learning, and in hindsight, I suspect the school's main purpose was childcare. My father also attended classes to learn English while my mother stayed home with my one-year-old sister. On most evenings, my family would spend a few hours at the Ostia post office, where the Soviet emigres would gather around the circular fountain to exchange the latest news and gossip. We also took time to visit all of Rome's historical attractions, including Vatican City and the Coliseum. My father, 13-year-old brother, and I even took a bus tour of northern Italy to see Florence, Milan, Pisa, and Venice. My few memories of Italy are happy ones. Despite the considerable uncertainty and hardship, my parents and the other Soviet Jews in Ostia were brimming with hope and optimism as they stood on the precipice of a new life in America.

FIRST DAYS IN AMERICA

Like the many millions of immigrants who preceded us, my family's first steps in America were on New York City asphalt. I don't remember much about our Alitalia flight from Rome or that first night in New York, but I have since felt a special affinity for both the airline and the city. While I have yet to fly Alitalia again, I have spent most of my adult life living or working in New York City.

Unlike the prior night's arrival into a cold and dark New York City, the following day lives in my memory as almost blindingly bright and sunny. When we stepped through the double doors of Miami International Airport and into the Miami sunshine, I was overcome by a wet and heavy blanket of heat. The weather wasn't unusual for a late December Miami day in the low 80s. But the warmth and brightness were so foreign to the lives we had lived, in which Decembers were always dark and cold, that it served as an appropriate epilogue to our past and prologue to the future on which we were embarking.

Our first days in Miami were spent at the Carlton Hotel in what is now South Beach. As it so happened, the Carlton was yet another link in a long chain of support and beneficence that helped families like mine get resettled in a new country and without which Soviet Jewry may well have not gotten a foothold in the United States. I know this because, as it so happened, the Carlton was owned by a man whose son would one day become my friend and explain this to me. But that was still 10 years away. When we arrived in Miami Beach, it was 10 years past its former prime and another 10 years from becoming South Beach. In 1978, Miami Beach was a haven for senior citizens and, increasingly, newly arrived immigrant families from the Soviet Union and Cuba. English was spoken primarily by the very old and the very young.

Thanks to the efforts of the Jewish Federation and its extensive support network, we moved out of the Carlton Hotel and into more permanent lodgings within days. We settled at 1361 Meridian Avenue—directly across the street from Flamingo Park and in the heart of the Russian Jewish community. With only 1.5 bedrooms, it was a small apartment for a family of five, but we were very grateful to have it. The Federation soon helped my father find his first job in America and helped my mother enroll in community college to adjust her computer programming skills to the demands of the American marketplace. To make ends meet, my parents also cleaned a medical office at night. On weekends, my brother and I would distribute flyers for that same medical office (until I got fired one day for not doing it with sufficient enthusiasm). Although my parents worked hard, we were also fortunate that the opportunity to work hard, especially in those early days, was seemingly always available. A lot of people seemed to be rooting for us and vested in our success.

SCHOOL

Within days of settling into our new apartment, I was attending a small yeshiva at the southern edge of Miami Beach. It did not go well. My days were spent being mostly ignored by the teachers and teased by the children. As I spoke neither English nor Hebrew, my options for in-class learning were admittedly limited. Whether I could have learned something, anything from deciphering some worksheet or text remains an open question since I was never given a chance to do so. Worksheets never made their way to my desk, and I have no memory of ever handling a book. On the other hand, I clearly recall being reprimanded for rolling my pencil across my empty desk.

The kids were not much better, although they at least had the defense of youth. All my peers were six-year-old Orthodox Jews. Orthodox Judaism, more so than most other western traditions, commands practitioners to live by a strict code of conduct that permeates almost all aspects of life. There are lots and lots of rules, none of which I managed to pick up in Soviet Ukraine. So when I sat down to eat my lunch of chicken cutlet and chocolate pudding, thereby committing the grave offense of mixing milk with meat, I was not protesting religious doctrine or seeking to stir revolution. None of that mattered, of course. This was heresy! And my classmates were not standing for it. The pudding never made it into my mouth. Instead, it ended up on the ground and on the fringes of my tzitzit, the school-mandated ritual garment traditionally worn by Jewish males.

That experience, which lasted about a week, was my first direct contact with organized Judaism. Although it did not turn me off to Judaism forever, it tied, in my mind, orthodoxy (Jewish or otherwise) with rigidity of thought, intolerance, and illiberalism.

I completed the remainder of first grade and second grade at the local public elementary school. Leroy D. Feinberg Elementary could not have been more different than the yeshiva I had just left. The student population was entirely composed of immigrant children, almost without exception. The student body was poor and from somewhere else. I spent most of the remainder of first grade in the English as a Second Language (ESOL) class with other Russian kids and a Russian-speaking teacher. The Cuban kids had their own ESOL class with a Spanish-speaking teacher. It was a loud and rowdy place, but one that was also vibrant and comfortable.

Leroy D. Feinberg Elementary was the second of five elementary schools I would attend. The nearly annual changes resulted from the Federation's efforts to provide Russian immigrants with a Jewish education and my parents' steady climb up the economic ladder. The third and fourth grades were spent at two different Jewish day schools. These were the places where I had my very first taste, albeit in very small bites, of academic success. These were also the places where I was first exposed to wealth and inequality. It wasn't until I returned to public school in the fifth grade, this time at Greynolds Park Elementary in North Miami Beach, that I finally started to feel the puzzle pieces coming together. That was where I first found lasting academic and social success and the place I stopped feeling like an immigrant.

SETTLING IN

Our first years in the United States were difficult but ultimately manageable thanks to the kindness of strangers. Like many other immigrants, my brother, sister, and I relied primarily on donated clothing provided by the Jewish Federation. One of my best friends (also named Alex), who is now a successful physician in the suburbs of Washington, D.C., received most of his clothing from a family with a child named Eric. Many of Eric's t-shirts had his name emblazoned on the back. So much of Alex's clothing was marked that he came to adopt Eric as his own middle name in an attempt to explain the inevitable questions that arose whenever he wore one of Eric's t-shirts.

We also benefited from government support, including food stamps, free school lunches, and subsidized rent. Government assistance, along with the support of the Jewish Federation, gave my parents the space they needed to acquire the skills to succeed in America. Before long, my mother had graduated from community college and boasted a good job at Flagler Federal Savings & Loan as a senior programmer, where she would remain until the early 1990s when Flagler fell victim to America's savings and loan crisis. At the same time, my father would take odd jobs when he needed to and until something more stable became available, which eventually it did.

We were surely poor, but I was also largely ignorant of that fact, at least during those first years in America. All of my friends and peers were similarly situated. We all wore secondhand clothes, and practically everyone at my public elementary school carried the same 7x5 green card marking them free lunch eligible. The world described in television commercials, with McDonald's and first-run movie theaters, was simply outside the realm of my experience and so was not something I felt deprived of.

Sometime in 1979, we bought our first automobile. It was a 1971 Pontiac Grand Safari station wagon, white with wood paneling along the sides. Its third-row bench seat faced the back. If it had seat belts, they went unused. Car ownership was a realization of a dream for my father, brother, and me. It was a palpable step, along with U.S. citizenship and homeownership, on the path to becoming American. It also represented a kind of freedom that we had never known before. With a car, all of America was open to exploration. Over the next few years, we would explore Florida and eventually make our way up and down the East Coast.

JUDAISM

I have had a complicated history with Judaism. Before coming to America, my parents were avowed atheists. Although my family had a strong Jewish identity, it was forged mostly by the centuries of persecution that predated them, and more recently, by the Shoah. We were Jewish, in part, not because we chose to be Jewish, but because Judaism was thrust upon us by the outside world. Even within the Soviet Union's so-called "socialist utopia," with its appeals to equality and brotherhood, our Jewishness was marked on our passports, if not on our faces. Judaism, or more precisely, Jewishness, was the reason for our fleeing the USSR, but also the reason for our being able to do so. Jewishness was at once the cause of our despair but also the cause of our salvation.

As noted earlier, my first contact with Judaism in America did not go well and left me with a deep distaste for the entire enterprise. My brother's bar mitzvah later that year (1978) did nothing to change my mind. Gary (then Igor) was 13 when we stepped onto the tarmac at JFK. Jewish tradition dictates that a boy becomes a man at 13, and usually marks this seminal event with a religious ceremony and celebration. The rabbis at my brother's Mesivta Yeshiva in Miami Beach were not about to let this opportunity slip by.

Mesivta was an interesting place. It was an Orthodox Jewish yeshiva in a seemingly perpetual state of financial despair and physical disrepair. Its school bus had been dredged out of the Miami River, and its physical plant might as well have been. Mesivta's primary mission was to train Jewish boys and young men for a life of Torah study. The recent influx of Soviet Jews into the Miami Beach community posed a true dilemma for Mesivta. On the one hand, the Russian boys and the tuition dollars accompanying them were a much-needed financial lifeline. On the other hand, few, if any, of these immigrant boys had either the academic background or the inclination to devote their lives to the Torah. The result was that Mesivta did little more than warehouse these Russian boys until the Federation stopped paying tuition. At that point, almost without exception, the Russians enrolled in public school.

Gary's rabbis scheduled the bar mitzvah on the Sabbath at a synagogue two or three miles from our apartment. Given the prohibition against mechanized travel on the Sabbath, the rabbis had arranged to pick up the entire family on Friday afternoon and host us overnight near the synagogue. After the ceremony was over, we were bid adieu, instructed to make our way home, and reminded to avoid using any form of mechanized transport on the Sabbath. For reasons I will never understand, we did just that. We walked the several miles to our apartment, in the Miami heat, all while carrying a baby without a stroller.

I still get angry whenever I am reminded of this episode. I am angry at the rabbis who lacked the simple decency to offer to drive our family of five, including two small children, home after the Sabbath ended. And I'm angry at my parents for lacking the self-dignity to set matters right or at least refuse to be bullied or guilted into arbitrarily obeying some religious prohibition.

And yet, despite these initial setbacks, I had never thought of turning away from my Jewishness and even kept finding my way back to Judaism. My third and fourth grades were spent in Conservative Jewish day schools, markedly more liberal than my brother's Mesivta or the Torah Academy, which was my first introduction to Judaism in America. The Jewish values taught at those Conservative schools were more familiar and sensible. And those schools also offered a relatively good secular education.

As an adult, my wife and I embraced Modern Orthodox Judaism for many years and raised three of our four kids at least partially in that tradition. Although it was much more liberal than the "black hat" orthodoxy of my youth, we ultimately found it incompatible with the life we wanted for ourselves and our children.

Through all of my various experiments in Judaism, I have never wavered in my Jewishness. In terms of self-identity, Jewishness has been the one constant throughout my life.

FINAL REFLECTIONS

Though I was born in the Soviet Union, I lived there for less than six years. I cannot read Tolstoy or Dostoyevsky in the original, and my native Russian is useless for anything other than the most perfunctory conversation. My memories of the "old country" are few and sporadic. For centuries, life in Ukraine and Russia had been difficult, and for Jews, at times, impossible. Life would surely have been hard if I stayed in the Soviet Union and possibly made harder because of my Jewishness.

In contrast, the United States has embraced me and welcomed me into its fold. I have lived in the United States for almost 45 years. My American English has no traces of any foreign accent. I first met my oldest friends on American soil. My vernacular is American, replete with references to American music, television, and movies. America is truly the only home I have ever known.

The same cannot be said of my parents. While my mother has a strong command of English, my father does not. Starting life anew in a foreign country is exhausting, and it continues to be so for the rest of your working life. Now that my parents are retired, I see those efforts starting to unwind. Their interests are shifting decidedly back to Ukraine. Most of the media they now consume is once again in Russian. Despite nearly 45 years in America, even my father's iPhone is set to Russian.

My brother, too, retains strong ties to his Russianness. He was already a teenager when we arrived in America, with a strong command of the Russian language and a love of Russian literature. Unlike my sister and I, he had ingested a large dose of Soviet popular culture. Growing up in America through the present day, my brother's closest friends are native-born Russians, as are his ex-wife and current wife, both of whom are committed to raising their kids with a strong Russian identity and Russian fluency.

Not so for my sister and me. My sister, Elaine, who was just a baby when we left Russia, has no Russian friends. She married an American Jew and raises her two children without regard to Russian fluency or culture. None of my four kids speaks Russian either, although two of them can read Hebrew reasonably well. I never dated any Russian women and also married an American Jew. Most of my friends are American-born, although several of my closest friends share the same Soviet emigrant narrative.

I am proud to have made the journey out of Soviet Ukraine to America and to have had my life shaped by that experience. Immigrants to this great country have a unique love for America because they experience American values and ideals in a very tangible way, much like our Founding Fathers did. Bedrock American principles like limited government, freedom of expression, and the right to privacy are mostly taken for granted by native-born Americans. But to immigrants like my parents and me, who lived under a government unconstrained by any limits to its authority, that had no tolerance for unsanctioned expression, and encouraged its citizens to inform on each other, the existence of these bedrock American ideas would impact their quality of life in very concrete ways, from their very first days in America to their very last. ■

ANNA ABRAMZON

NOW

I am 39 and live in Los Angeles with my husband and two daughters. All four of us were born in different countries. Growing up as a young immigrant in Chicago planted the seeds for a nomadic life. After going to art school, I picked up my suitcases and haven't put them down in any one place for long. Since college, I have lived in two countries, four states and six cities, including four years in Israel. I am a painter, specializing in figurative art with a Jewish soul. In my work you will find echoes of my immigrant experience - my grandmother's teacups, lace from the curtains of our Kiev apartment, and the wonder of being a newcomer.

I was born in 1981 in a country that no longer exists to a family that no longer exists. For my first seven years, I lived in an 800 square foot apartment with my mother, father, and paternal grandparents in Kiev, Ukraine, then a part of the Soviet Union. Our apartment had three rooms—my grandparents' room, my parents' room, which doubled as a dining room, and my room, which doubled as a living room. Connecting the rooms was a hallway, off of which there was a bathroom split into two rooms: one for the toilet and one for the sink and tub, a small kitchen, a balcony that ran the length of the apartment and at the end of the hallway a closet, which served as my father's sculpting studio. I could sit for hours smelling the plasticine and watching his sculptures turn from wire skeletons to fleshy, muscular figures. I loved life in that apartment.

Anna 1987.

One of my favorite childhood memories is waking up to the smell of fried potatoes on Sunday mornings. I would follow the smell to our kitchen, where my grandmother would be busy at the stove, light pouring in through lace curtains. As the only child, I took for granted my effortless ability to delight all the adults in our family and the unabashed attention they poured on me. I would enter the kitchen like a long-awaited guest, and they would greet me with their embraces. We would feast on herring with onions, oily fried potatoes, crusty Ukrainian bread, and a salad of tomatoes, cucumbers, green onions, and dill. To this day, this is my favorite breakfast. Later, I would often spend hours in my room, drawing and listening to stories on my record player.

Despite the tight quarters and the scarcity of food and other resources, my grandparents would host dinner parties regularly. Weekend evenings were often spent around a long, beautifully dressed table that would be pulled out for the occasion and set up in my parents' room. Long after I would go to bed, I could hear laughter and the clink of crystal glasses.

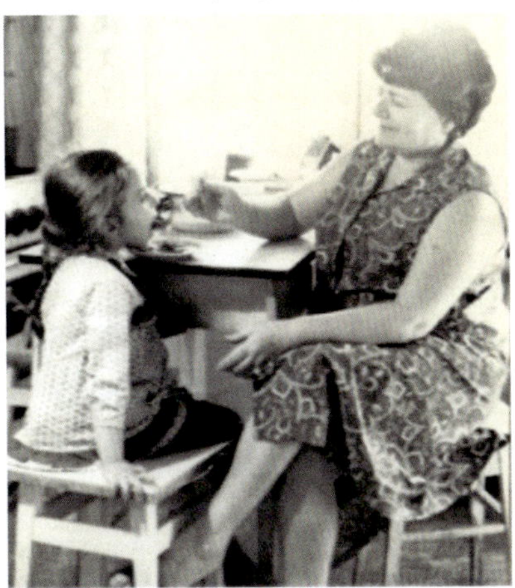
Babushka Mayya feeding Anna in Kiev apartment.

My family kept me sheltered from the hardships they endured. My parents had tried to leave the Soviet Union years before I was born and were refused, which categorized them as "refuseniks"—a label that came with all sorts of repercussions in the Communist country. As dissidents, they lived in a constant state of fear. Later I would learn that my grandparents used to follow my father wherever he went, walking several meters behind him, so they would know if he had been picked up by the KGB. He would disappear into unmarked cars and secret passageways off the street, or in the subway tunnels, or train stations, the rest of the family not knowing where he was taken or whether or not he would be released.

I also know now that there was constant tension and fighting between my parents, even back then, but under my grandparents' tight reins, it happened in silence. Silence was a recurring theme of my childhood. I knew from a very young age that anything said at home was a secret not to ever be repeated. Nothing of consequence was ever to be said on the phone. "I don't know" was my default answer to everything. Silence and secrecy were mandatory for keeping our family safe.

I understood that our family was different and that this kind of difference was due to our being something called "Jews," though I had no idea what this meant. I was always trying to pinpoint the difference. I noticed that my grandfather swung his arms when he walked more than most people, and I hypothesized that maybe this was Jewishness. I also knew that Jews had their own country, it was called "Israel," but I was never to mention it, and our own songs like "Chava Nagilla" and "Shalom Aleichem," with words that were as mysterious as the entire concept of Jewishness, which I was never to sing outside our home. Once, while walking down the street, I asked my mother if there was such a thing as a Jewish star. Since I was familiar with the five-pointed Soviet star, she hushed me and said yes, but she would show me at home.

When the Chernobyl reactor exploded, about 100 kilometers from our home in Kiev, I remained mostly oblivious to the fear and danger surrounding me. Cans of food began arriving from friends in Moscow, and I was not allowed to touch any leaves or play outside. Eventually, my family members all took their vacation times one by one to evacuate me from Kiev, and I spent months on an adventure staying in the homes of my grandparents' friends in Lithuania, Moscow and Leningrad. In the meantime, my father went to Chernobyl to help design transitional housing there, and my cousin, Ilya, the only cousin I had my age and the closest thing I had to a sibling, spent months in and out of hospitals with radiation poisoning. My Uncle Arkadiy, my grandfather Lev's youngest brother, suddenly got sick and died just months after the explosion. But I wouldn't realize any of this was due to Chernobyl until I was much older.

The closest thing I experienced to a Chernobyl-related trauma came from my first-grade teacher. Teachers in the Soviet Union could be notoriously cruel, but I was lucky. I had gotten the young, new teacher. She was sweet and gentle and I loved her. Early in the school year, our homework was to make a collage about fall. Art was always my thing, so I took the assignment very seriously. My preference had been to go outside and gather leaves for the project, but touching nature was out of the question. Instead, I spent hours laboriously cutting up leaves out of construction paper and making an elaborate, intricate design, which I proudly handed in in the morning. The teacher gathered all of our assignments and then stood in front of the class holding up two of them. One was by Olya, the best student in the class and the object of my obsessive competition, and the other was by Boris, the boisterous class clown. Olya's was busy and clearly labor-intensive, made entirely of real leaves, while Boris's was just three found leaves glued to a white sheet of paper. "These are the only students who thought to use real leaves," the teacher said, "and these are the only true artists in the class." She then held up the rest of our projects in one stack and calmly ripped them up into four neat pieces in front of us and tossed them into the wastebasket. It took all my strength to hold my tears until I came home. That night I cried myself to sleep.

When I was five or six, an old friend of my grandmother's came to visit. Her name, like my grandmother's, was also Maya. She had left the Soviet Union years before and now lived in America in a place called "Chicago." She had been a railroad engineer alongside my grandmother in Kiev. Now, in Chicago, she worked as a manicurist. She told wondrous stories of America, of strangers smiling at each other on the streets. She said she was dismayed that when she smiled at a teenage girl in the elevator of our Kiev building on the way up, the girl looked back at her like she had two heads. I wondered why anyone would smile at someone they didn't know.

She brought gifts for everyone. Pantyhose for my grandma, for my mom a set of eyeshadows with more colors than any of us had ever seen, and for me she brought the most beautiful gift of all—a tiny little silver bell filled with chocolate. It was so precious that rather than eat it, we proudly displayed the treasured gift in our china cabinet along with my grandparents' wedding tea set and crystal glasses for all our guests to see. Years later, in America, I would learn that the precious bell was called a Hershey's kiss.

About halfway through first grade, I began hearing talk at home of "leaving." Like all the other mysteries surrounding our family, this was another abstract concept that I knew I was not allowed to speak of. The biggest suitcases I have ever seen appeared in our hallway. Books and toys began to disappear into them. My favorite baby doll, Tzinzenella, had to go in the suitcase also.

As our departure date came closer, my grandmother came to school and talked to the teacher, who cried as she looked at me, "But she is my kolokolchik," she said, using the Russian word for "little bell." And then the day came. My parents and grandparents carried the suitcases down the steps of our apartment building. My friends from the neighborhood were playing hopscotch in the courtyard. I waved to them casually, and they waved back. I don't think I fully realized that I would never see them again.

Before we were allowed to board the train out of the country, the border patrol officers were to inspect all of our belongings to make sure we were not smuggling any Soviet property out of the country. All artwork was considered property of the state, but through a connection, my father had gotten permission to take a handful of his sculptures with us. The officer inspected everything, including squeezing a bit of our toothpaste out of the tubes.

It wouldn't be until months later, unpacking our baggage in our sponsor's apartment outside Chicago, that I would find out what the inspectors did to Tzinzenella, my lovie. I would pull her out of the suitcase, eager to be comforted by her smell and the texture of her hair, matted by years of snuggling, only to see her head fall back at an unnatural angle, hanging on by a thread, her plastic eyelashes clicking open and shut. The Soviet inspectors had slit her throat before putting her back in the suitcase. What I remember most about that moment was realizing that she didn't smell like home anymore.

The journey out of the Soviet Union lives in my mind as a set of images. The menacing teeth of the barking dogs, the uniformed officers, my father pressed against the glass window of a train car so full that there were people squeezed into the nets on the ceiling, struggling to breathe and letting out what I remember as a silent scream. My mom dragging me along the platform, begging the officers to let us walk through the empty cars in which we were not allowed because the refugee car was so full there was no way to get in through the doors. Nodding off and jerking awake over and over while sitting on a suitcase on the train. But most of all, my grandmother's tear-streaked face as we said goodbye.

The packed train stopped and unloaded all of us, exhausted and disheveled, onto the platform in bordering Czechoslovakia. From there, we boarded another train. This time we were allowed to spread out like human beings. At the Austrian border, uniformed officers went through the train checking everyone's documents, and eventually, we arrived in Vienna, where minivans drove us through the immaculate, beautifully lit streets to our transitional housing. We had never seen a minivan before. The next morning, in Vienna, we awoke to the sound of birds chirping for the first time in our lives.

The route to America was organized by refugee aid organizations. First, we would spend an unspecified amount of time in Vienna and then in Italy. During this time, we could lobby governments of the countries we hoped to immigrate to prove that we were, indeed, refugees who had suffered persecution. Some of our fellow travelers ended up going to Australia, some to Israel, and many of us would go to the United States. Some families would spend up to 18 months in limbo in Europe, waiting to find out their fate. For us, the journey would be relatively short. We spent 11 days in Austria. My mother marveled at how easily one could buy pantyhose. I fell in love with the Barbie dolls I saw in store windows. I had never seen anything so beautiful, and I wondered if I could ever have one of my own.

Eventually, we moved on to Italy, where in a beachside town outside Rome called Passaskuri, everyone rented small villas, packing in as many families as could possibly fit. We shared ours with two other families, each with boys my age. Our parents would go off in the mornings to sell decorative matchboxes and hand-painted spoons and playing cards they had smuggled out of the Soviet Union at the Italian market. The time in Italy was the most freedom I had ever felt to that point in my life. While our parents were off, we kids had the run of the place. We would spend time looking for cool rocks at the beach, peeking into courtyards to watch Italian boys playing soccer, making up elaborate games, and I would always be drawing. Still, I dreamed of a Barbie.

One night, as I was drifting off to sleep, I decided to talk to God. I didn't know who God was, but I would hear my mom asking him for things with phrases like "Dear God, please let us get through this." I decided to try it too. With all my might, I asked him to please, please bring me a Barbie doll. The next day, as I was walking down the street with my mom and my dad was off at the market, a car pulled over next to us. An Italian man got out and started gesturing wildly, explaining something about a "bambino." He motioned with his arms that this bambino was small and is now big. Then he went into his trunk and took out two life-size colorful matching boy and girl gnome dolls and handed them to me. I was overjoyed. That evening, my father came home from the market carrying a special box. Inside was not only a Barbie, but a Barbie with about 10 different outfits to change her into. I didn't know who God was, but he sure could deliver.

In Rome, my parents took me along to what I understood to be a very important meeting, during which they were to share their experience as dissidents in the Soviet Union. They spent time preparing and discussing which stories they would tell and how they would answer potential questions. What I remember most clearly that day is not the person interviewing them or what was said during the meeting itself. What I remember vividly is my parents fighting after. "Why did you tell that story about the subway tunnel?" my mother yelled at my father. "That was nothing! You should have told about the time we were arrested at the train station!" In the end, apparently, the subway tunnel detainment story was enough to get us refugee status in America.

We arrived in the United States on June 1, 1989. I was seven years old. There is a faded photo of my parents and me walking out of the terminal at O'Hare Airport in Chicago. My father with his thick halo of hair and Abraham Lincoln beard, dressed in stonewashed jeans and matching jacket, my mom in a skirt, holding a bouquet of flowers, and me with big Soviet bows in my hair, clutching the Mini Mouse doll my grandmother's friend Maya and her husband Rudik brought me.

My parents were younger then than I am now. Ahead of them was a small apartment, with wall-to-wall long-haired mint green carpeting that would leave balls of green fuzz everywhere, a table with three chairs, one of which had a broken leg and had to be propped up on a book, and two mattresses. Then there would be more apartments, each a little nicer than the one before. Ahead would be my father setting off for job interviews in his acid-washed jean outfit, carrying a shoebox full of photos of his work, my mother coming home exhausted from long days of working in a curtain store. There would be the three of us listening to the phone ring over and over and waiting for the answering machine to pick it up so that my parents wouldn't be ambushed into having an impromptu conversation in English.

Coming to America.

Immigration would prove to be too much for their fragile marriage to withstand, but they both forged their own paths in America and built new families. My father opened an architecture firm in Chicago, my mom got her PhD in education. In the last twenty-five years, they have only occupied the same space a handful of times—my bat mitzvah, my wedding, occasional drop-offs or pickups of their shared grandchildren during our visits to Chicago.

Every story from my childhood has two different, and often opposite, versions when told by my parents. I have spent the last 30 years piecing them together, both in painting and writing. June 1 is the only day in the year when I text both my parents the same thing: "Happy Coming-to-Americaversary!" Neither of them ever remembers the day before my text, but I keep it up year after year because that was the day my parents, through their strength, courage, and resolve, made sure that where I come from would empower my future, not limit it. And that they did together. ■

DAN ZILBERMAN

NOW

I am 48 years old, and after spending most of my career living in New York and London, I now live with my family in Aspen, Colorado. I am married, and we have three children, ages 14, 12, and 10. I have worked in private equity for over 20 years, and I am a senior partner and part of the executive management team at one of the largest private equity firms in the world. Amongst other senior roles, I have run my firm's European operations and built our financial services and special situations investing businesses. I am also a professor and Senior Fellow at an Ivy League university teaching classes in Finance.

Q: TELL ME ABOUT YOUR FAMILY'S BACKGROUND AND THEIR PATH TO AMERICA.

I would venture to guess that my family's path to the United States is pretty different from that of a lot of other people you may have spoken with. It's a story of twists and turns, major setbacks, but ultimate American triumph.

My mother's family is from Riga in Latvia. My father's family is from Tbilisi, Georgia, although they were originally from Odessa, and they ran to Tbilisi when the Nazis came. I would say my mother's side of the family was fairly simple. They came to Riga from Belarus, where they lived in a late 19th-century type shtetl. They were simple peasants but nice smart people. My grandfather (mother's father) had a full different family prior to the war. Tragically, however, while he was away fighting in a Russian tank division during World War II, his wife died of starvation during the multi-year blockade of Leningrad (St. Petersburg), where they lived at the time. She rationed any food she could find (including eating dogs, cats, rats, and insects) to her three young children. Upon returning from the war, my grandfather collected his three young children from orphanages across Russia and moved to Riga, where several of his relations from Belarus had settled postwar. There he met my grandmother and proceeded to marry and have three more daughters (of whom my mother was one). Thus, his three children from his previous marriage, his new wife, and three new children formed a Soviet postwar type Brady bunch.

Coming to America.

My father's family was a bit different. Both sides of the family are from Odessa. On my grandfather's side of the family, his grandfather emigrated to the United States in the early 1900s. He aimed to make some money, send it back to Odessa, and have the family join him. But the tsar changed the rules and stopped allowing Jewish families from Ukraine to emigrate to the United States. Tragically, they never saw each other after he left. Family lore is that the grandfather ultimately remarried, started another family and became a millionaire, but there was no further direct link to him (besides some letters), so I'm not sure how true this is. My grandfather's father grew up to be a fairly high-ranking person. I believe, he ran maritime trade for the Soviet Union. Ultimately, his level of influence led to his arrest and murder by the KGB when my grandfather was a young boy. There was a point when Stalin looked to eliminate anybody in a position of power and could become a threat. And while I would suggest that somebody in charge of maritime trade isn't a threat to the Premier, Stalin clearly had a different opinion.

At the start of World War II, my grandfather joined the Soviet Navy at age 16 (he lied about his age to do so) and became fairly decorated, with more brass medals than his lapel could fit. However, to his chagrin, when he returned to Odessa after the war, he found that the Nazis murdered his mother and grandmother on a fateful night when a meaningful proportion of the Jews in Odessa were marched barefoot through snow-covered streets into the woods, shot and dumped into mass graves. My grandfather was now truly alone and, on a whim, made a trip to Tbilisi, Georgia, with a friend, where several Odessa Jews had run to hide from the Nazis during the war. This is where he met my grandmother and settled to form a family.

On to my grandmother's side of the family. Her father was a very successful entrepreneur, first in Odessa and then in Tbilisi. I never quite understood how he did this, but under communism, there was some underground private enterprise. It was mafia-type stuff, under the radar and involved corroboration from corrupt Communist Party officials. In this construct, my grandmother's father was very successful, wealthy (by Soviet standards), and influential, even during communism. He and several of his partners became the elders of the Tbilisi Jewish community and led much of the commerce and activity of Ashkenazi Jews in that town. Given this positioning, my grandmother and her sister both became doctors, which was unusual for women in the 1940s and 1950s. Ultimately, my grandmother became the team doctor for the Soviet Olympic team in wrestling and judo and traveled extensively across the world with the team.

My parents met when my father's family vacationed on the Baltic coast and ultimately married. I was born in Riga, but we moved to Tbilisi shortly after my birth, where my father's family is from. I also have a younger brother, four and a half years younger than me, who is a senior partner at a leading Silicon Valley venture capital firm.

Q: SO WHY DID YOU DECIDE TO LEAVE?

Well, this is where the story starts to get a little interesting. My father was an aerospace engineer and worked in the Soviet Space Program, where he designed propulsion systems for rockets that went to outer space. He was a relatively young guy, so I wouldn't say he was especially senior, but he had top secret clearance and all the access and knowledge that came with it. By Soviet standards, we probably lived better than most because of my grandmother's family. By Soviet standards, my great-grandfather was highly accomplished and affluent. Thus, we owned a sizeable house and didn't want for too much. In fact, when we first moved to the U.S., our standard of living declined materially from what we had experienced in the U.S.S.R. Thankfully, this would ultimately change through hard work. While many Russian emigres complained about life in the U.S.S.R., our life there was decent by Soviet standards. Still, this was communism.

A young communist in training. Wearing the ceremonial hat of the head of the Tbilisi police department, who was a family acquaintance.

So the story gets interesting around 1975 when my mother's parents and my mother's sister emigrated from the U.S.S.R. to Israel. Once they emigrated, the KGB immediately showed up. They told my father, "You work in the space program. You have top secret clearance, so don't bother to show up for work tomorrow because you now have family beyond the Iron Curtain." He tried to persuade them that he had no connection to his wife's family. All he knew was physics and engineering, and he loved the motherland, but to no avail. He asked the KGB and the Space Program what he was supposed to do to feed his family if he could not work in his field of training, but the reply was basically that they did not care. With family behind the Iron Curtain, he could no longer work at a top clearance job. So my family had never actually looked to leave the U.S.S.R., because life was pretty decent in Tbilisi. But with two kids and a wife and unable to work at his trade, my father and mother (and ultimately my grandparents) decided to emigrate.

They applied to leave, but because of my father's former top security clearance, the Soviets wouldn't let them leave. They didn't want his knowledge base in the hands of the West.

Q: YOUR FATHER BECAME A REFUSENIK?

Yes. You may recall there was a group of Russian Jewish scientists in the 1970s who were not permitted to leave, and they got the name "refuseniks." They held demonstrations, gave speeches, and held hunger strikes to gain attention for their plight. My father was such a refusenik, albeit a less active one for fear of arrest. My family tried to leave for five years, but the Soviet government refused to let them go. Leaving became an all-encompassing mission. We wanted to get the hell out of there, at any cost.

Q: SO HOW WERE YOU ABLE TO LEAVE?

We had been denied for five straight years, after numerous applications every year. It ultimately got resolved when my grandmother, a very strong woman, strategically developed a close friendship with a woman who was the wife of the top Soviet general in the Caucasus region. She had ulterior motives, and through this woman, she got to know the woman's husband—the general—a very influential person in government. After carefully developing the relationship and dialogue over years, my grandmother showed up at this general's house one night at 3 a.m. with a suitcase full of money—James Bond style.

I don't know the amount, but it was reputedly millions from my great-grandfather's estate. She showed up with a suitcase at 3 a.m., she left the suitcase, and left the house with fabricated emigration visas and paperwork for my entire family. So we wound up leaving the country under false pretenses. Even leaving was really frightening. I was eight years old when we left via Sheremetyevo Airport in Moscow. My grandparents got through, but then they started looking at the paperwork from my immediate family, including my father, my mother, and my three-year-old brother. They saw something suspicious with the paperwork and wouldn't let us board the plane to freedom. So my grandparents got on the plane, and we stood there at the airport, watching them leave. My brother and I were crying because we were being separated from our grandparents. My mother and father were sobbing because they thought the jig was up, and the Soviet authorities figured out that we had fake paperwork and that they would end up in jail or even be executed. Somehow, however, we called this general, he pulled a couple of strings, and we were allowed to leave the next day. And we flew to Vienna, Austria.

Just a last piece of pretty interesting background. From Vienna, we went to Ladispoli, a little coastal town in Italy, which I'm sure a lot of the people you've spoken to went through on their way to the U.S. In Rome, we were interviewed by the U.S. Consulate or Embassy (I'm not sure which one), who interviewed all the Russian emigres to make sure they were fit to enter the United States.

And at that point, they realized that the visa we had to come to the United States had some inconsistencies with our actual identities. The U.S. authorities figured out who my father was, what he did for a living, and that we left under false pretenses. To them, harboring an escaped Soviet rocket scientist in the midst of the Cold War was really problematic. So they told us that the U.S. couldn't accept us and that we had to go back!

To this, my father said to them that if they sent the family back to the U.S.S.R., the Soviets would execute not only him but perhaps the whole family. So they made a deal that my father would work with the U.S. government for a period of time, and we would spend the next number of months living on a U.S. army base in Bamberg. My father worked with the CIA being debriefed. I was an eight-year-old kid, and every day I had these nice Americans show up at my house on the base bringing me presents and speaking fluent Russian with me. With the benefit of hindsight, these nice Russian-speaking men were clearly CIA agents that my dad was working with.

"Wow, you mean we can buy any of this stuff without standing in a long line?" Standing with my mother and brother on a typical shopping street when we first got to Rome.

Interestingly, my father would tell you (he has passed away since) that he didn't believe the CIA learned much from him in that year that they didn't know already, meaning that there were likely U.S. spies in the Soviet Space Program more senior than my father, and with greater access than he had. The CIA knew details that my father didn't know, even though he worked on these rockets and projects for years.

We then moved to Brooklyn, like most Russian immigrants. My mother went to college to become a nurse, just because she needed a job. My father started a couple of businesses and had some success and some failures. For most of his life in the U.S., he ran an auto body repair shop with a partner in Brooklyn. The life of an immigrant—he went from rocket ships to fixing broken Buicks. My father also wound up going back to the Ukraine after the fall of communism, bought some businesses there in import/export and nickel (the metal), and had considerable short-term success until the Ukrainian authorities took away much of what he had created during a regime change.

My brother and I had relatively normal American lives after age nine. We lived in Staten Island in a small semi-attached home that our parents purchased and went to normal American public schools. We excelled in football, the ultimate American sport, and I played for my high school and college football teams. I say after age nine because my life was fairly mundane. Prior to age nine, it was quite tumultuous.

So that's our background. I suspect most people didn't leave the country using fake paperwork and didn't work for the CIA on the way here, but ultimately we got here. It was total cloak and dagger though.

Q: WOW, THAT IS AN INCREDIBLE STORY. WHAT DO YOU REMEMBER ABOUT THE U.S.S.R.? YOU WERE EIGHT. DO YOU REMEMBER ANY SMELLS, FOODS, ACTIVITIES?

We lived in Georgia, which, as you know, is ethnic and is quite different from the rest of the Soviet Union. The food was amazing. I still think it's some of the best food in the world. My great-grandfather was like the scion of the Ashkenazi Jewish community in Tbilisi (I say Ashkenazi because there were also Georgian Jews and Mountain Jews, but these were very different sects that didn't mix much with the Ashkenazis). If there was a dispute in the community, they would come to him, and he would arbitrate who was right and who was wrong. So it was a fairly prominent household while he was alive.

One memory my mother always talks about, and it just speaks to what a screwed up place the Soviet Union was, is that they used to give out coupons to kids in schools, and families used those coupons to get food at home for the kids. So in a sense, because there was a shortage of food, they would give out coupons to kids in school so that young kids would be nourished at home. When we announced that we were leaving, I was probably in the third grade. My mother remembers my third-grade teacher making a special trip to our home and saying, "I understand you are leaving. I just gave your son coupons for food. If you're leaving, you're not eligible for the food. I want the coupons back." We later heard that the teacher kept the coupons to make sure she had enough to eat. This spoke to how screwed up the place was.

Our home was also robbed. Three guys with guns came into our home and said, "We know you're leaving the country. You must have something in the house that you intend to take with you. We want it all." Luckily I wasn't there, but my mother and brother were there. They ransacked the house and took a lot while my mother and three-year-old brother watched under gunpoint.

Q: HOW DID YOUR PARENTS FEEL ABOUT COMMUNISM? STALIN MURDERED YOUR GREAT-GRANDFATHER, SO I IMAGINE THERE WAS SOME ANIMOSITY. DID THAT COME THROUGH IN YOUR CONVERSATIONS WITH THEM?

Most definitely. But remember, my family had no intention to leave until my mother's family left, and my father was told he couldn't go to work anymore. But I would say my father was a borderline patriot. And he actually believed the hype until the KGB showed up one day and said that he was no longer part of the system. On an absolute basis, our life was poor. On a relative basis, our life was better than many other people in the Soviet Union. So my father was a semi-patriot. It's all he knew and believed in, and inertia just set in until the KGB told him he couldn't work. Then he soured on the place, and they desperately wanted to leave.

Q: DO YOU REMEMBER ANY ANTI-SEMITISM?

I would say we were very fortunate. Georgia was a lot more accepting than other places across the Soviet Union. Given its history, it was definitionally a very diverse place. So I would say, no, I don't believe we were exposed to much anti-Semitism. And again, because my great-grandfather and grandmother were such accomplished people in that community, the family was pretty well-positioned.

Q: AS YOU WERE LEAVING FROM GEORGIA, WHAT DID YOUR PARENTS TELL YOU ABOUT WHAT LIFE WOULD BE LIKE IN THE WEST?

I distinctly remember a comment that was akin to "the streets are paved in gold." Living in the West, we all know they're not, but the belief of something better on the other side was so profound that the best way to describe it was with this kind of imagery, such as the streets being paved with gold.

Remember that while we were not allowed to leave for five years, my mother's whole family—her parents and sisters—were all living in Israel at the time. So we did have some connectivity to family members on the other side of the Iron Curtain and had some visibility. Also, because my grandmother was a Soviet (and Georgian for domestic competitions) team doctor for various international sporting competitions, she would travel a fair bit abroad even when we lived in the U.S.S.R., and every time my grandmother would come back from an international sporting event, whether it was the Olympics or some other international competition, she came back with the most amazing goodies—Wrangler and Levis jeans, Marlboro cigarettes, Coca Cola, M&Ms—stuff that was amazing for those of us living in the U.S.S.R. The fact that we knew that this stuff existed in these other parts of the world made us pretty excited to get over there.

Q: WHAT WAS YOUR FIRST IMPRESSION OF VIENNA WHEN YOU GOT THERE?

That actually is a more vivid memory than most other things from my childhood. We were blown away! I remember walking the streets and seeing stores full of merchandise—foods galore. There are two distinct memories I have. Remember that I was barely eight years old. I remember walking down the street, and there was a vendor selling coconut chunks. Living in the U.S.S.R., I didn't know what a coconut was. I'd seen it in books. So I was blown away. My parents bought me a piece of coconut. It was like the most amazing thing I'd ever eaten. The other vivid recollection I have is walking by a jewelry store, or maybe a watch store. And there was a diver watch in an aquarium full of water and goldfish. So there was a watch sitting in the corner with these goldfish swimming around it, and I was just blown away that a watch could work underwater. My dream was to one day have a watch like that! The American dream to achieve and have the ability to acquire has driven me most of my life since then. So I would say the Vienna experience was particularly impactful because it was such a day and night comparison for an impactful little boy.

Q: AND AFTER VIENNA, YOU WENT TO ITALY?

We flew to Rome, and they put us in this town on the coast called Ladispoli. I believe a lot of Russian immigrants were put there. And that's where we were waiting to come to the U.S. until the U.S. government told us to take a different path.

I remember my parents hired some Russian emigre, who was living in Italy and had a car, to give us a tour of the country. My parents did the whole trip, whereas I think I might have done only half. I was little but still have some recollection of the beauty.

Q: THEN YOU WENT TO GERMANY?

Yes, we went straight to Germany, and even that was a bit of an adventure because we didn't have the paperwork to go to Germany. We had Soviet passports and no German visas, so the CIA basically snuck us into Germany.

Q: WHAT WAS LIFE LIKE IN GERMANY?

We lived on a U.S. Army base, and we were encouraged not to leave the base too often because there was concern that the Soviets would figure out what was going on with my dad. While at the base, the whole family took English classes to prepare for our new life once we got to the U.S. In the meantime, my dad went to work every morning to be debriefed and help the CIA representatives assess the designs of Soviet space apparatus, where certain facilities were located, logistics, etc.

Because I was so young, it almost felt like we were in the United States. It felt like we were in Indiana or somewhere else in middle America. These bases were so immense, with supermarkets, it felt like a small town that just happened to be in Germany, and all the people were in the military.

Q: SO THEN YOU MOVED TO AMERICA—BROOKLYN, RIGHT?

We moved where we did because we had some family friends from Georgia who had settled in Bensonhurst, Brooklyn, and they were kind enough to find us an apartment there. I have one distinct early memory: We were in one crappy apartment, and my grandparents had a crappy apartment right above us. This was a crappy tenement building, and no matter what the superintendent tried to do, the elevator always stunk of stale urine. Specifically, I distinctly remember being woken up my first morning in the United States and my father saying, "We are going to garbage."

And I'm thinking, "What the hell is garbage?" As far as I knew, we were going to a store called Garbage. As it turned out, we literally walked the streets of Bensonhurst, Brooklyn, early in the morning, picking up stuff that people had thrown out. I remember walking and lugging a rotten couch that somebody threw out and then walking around to find a lamp and a small table. That was pretty sobering, but a fruitful expedition to that mythical "store" called Garbage. In the U.S.S.R., we lived in squalor, but on a relative basis, we lived better than most. Now, all of a sudden, we show up to this place which was supposed to be paved with gold, and the first thing we do is go pick up someone else's trash as furniture. So that's my first memory of the United States.

Q: WAS IT DIFFICULT FOR YOU TO LEARN ENGLISH?

No. It's remarkable. We got to the States in the summer, and I literally sat there all day and watched cartoons—*Tom & Jerry, Looney Tunes*, etc. That's all I did all summer. Between the English classes I took at the army base and watching the cartoons, I was very proficient in English by the time school started in September. I imagine I probably wasn't fluent, but I had zero difficulties, as I recall.

Q: THAT'S INTERESTING AND VERY DIFFERENT FROM WHAT SO MANY OTHER RUSSIAN IMMIGRANTS EXPERIENCED. DID YOU EXPERIENCE ANY BULLYING FOR BEING RUSSIAN?

A clear mistake my parents made was where we began school. When we got to the States, I started school in a highly religious yeshiva (orthodox Jewish school) called the Yeshiva of Kings Bay, Brooklyn. The school was odd because it had a very sizeable Soviet immigrant population, but of course, it was also highly orthodox. On my first day of school, my mother sent me to school with a typical Russian sandwich: bread, butter, and sausage. And when my orthodox teacher saw me eating butter, which is dairy, and sausage, which is not only meat but happened to be pork, she flipped out, grabbed it out of my hand, and threw it out. On the second day of school, my mother gave me the same sandwich, and the teacher threw it out again. So for the first three or four days of school, I did not eat lunch because it ended up in the trash. Finally, my mother called the school in her incredibly broken English and said, "You're not letting my son eat. What's going on?" And they explained to her what kosher was. She literally did not know!

So I didn't experience any anti-Semitism because I went to a yeshiva and didn't feel anti-Russian discrimination in school because there was a sizeable Russian community there.

By the way, I was nine and should have gone to fourth grade, but the yeshiva put me in second grade. The logic was that I had not had any past Hebrew, religious, or English training. It was absurd. The next year, I moved to a local public school in Bensonhurst, which at the time was a very Russian community. So again, I didn't find any anti-Russian sentiment because there was a very large Russian cohort there. And I ended up skipping a grade there because they saw that I was too old to be in the grade the yeshiva had assigned to me, and I was overachieving academically.

Even though I didn't experience anti-Russian sentiment at these schools, I really, really, really wanted to be American. I was ashamed of being an immigrant and different (not sure why). So any time my parents spoke Russian to me in public, I spoke back to them in English, or I just ignored them. It was quite juvenile, but I desperately wanted to be an average American kid. I just wanted to be like everyone else. I didn't want to be different.

Q: YOU MENTIONED YOUR MOM WENT TO NURSING COLLEGE. WAS THAT A SHOCK, BECAUSE SHE HAD NOT BEEN WORKING IN GEORGIA?

Yeah. She worked her butt off. Her English was not terrific. She was about 32 years old and in school with 19-year-olds. She couldn't follow the teacher, so she would come to class every day with an old-school tape recorder, record every class, and then come home and listen to the class over and over with a dictionary in hand. That was the only way she could follow because the class was too quick for her language skills. She got a degree in nursing and became a registered nurse. My father worked as an engineer in some hole-in-the-wall engineering company for a very short while and then designed a pretty innovative auto alarm.

He was pretty handy as an engineer, and the alarm he designed gained some popularity. He ultimately used the money he made from selling the alarm to purchase (with a partner) his very own auto body repair shop in Brooklyn. So he went from designing rocket engines to fixing car engines.

Q: DID THAT HAVE AN EMOTIONAL TOLL ON YOUR FAMILY, OR DID YOU NEVER REALLY SPEAK ABOUT IT?

I'd say my mother did a good job acclimating and accepting the United States and becoming very Americanized. And maybe it's because she worked at a hospital where there was a large American contingent. My father never really left the Soviet contingent. He owned an auto body shop in Brooklyn. All of his cohorts were Russian emigres.

Everybody he associated with was from the U.S.S.R. His English never got as good as it should have because he never really had a reason to. He just kind of got stuck in the Russian immigrant community of Brooklyn. He loved America more than anything, but it felt like he deteriorated over the years in that community, both from a health, mental development, and emotional stability standpoint. While my mother excelled through immigration, my father deteriorated and ultimately died relatively young at 67.

Q: DID YOU GET ANY HELP FROM JEWISH OR WELFARE ORGANIZATIONS?

Yeah, there was a group called Rov Tov. They were a charity whose mission was to help settle Russian immigrants in the United States, and they were quite supportive.

I should also mention how you send money from the U.S.S.R. to the United States. There were a bunch of black market ways to do it. Again, by Soviet standards, my family was well-to-do. So they sent whatever they could at absurd exchange rates via the black market. But the other thing they did, which worked out poorly, is they went out and bought a lot of valuable art, rugs, and antiques. The plan was to ship this to the U.S. with their personal items and sell them in the U.S. to help support our new life. I don't know if you ever heard of a Russian painter called Wassily Kandinsky, but one of his paintings was included. He was a truly great Russian expressionist and highly valuable. So they filled a large shipping container with a collection of artifacts representing much of my family's Soviet assets. When the metal shipping container, which contained the antiques, jewels, rugs, and paintings finally arrived in the U.S., my grandfather almost had a heart attack when he opened it. The vast majority of the contents were stolen, likely in Soviet customs—paintings, jewels, rugs, antiques. Remarkably, the Kandinsky was well hidden in the container and arrived. Still, sadly after many trips to the Sotheby's and Christie's auction houses, my grandfather did not have the paperwork to prove that the painting was authentic. They thought it could be a counterfeit. (We still don't know if it was real or a pricey fake.) With most of the shipment being stolen in transit and the Kandinsky failing to bring value, our family basically had to start all over financially.

Q: DID YOU EVER TAKE A JOB AS A TEENAGER TO HELP YOUR PARENTS, OR DID YOU MOSTLY FOCUS ON SCHOOL?

My parents were incredibly generous for people who didn't have a lot, so I never wanted for much. I think the way they lived their lives was focused on the kids. They would sacrifice whatever it took for their kids. So ironically, in fourth or fifth grade, I always had more money in my pocket than any of my friends whose families had more means.

I remember my friends saying that they had never met a "rich kid" like Danny, even though I actually had less than anybody. Many Russian Jews tend to spoil their kids by giving them what they themselves didn't have. I did have jobs. I worked at Pizza Hut and an Italian deli, but that was more to have some spare cash to do what I wanted to do. But I'd say, given that my family didn't have much, they probably were more generous than they should have been.

Q: LET ME ASK YOU ABOUT TODAY. TO WHAT EXTENT DO YOU THINK YOUR IDENTITY IS A DUAL IDENTITY TODAY? WOULD YOU SAY THAT YOU'RE RUSSIAN-AMERICAN, AND HOW MUCH DOES IT INFLUENCE YOU?

I don't think I have a dual Russian-American identity, and my brother doesn't either. Clearly, we have that heritage, and we have that memory, and it is a meaningful portion of who we are and our makeup, but the identity isn't there. Remember when I told you that I was ashamed of being a Russian imigrant? I don't know why that was. I kind of wish that wasn't there, but I desperately wanted to be American when I was 10 or 11. I was ashamed of being an immigrant. In retrospect, that was silly. But when you're a 10-year-old kid, you don't know what drives your perspective. I just wanted to be like everyone else and wanted my family to be like everyone else. I didn't want to be different. While I speak (and read and write) Russian fluently, and it's a part of who I am, I wanted to be American and formulated my life in a manner where it's a much smaller part of my life, for better or worse, than it is for a lot of my friends who have a similar background. My brother is not too dissimilar, which is interesting.

Q: HAVE YOU EVER GONE BACK TO VISIT GEORGIA?

I have. I've tried to do some business in Russia, so I spent some time there professionally. We lived in London for a long time, so we've made many trips around the world. One of my favorite trips was where we spent 10 days in Tbilisi with my kids. So I have been back to Russia a number of times, and I've been back to Georgia. It's a part of who I am, but I don't really identify with it. As far as I see it, I am an American who lived in Georgia/U.S.S.R. when I was little, not more, not less.

Q: DID YOU TEACH YOUR KIDS RUSSIAN?

I haven't. And perhaps it's a shame. Maybe what I am about to say is just a cop out because, ultimately, I was probably just lazy in not doing so, but I still have some difficult memories from my time in the U.S.S.R. and didn't necessarily want to revisit those in teaching my kids the language—life under communism, anti-Semitism, my great-grandfather being murdered by Stalin, living as refuseniks, our assets being stolen in transit, etc.

But because I consciously made an effort not to teach my kids Russian, they have made an effort to learn it. They've gone to my mother. They have gone to Duolingo. So my kids can speak a little, poorly, but I had little to do with it. It's purely of their own volition. Kudos to them!

Q: DO YOU FEEL ANY RUSSIAN PRIDE, FOR EXAMPLE, WHEN YOU'RE WATCHING RUSSIA IN THE OLYMPICS?

No. I am American, I root for the United States. I have no special feelings about Russia today. It may as well be any other country. I spent about seven years of my life living in Georgia/U.S.S.R. when I was young, and the U.K. more recently (for business). In both cases, those are countries that I happened to live in, not more. I am an American through and through.

Q: IS THERE ANYTHING YOU WANT TO ADD?

We came to this country with nothing. We had nothing, but we have made something of ourselves, and today my kids live the life my parents dreamed of for us. The streets may not be paved with gold, but if you are motivated and passionate, you can pave your own path in gold through hard work. Thus, I think this is the greatest country in the world. It gives anyone a platform to do what they want if they work hard. Is it perfect? No. But for anyone hard-working, talented, and motivated, this country gives you incredible opportunities. I have had considerable success. My brother has had considerable success. Being an immigrant, you kind of have this insecurity. You feel like a second-class citizen. Your parents don't speak the language, and you don't understand the system or how it works. When I applied to college, my parents couldn't help me with direction. They didn't even know what an SAT score was. But that motivates you to pick yourself up by your bootstraps. And if you look at how many successful Gen 1.5 people there are, that speaks to this. On the other hand, others in that generation, who hung around Brighton Beach, didn't truly pursue an education, got stuck in the Soviet mentality and haven't taken the advantages that this country affords. There are two very different divergent paths. This country allows you to pick which path one wants to take—all it takes is hard work and dedication. This is pretty interesting to me. ■

MILA GOTTESMAN

NOW

My name is Mila Gottesman. I was born in Kiev, Ukraine, on August 20, 1964. My full name was Ludmilla, but my mom and all our family and friends called me Mila. Now I live in Westport, Connecticut, where I raised my three children. I teach piano to children and adults and have received a BM and MM in music performance at Manhattan School of Music. I'm going to tell you the story of how I came from the U.S.S.R. through Czechoslovakia, Austria, and Italy to live in the United States.

My mom and my grandfather (my mother's father) were musicians. My grandfather used to accompany the Kiev Ballet, and my mom worked as a piano teacher in Kiev's music school. My father worked as an electrical engineer. Unfortunately, he developed leukemia and passed away at the age of 32. I was only five years old and do not really have any recollection of him.

My life was pretty normal. I went to nursery school at the age of 12 months and then school at the age of seven. Since I was very little, my dream was to become a ballet dancer. But my grandfather told my mom, "Over my dead body she will go into ballet!" Unfortunately, in the '70s in Russia, ballet was taken very seriously, and if you took classes, you were expected to practice many hours a day. So, my mom decided I should take piano lessons instead.

From age five and on, I was enrolled in music school. Throughout the years, my life was basically the same as all the regular kids in my city. I became a Pioneer and went to Pioneer camps every summer. I lived in a communal apartment with two other families until the age of 10. My family had two rooms. My mom's parents occupied one room. The second room was divided into two rooms by a heavy curtain. My parents and I occupied one side of the room, and my aunt occupied the second part. All three families used the kitchen, but each family had its own kitchen table. We had to share a bathroom and bathtub.

Mila in Kiev, Ukraine.

At the age of 10, I moved to a newly developed part of Kiev. Before my father passed away, my parents had bought a three-room condominium. From age 10, we lived in our own apartment, and I had my own room. My mom remarried around the same time. My stepfather also had a one-room condominium apartment and decided to rent it out.

My life was pretty normal, except when I moved and attended a new school, I started to feel anti-Semitism. My classmates started to ask me if I was a Jew. When I answered them, "Yes, I am a Jew," they told me, "We do not have any Jews in our class, and you should move to the class with Jews." I told this to my mom, and somehow, she was able to move me to another class.

Mila in Kiev, Ukraine.

In the 1970s, a lot of our friends and a large population of Jews left the country. American President Jimmy Carter made an agreement with the Soviet government to exchange Jews for wheat. These Jews were considered refugees. Almost everyone got permission to leave unless you worked in a secret job. I remember my stepfather telling us a story that after the 1917 Revolution, his parents decided to leave Russia. By the time they collected all of their documents, the Russian government had closed the border, and his parents lost the opportunity to leave the country. So, my parents decided to immigrate because of anti-Semitism and to seek a better life with more opportunities and freedom of speech. I remember my stepfather telling my mom and me, "This country is not for Jewish people. If there is an opportunity to leave, we should take it." So, my parents applied for immigration. In order to receive a visa for immigration, my parents had to provide papers from their jobs that they did not belong to the Communist Party. They immediately got fired as "enemies of the state." My stepfather came to my school to collect documents stating I was not a Komsomol member. Fortunately, I was not. Otherwise, I would have gone through a very painful meeting with Komsomol members to reject me from the Komsomol Party. After that, I stopped attending school because my parents decided they did not want me to experience any threats or bullying from other children.

Once, my mother stopped back to work to take something she had forgotten. Some of her colleagues and work friends who were very close to her did not even acknowledge her presence and were afraid to speak to an "enemy of the country." However, some people she barely knew approached her and wished her good luck in her new life. She was very surprised by all these reactions from people.

We were lucky to survive for over six months while waiting for permission to leave the country. What mostly helped was the money we got from selling two of our condominium apartments and many valuable books. While we waited, we took private English lessons. Looking back, my parents' knowledge of English was much better than other immigrants leaving the Soviet Union. After over six months of waiting, we finally got permission to leave the country. I was constantly afraid that something would happen and the border would close since I remembered my stepfather's story of his parents not being able to leave the country. We left the country on November 2, 1979, and the border of Ukraine closed two weeks later. The government stopped immigration in Ukraine due to the 1980 Olympic Games in the U.S.S.R. At least that's what they said. All the people with immigration visas had sold their apartments, lost their jobs, had no money, and had to start their lives all over again. We were very, very lucky. While waiting for permission to leave the country, my mom gave 100 rubles (an equivalent of one month's average salary in Russia at the time) to a person in charge of the waiting list to receive visas. He moved our names much closer to the top of the list. I can't imagine what would have happened to us if she had not done that.

Until we passed the Iron Curtain from Czechoslovakia to Austria, I felt very uneasy thinking that something might happen and we would be turned around. Once we arrived in Vienna, we were asked where we would like to immigrate. We had a choice between Canada, the United States, Israel, South Africa, and Germany. My parents had decided to move to the United States a long time ago. Perhaps my mom would have a great job being a musician in Germany, but she felt very uncomfortable living among Germans. We declined to go to Israel due to constant wars, a lack of jobs, and a difficult climate. My parents felt that the United States was a country of more opportunities than Canada. Whoever wanted to go to Israel was taken right away on a plane. We were moved to a hotel with the other immigrants who had decided to go to the other countries.

After leaving Ukraine and arriving in Vienna, everything looked colorful, clean, and beautiful. I was walking around thinking I was in a movie. Everything was unreal. I remember my parents went to the supermarket next to our hotel. My mom almost fainted seeing all the varieties of cheese, meat, salami, etc. She came out of the supermarket shaking.

We stayed in Vienna for 10 days and then were moved to Italy, where we stayed a month. The first couple of days we stayed in a hotel. Then we moved to the suburbs of Rome to a little town called Ladispoli. The Soviet government gave each of us $100 plus one suitcase. Before leaving the U.S.S.R., we bought some Russian souvenirs to sell on the market in Italy to have some money for traveling. I remember my mom, stepfather, and I would go to the market and sell things like classical records, Russian souvenirs, and coffee. That's how we got some money to travel while in Italy. At the end of the month of our stay, we found out that we would be flying to New York. We had no relatives in the United States, and we knew that families without any relatives would usually be moved to big cities because of job opportunities.

I remember flying into JFK Airport in New York on December 27, 1979. It was very, very cold. I remember waiting a long time in the airport after we landed and sitting in the bus. It was very cold and dark, and when I looked out of the bus, I saw a woman sitting in a car. She turned the key and drove away. It struck me that this was the first time seeing a woman drive a car. I was very surprised. The bus driver took us to Brooklyn to an Orthodox neighborhood. I later found out that the neighborhood was called Crown Heights. The private house we moved into had not been lived in for a long time and had accumulated a lot of dust and mice. Four families moved into the house with us, and we each had a room. Our room had a broken door off the hinges, and we had to pick up the door to close it. Our room had three beds with dirty sheets and nothing else, not even one chair. The owner of this house was almost not heating it. We had to stay in coats because it was so cold. My stepfather met the owner of this house and told him he should heat it better because it was freezing outside. But the owner didn't do anything. The next time my stepfather met him, he said, "If you don't heat the house, I will go to the synagogue and tell everyone that you love money more than G-d." After that, the owner started heating the house well.

We lived in this house for a month, and then the Jewish Organization NYANA helped us find an apartment in Queens, New York. We moved to Lefrak City, Queens. It was a complex of 20-story buildings. We got the apartment half price because the Lefrak City owner or management wanted to gentrify a rough neighborhood by bringing in Russian immigrants. Unfortunately, we were not welcomed by the current residents, and after nine months, all of the Russian families had left.

One month after living in the United States, my stepfather found a job as a draftsman, and NYANA stopped helping us. My mom knew back in the Soviet Union that she would study computer programing because in the late '70s and '80s it was a good field to support a family financially. She knew she would not be able to support her family as a musician. She went to a nine-month programming school and found her first job in the United States by saying that she used to work as a computer programmer in the Soviet Union. Of course, they couldn't check her background, and she started working in a field she never knew before. It was very difficult for her to work as a computer programmer without any experience in a new country, culture, and foreign language. I remember her telling me she would go out during lunchtime and walk around the building thinking, "Should I leave the job now or wait until they fire me?" She had never seen computers before! She was very brave. And little by little, by asking different people, she managed to work in this field for 12 years until 1992 when the bank she was working for closed. The same year, my stepfather passed away from colon cancer. After losing her computer programing job and her second husband, my mother decided to go back to teaching piano.

Going back to January 1980, my parents enrolled me in Forest Hills High School in tenth grade. During the enrollment, I found out there were a lot of Russian immigrant kids enrolled in the school. We had so many Russian kids that the school principal decided to make a Russian room we could go to when we were free or needed help.

What struck me the first days of high school was my math teacher sitting on the top of a desk, which would be unthinkable in Kiev, and

Forest Hills School field trip, 1981-1982.

just talking to kids. It also surprised me that kids in high school were much more polite and well-behaved than the school I'd come from in Kiev. I felt the teachers in the United States were much friendlier and more understanding.

We had two Russian teachers. Because I was new at school, it was so much easier to make friends with Russian immigrants like me because we had so much in common. What brought us together was that we had the same background and issues with assimilation to a new culture and environment. All of my friends and my parents' friends ended up being Russian. I made friends with a couple of girls who also studied piano back in the Soviet Union. We even ended up having the same piano teacher during our high school and college years. We were admitted to the same college, Manhattan School of Music, in New York. I decided to go into the music field, aware that it was not the most profitable profession in the United States compared to the Soviet Union, but I had no interest in anything else. I also felt that teaching piano would be the best career choice for me. The same thing happened in college. I ended up living in a Russian bubble because we had no dorms, so I lived with my parents. A lot of Russians attended the Manhattan School of Music. Also, my parents and I lived in a Russian community in Jackson Heights, Queens.

Looking back, the people I spent time with during high school and college had a lot of fun together, going to the movies, having parties, and going on blind dates. I'm sure we all had different values from the American generation of our age, and we were growing up very differently from them.

Five years after moving to the U.S., my parents and I got American citizenship. I formally changed my name from Ludmilla to Mila. My college piano teacher warned me I was making the biggest mistake of my life and said, "Ludmilla is such a pretty name!" However, I was tired of people constantly misspelling my name.

After getting my bachelor's degree, I took a one-month trip to Israel to visit my parents' friends, and there I met my future husband, who was born and raised in Israel. His parents came from Iran and had come to Israel in the early 1950s. We fell in love, and after my master's graduation, he offered to get married and stay in Israel. I rejected this idea because I realized Israel was too small for me. I did not want to raise kids amidst war, and I didn't want to start the immigration process for the second time in my life and learn a new language. I felt if we lived in the United States, it would be a home for us as new immigrants on both sides—his side and my side.

In 1991, we decided to move to Connecticut because of my husband's job. In 1992, my daughter was born, and we decided to name her "Ilana." "Ilan" means oak tree in Hebrew, and she was the first generation born in the United States, so her name had a deep meaning. Later on, we had two more kids, Alexander and Eric.

My kids were raised in three different cultures: Russian, Israeli, and American. Unfortunately, they don't speak Hebrew and Russian as well as they speak English because my husband didn't speak Russian, and I didn't speak Hebrew, so he and I communicated in English. My kids grew up in a completely different environment from mine or their dad's. They grew up in Westport, Connecticut, and went to one of the best public schools in the United States. They grew up being Americans, but at the same time, they were still connected to Russian and Israeli cultures. They went to visit their family in Israel numerous times. They also had a connection to the Russian culture because their grandmother spent a lot of time with them.

Mila's three children: Ilana, Alexander, and Eric.

I never had any siblings or young relatives, and it was not easy to raise three kids. I was faced with different cultures of raising kids (Russian, Israeli, and American). My mother thought that my husband and I were very, very soft with our kids. I remember her saying many times that my kids were "growing as a weed." It created some tension. Because my mother came from a completely different culture, she tended to interfere and give too much advice on how to raise our kids. She did not agree with many ways American kids were raised.

I had to deal with my mom's opinion because my kids didn't have any other relatives in the United States except for her. All the relatives on their dad's side lived in Israel. We also had Russian au pairs, and my kids were exposed to the Russian language and culture. My children went to regular public school, but at the same time, they attended Sunday Hebrew School, and they all got Bar/Bat Mitzvah'ed. They grew up in a very American environment without having any Russian friends.

From 2003 to 2010, I seriously got involved in ballroom dancing. My dream of becoming a ballet dancer never became a reality, but I tried to enjoy dancing in my adult years. I was so much into ballroom dancing that I decided to compete. I even got third place in one of the amateur competitions on the East Coast.

In 2014, my marriage fell apart, and I got divorced. After a while, I decided to go online to find a person to share my life with. Three years later, my dream came true, and I found a wonderful person. My boyfriend is American. His family came to America pre-Civil War. I am happy that he is Jewish, but for me, it is not as important as having a wonderful person around me, so it doesn't make a big difference if the person is Jewish or not. What is most important is that the person is happy, cheerful, educated, and has respect for women. My boyfriend is totally nonreligious, including all his friends and family. I never felt very comfortable in a religious environment, even going to synagogue on the high holidays. It reminded me of Soviet propaganda and brainwashing. A lot of people disagree with me, but I very strongly believe religion separates cultures rather than bringing them together. Although we have completely different backgrounds, my boyfriend and I have common interests and the same life values, passions, and hobbies.

Every day, I feel that I am becoming more American, especially by living with my American boyfriend, meeting his friends, and spending time with his family. It's a lot of fun. A lot of people ask me if I want to visit the city and country where I was born. I'm not sure I will ever go back. I still have the fear that if I go back, I will not be able to leave. For years after I moved from the Soviet Union,

Mila with boyfriend Dickie, Westport 2018.

I had nightmares that I would go back and not be able to return to the United States. It's silly because things have changed, but I can never trust the Russian government. After over 40 years of living outside of Ukraine, I am pretty sure that returning to the country of my birth would make me feel like a foreigner. I do not feel any desire to visit. However, I would love to travel to countries I have never visited before.

If I gave advice to anyone coming to the United States, it would be the American tour guide's advice in Italy during our immigration. The advice was, "Never compare yourself to anyone in the United States." I am very happy I live in this country. I will always be thankful to my parents for bringing me to the United States. I'm particularly happy and grateful that I live in the tri-state area, have a successful career teaching piano, and that my kids live in this country.

While I was writing this essay, my 82-year-old mother passed away. She was buried at the Mt. Hebron Cemetery, in Flushing, New York, next to my stepfather, on March 18, 2021. I realized nobody has my family's immigration story except me. Just me. How strange. That is why it's important to write our memories for our children and grandchildren so they can pass them on to future generations. ■

LISE FALALEEV

NOW

My name is Elisabeth Miranowski, but I was born Elizaveta Andreevna Falaleyeva (Elisabeth A. Falaleev) in St. Petersburg, Russia, in 1977. When I became a U.S. citizen in 1995, I dropped the patronymic. I live in Riverside, Connecticut, with my husband and our three children. I'm a lawyer by training but am staying home for now to raise my three children. I definitely drink more coffee and win fewer arguments now than I did when I was practicing law.

Q: TELL ME ABOUT YOUR FAMILY'S BACKGROUND IN RUSSIA.

My mother's father was a communist official in the army, and her mother was a surgeon. Bear in mind when you read "communist officials," we are not talking about a time or place that gave them much choice in the matter. They were very busy, so my mother, Marina, was essentially raised by her paternal grandmother Elisabeth, who managed to stay out of the communist propaganda machine, and retained the beliefs and culture of pre-revolutionary Russia. This made for an interesting upbringing for my mother in mid-20th century Russia (or rather, the Soviet Union). Despite embracing the anti-communist views shared by my great-grandmother, my mother still had to follow the protocols set forth by the communist regime, attending scout camps, working at a kolkhoz (communal state farm) in the summer, etc. But my mother's impetuous nature bubbled up regularly. I love the story of her best friend, Nikita's, birthday one summer when they were in college. My mother and Nikita were at two separate kolkhozy, but that didn't stop her and her friends from celebrating Nikita's birthday in St. Petersburg by attending an underground art exhibition. They snuck out of their farms under some sacks of potatoes in a wagon, went to the city, and were back by dawn! I think my mother instinctively knew for a long time, long before the actual thought took hold, that she would not stay in the Soviet Union.

My parents met at university. They were both students in the Linguistics Department at Saint Petersburg State University. My mother was majoring in English and my father in Norwegian and Swedish. They married during their senior year, at the end of which I was born. They were part of the '60s and '70s generation, involved in the underground rock and art movements and curious to learn about the world beyond the U.S.S.R., constantly mingling with foreign students. Boris Grebenshchikov, widely considered one of the "founding fathers" of Russian rock music, was their close friend and briefly lived and played in my father's home on Kamenny Ostrov (Stone Island) in St. Petersburg. If you look in *The Village Voice* archives from 1989, you'll find an article entitled, "The Rooms off Nevsky Prospect: A Decade in Aquarium." Aquarium was Grebenshchikov's band, and the article talks about my father and our house and mistakenly refers to me as Boris' daughter (we were the same age, but her name was Alisa). It even mentions my pet donkey, Bibi-Khanym, that my parents had smuggled back from their honeymoon in Tajikistan. I've yet to meet another person whose first pet was a donkey.

Since my parents were both completing graduate degrees during my earliest years, I often stayed with my mother's parents a couple of miles down the road from the smoky music-filled house on Stone Island. My maternal grandparents helped raise me, my grandfather standing in long lines to get me fresh berries or the state-provided formula while my mother attended classes, eventually completing her master's in linguistics and comparative literature.

We left Russia when I was three, so my memories are few but precious—our apartment, my paternal grandmother's home on Stone Island and, of course, my pet donkey. I was distraught to leave Bibi when we left Russia and cried when he was taken to the Leningrad Zoo.

Q: ARE THERE TIMES WHEN MEMORIES COME BACK TO YOU? ARE THERE ANY SIGHTS OR SMELLS YOU ENCOUNTER NOW THAT TRIGGER SOME OF THOSE MEMORIES FOR YOU?

You know those Russian deli shops that seem to occupy half of Brighton Beach (Brooklyn)? There aren't that many around here, but there's a Polish-Russian store in Stamford, Connecticut, called Warsaw Deli. I went in for the first time about a year ago, and my reaction to the smell floored me. "Oh my gosh, this smells like Russia," I thought. I couldn't tell you if that olfactory memory was from Russia itself or if it was from my time here, growing up and going to Russian school or Russian camp. But I can tell you that I started crying standing in that store, hearing a little babushka berate her husband for not grabbing the right jar of pickled herring. Sometimes I take for granted that I'm Russian, and I have done little to hold on to that heritage as an adult, which probably is not uncommon in this day and age when we are all so busy. But at that moment, I was so upset with myself for not having taken more time to hold on to more of my heritage over the years. The Russian language and culture are exceptional. Opinions differ on the country as it is now, but the Russian language and culture, and the Russian people, are wonderful.

Q: DID YOU STOP SOMEWHERE ON YOUR WAY TO AMERICA?

Yes, we spent a year in Vienna as political refugees with Caritas. We shared an apartment with two other families while Caritas was looking for a sponsor for us in the U.S.

Q: WAS IT A CULTURE SHOCK TO BE IN VIENNA AFTER RUSSIA?

Not really. You have to remember that St. Petersburg is more European than most Russian cities, so on the surface (i.e., architecturally), it was not shockingly different. But I do remember that I suddenly couldn't understand what people were saying and didn't know why. So in that sense, you can say, yes, there was a bit of a shock. Differences in lifestyles or politics were beyond me at that age, so those types of differences, including the availability of so many more items in stores, went over my head.

Q: WHAT HAPPENED WHEN YOU LANDED IN THE U.S.?

Eventually, Caritas sent us to San Francisco, since there was a large Russian community there, in the hopes that my parents might find employment in one of the universities, given their academic background. They settled in Berkeley, and my father began working at the Monterey Institute of International Studies (now Middlebury Institute of International Studies), teaching and translating. By then, my parents knew they were separating, and my mother didn't apply for jobs in California. Instead, she moved with me to the East Coast, where she had a few old friends. My mother was glad to have a small community in the tri-state area to become part of and reconnect with many friends from her university days. Many of the foreign students she had befriended in her country years before now welcomed her to their country.

I started school at Greenwich Catholic Elementary School. Since my mother was a single working parent, she signed me up for all kinds of after-school activities at the Greenwich YWCA—gymnastics, swimming, chess, cooking, arts, etc.—to keep me occupied until the end of the working day. Being Russian, she also made sure I studied piano and took ballet classes on the weekends. And most importantly, she signed me up for "Russian school" at the Holy Virgin Protection Russian Orthodox Church in Nyack, New York, where I studied Russian language, history, religion, and culture on Saturdays during the school year. In July, I attended a Russian sleepaway camp in the Catskills called Camp NORR, which stood for the National Association of Russian Explorers (in Russian: Национальная Организация Русских Разведчиков, or НОРР). These helped preserve the culture and language for me, and they enabled me to develop lifelong friendships with many other young Russians.

While I was starting school, my mother found an entry-level IT job with CBS Publishing in Greenwich and rented an apartment in Stamford. The owner of the apartment was from the old Russian emigration (so-called "White Russians") and had a son, Ivan, living in New York City who visited him often. Over time my mother and Ivan became good friends, and romance blossomed. They married in 1985.

Q: SO YOU MOVED TO SAN FRANCISCO WHEN YOU ARRIVED FROM THE SOVIET UNION. DO YOU HAVE ANY DISTINCT MEMORIES OF SAN FRANCISCO?

No, not really distinct. And again, there was less of an "I can't understand people" because my mom had tried to teach me some words of English and songs of English. We have recordings of me when I was a small child reciting *Humpty Dumpty*. So I think I started to assimilate there, but our living situation was unusual because we didn't have much money. We weren't allowed to take much out of the Soviet Union, and my parents had already separated, pretty much on arrival. So my mom found a room in a house with five other roommates, and children were not allowed. So I was basically hidden in her room. Luckily, we weren't in the Bay Area long.

Q: ONCE YOU MOVED TO THE EAST COAST, DID BEING RUSSIAN, OR FROM SOMEWHERE ELSE, AFFECT HOW OTHER KIDS TREATED YOU?

I didn't speak English well right away. I remember struggling a little bit in the early grades. It was obviously easiest when I was in Russian school or at Camp NORR. Kids in kindergarten don't label much. They sort of accept everybody. You can come in with three arms, and they'd get used to you. As you get older, probably around second or third grade, kids start to identify who's different and who's not. I'm seeing that again as a parent now.

I would say that probably in fourth or fifth grade it started being a "thing" that I was from somewhere else and had a bit of an accent. Occasionally having caviar sandwiches for lunch probably didn't help, but they were so good!

Then as you got into middle school—and I'm sure this is similar for everybody you've talked to—kids started to identify with what was happening in the world (or at least as they heard about it from others). The whole concept of the Soviet Union and communism entered the picture. As you know, Russia was always the enemy in movies, and that's where we were from. So yes, I got a good amount of "You're a commie" and all that other fun stuff.

The biggest long-term impact of this was linguistics. Russian is my native language, but I started intentionally not speaking it at home with my parents because I didn't want to be different. I wanted to assimilate. And for anyone who has ever studied Russian, it's a hard language to learn. I really do regret how much of it I've lost. Too much to pass it on to my children. I can still understand everything, and I can speak (although with an American accent and imperfect pronunciation), and my reading is okay but slow! My ability to write has almost completely faded.

Q: HOW DID THE DECISION TO DOWNPLAY THE RUSSIAN LANGUAGE AT HOME GO OVER?

Not well. My mom tried hard to maintain the Russian culture for us. We couldn't afford much, so she would volunteer to teach at the Russian school in return for me going for free. It was an hour drive each way and lots of class prep on top of her work, so no small undertaking. I didn't appreciate at the time how much she was doing. She didn't want me to be 100 percent Russian, but she did want me to keep a strong connection to where we came from. So it did bother her quite a bit. She was very insistent. "You have to do your homework. You have to go to Russian school. You have to speak Russian." I can still hear her saying, "No mixing languages!" when I'd try to slip in English words for Russian ones I didn't know. She tried very hard. But social pressure is powerful when you're a tween/teen.

Q: WHEN YOU WERE GROWING UP, DID YOUR PARENTS, OR DID YOUR MOM, HAVE MANY RUSSIAN FRIENDS?

In the beginning, my mom only had Russian friends, and that was why we came over here. And you know what they say: It takes a village to raise a child. They were her village at one point as she was juggling three jobs. So at first, it was only Russian people. But she later expanded her social circle beyond Russians, and that happened primarily through work.

Q: WHEN YOU WERE GROWING UP, WERE YOU INSPIRED BY THE IMMIGRANT WORK ETHIC?

I don't think I grasped it. I know other Russian immigrants are very aware of it, but I wasn't as much. My mom was in survival mode. I had a lot of after-school activities. I just wanted to be the best in my class but not because of being an immigrant.

Q: DID YOU HELP YOUR MOM OUT IN ANY WAY BY WORKING ODD JOBS, OR WERE YOU MORE FOCUSED ON SCHOOL?

No, I was more focused on school growing up. In fact, my mom wouldn't let me get jobs when I was younger—at least not during the school year—because she wanted me to prioritize schoolwork and grades. I babysat here and there, but no steady job.

Once I was fifteen, the focus shifted to internships in the summers, but it wasn't for pocket money. I think I was allowed to keep 20 percent of what I took home, and the rest went to savings for college.

In college, I worked for most of my spending money. I knew that the tuition at Middlebury College stretched us beyond what we could afford, and I was grateful my parents had let me go.

At one point, I had three work-study jobs. Speaking of college, I applied for a program at Middlebury called the International Major, which has since been discontinued. It allowed you to graduate in three years by taking an accelerated course load plus spending two summers at the famous Middlebury Language Schools. I thought this was a perfect program for me. Only a handful of students were accepted into this program each year, so very competitive, plus financially interesting in that not only did you pay less for college overall, you entered the workforce earlier. I was accepted and was one of the first graduates of that program. (Seven started my year, but only three finished.)

Q: WHEN YOU WERE GROWING UP, DID YOU CELEBRATE AMERICAN HOLIDAYS LIKE THANKSGIVING OR FOCUS MORE ON RUSSIAN HOLIDAYS?

At first, we focused more on Russian holidays. And because we are Russian Orthodox, we followed the old Julian calendar when it came to those holidays. Christmas for us, for example, was January 7. What we called "American Christmas" Eve was the day we got our Christmas tree. Yes, that did mean slim pickings for trees! But it was a fun tradition on a day that otherwise didn't have traditions for us. And once I started working, it was great not to compete for vacation days around American Christmas. I could always get time off during the week after New Year's.

Celebrating the Russian holidays was great at home, but also a fun time with other Russian friends. As you know, there is a significant Russian community in the tri-state area. Thanks to that, we were able to celebrate all the Russian holidays surrounded by other Russian Orthodox people. Just across the Tappan Zee Bridge lies a Russian Orthodox convent called Novo-Diveevo, and we would go there for church and religious celebrations. The church that ran our Russian School, Holy Virgin Protection Russian Orthodox Church, would host traditional celebrations, like Blini (the Russian Orthodox answer to Mardi Gras) and pelmeni to ring in Stary Novy God (Старый Новый год—the Old Russian New Year). Perhaps because we were "far from home," the Russian community also created semi-holidays—long weekends where everyone would go to the Tolstoy Foundation, retreats for youth to different Orthodox churches traditionally held on certain dates, etc. We all looked forward to these because many of us did not get to see each other outside of these events. Remember, this is pre-social media and cell phones! We wrote lots of letters!

But I am digressing. You asked about American holidays. We started celebrating Thanksgiving when I was in high school. At that point, most of our family was American (namely, my younger brothers, who were born here, and my stepfather, who had already been naturalized). And we loved going to the Fourth of July fireworks in Stamford. All in all, we were proud to live here, and I would say by that point, even though I was still not a citizen, I felt just as American as I did Russian.

Q: DID YOU RESENT THIS OR ACCEPT IT?

The emphasis on Russian holidays? To be honest, I feel that growing up, until probably eighth grade, my closest friends were my Russian friends because we had so much in common. And the funny thing is very few of them were born in Russia. Most of them were born here. But honestly, if you were at one of our friend catch-ups or dinners, you might not know if you were in the U.S. or Russia. Everyone was speaking Russian, and there were Russian icons up in the corner of the kitchen and so on. It was easy. We didn't have to think about anything. So when we did the Russian holidays, that was just normal.

It's funny because we're having these discussions now in our house that make me think about those things. With our oldest, we're getting to that "Is Santa real or is he not?" phase. And we have celebrated Russian Christmas (with my parents) and American Christmas (with my husband's parents). So how do you explain how that can all coexist? But for me, it was normal. I joked to my friends that I got to celebrate two Christmases. "I get yours off, and then I get to celebrate mine." And as I mentioned before, in the work world, it was great because everybody wanted Christmas week off. And marrying somebody who's not Orthodox is also great because divvying up the holidays is easy—no need to alternate the big ones!

Q: DID YOU AT SOME POINT GRAVITATE AWAY FROM YOUR RUSSIAN FRIENDS TOWARD AMERICAN FRIENDS?

I don't know if I wanted to gravitate away from my Russian friends. I really enjoyed both groups, and they were so distinct. I actually had two sweet sixteens, a Russian one and an American one. But I will say that I was probably the most American of my Russian friends. For example, I was a cheerleader, and no one else was. So I think it was inevitable that I kind of separated more than the others. I'd say the rest of my friends have remained tighter with each other than I have with them. Then once you go to college, it gets much harder, regardless of what backgrounds or origins your friend groups have. You're living far away, so you can't just catch up on Friday night. Your interests shift, and you focus on summer internships and your career goals and where you end up in grad school. It gets harder to maintain friendships that don't have as many commonalities as they did 10 years before.

Social media has a lot of pros and cons, but one pro is that you can still stay abreast of what folks are up to. It makes it easier to reconnect in little ways when you can't in big ways. I love "seeing" my childhood friends with their spouses and children, and dropping each other little comments here and there feels like a quick little hug from far away.

Q: HOW DID BEING RUSSIAN AFFECT YOUR COLLEGE EXPERIENCE? DID YOU FEEL AS IF YOU WERE DIFFERENT FROM THE TYPICAL MIDDLEBURY STUDENT IN ANY WAY?

Oh goodness, no! At Middlebury, I was so boring. I remember my first class on the first day. I sat between a girl who had skied for the Norwegian national team and another girl who had taken the previous year off to do volunteer work in Africa. If you have an interesting or international background, I'm not sure you could end up at a better school. I don't know if you know about the language schools at Middlebury in the summer. I did the French school, which is a seven-week immersion course. I loved it. It was also a small world. It turned out one of the professors at the Russian school had a daughter my age, and we had overlapping friend groups. We had been at the same parties, etc., so we would meet up now and then to hang out (which was against summer school policy, as I had signed an oath to only speak French during my summer, and we would speak English and Russian).

One summer, it happened to be the 50th anniversary of the Russian Language School. As part of the 50th-anniversary celebrations, the famous Don Cossack Choir came to perform at Middlebury, and my friend snuck me in to see them perform and attend the after-party, where we sang Russian songs and performed Russian dances with them. While I was taking a break from doing the traditional Russian dances, I felt a tap on my shoulder. I turned around to find the head of the French school who asked me, in French, what I was doing there, and did I not recall I had signed a pledge to speak no language other than French? Caught red-handed! I was given an official warning and told to go back to the French dorms. It was past midnight at that point, so I didn't have any complaints. It had been worth it to sing and dance with the Don Cossacks!

Q: WHERE DID YOU CHOOSE TO LIVE AFTER COLLEGE? WAS IT IMPORTANT FOR YOU TO LIVE NEAR YOUR FAMILY?

You know, not really. Growing up in Connecticut, Manhattan was the obvious choice.

Q: SO WHAT PORTION OF YOUR SOCIAL CIRCLE RIGHT NOW IS MADE UP OF RUSSIANS?

Close to zero, which is funny because it was probably 30 percent in college and 50 percent in high school, increasing as you continue in that direction. Geography is part of it. If Natasha hadn't moved to Switzerland, if Tamara wasn't in Minnesota, and Katya wasn't in Sea Cliff, we'd probably see each other much more often. The four of us were best friends when we were seven years old.

Tamara is the best at keeping in touch. I love her for it. And it was wonderful going to Natasha's wedding just a few years ago. One of my resolutions for next year, when all three kids will be in school five days a week, is to make more effort. It's amazing how much time just disappears when you're raising kids! But thank goodness for social media, cell phones, and email. It allows us to hang on to friendships that would be otherwise hard to maintain, even in a limited fashion.

Q: YOU MENTIONED THAT YOU STILL CELEBRATE ORTHODOX CHRISTMAS IN ADDITION TO AMERICAN CHRISTMAS. ARE THERE ANY OTHER UNIQUELY RUSSIAN TRADITIONS THAT YOU FOLLOW RIGHT NOW?

Sort of. We occasionally make pirogi—only the meat ones (I'm not a huge fan of the other options!—and join my parents for blini when we can.

For International Week of the Child, I enjoy going into my child's preschool classroom and talking to them about being from Russia. I bring in my old БУКВАРЬ (Bukvar Russian Alphabet Primer), some matryoshka dolls, and a picture book of St. Petersburg. I think I will keep doing that after my children graduate. It's fun to share.

Other than the double holidays, that's about it unless you count the fact that each kid has a matryoshka doll!

I will say that being Russian is akin to being Jewish for some people in that it's as much a cultural identity as it is a religious belief. And so, for me, even though we are raising our family Episcopalian, I will always be Russian Orthodox. So if I'm in a bind or I'm worried, I'll pray in Russian. Sometimes when I'm up late working on some volunteer project, I'll play Grebenshikov in the background. These are little things, but I try to hold on to them for myself. I'll watch Russian TV and stuff. I very rarely go to church, frankly, in large part, because there is no Russian Orthodox church. It's a road trip.

I am distinctly more American right now. I love to reminisce about the Russian experiences I was lucky enough to have when I was younger, doing traditional Russian dances with the Yale Russian Choir (and, of course, the Don Cossacks!), presenting bread and salt to the Romanov descendants when they came to New York, attending Russian balls at the Plaza Hotel, performing in traditional Russian plays and musicals with friends. These were highlights of my childhood.

Q: ARE THERE ANY RUSSIAN VALUES YOU WANT TO PASS ON TO YOUR CHILDREN OR HAVE ALREADY PASSED ON?

It's hard for me to define what's really a Russian value. Take frugality or not raising spoiled kids. I feel like we try to drill that into our kids, and my husband is not Russian despite having a very Russian-sounding last name. We definitely teach our kids not to waste. My kids have known what a short-order cook is since they were little because I keep telling them, "Mommy is not a short-order cook. If you don't like what's for dinner and you're not hungry, you can go upstairs. If you're hungry, you'll eat it." My mom was a single mom for a very long time. And even when she met my dad, it wasn't like there was an influx of money. She was very big on not wasting anything, from food to clothing and everything in between. Especially raising kids in Greenwich, it's easy to lose your perspective. So I'd say the "don't waste it" mentality definitely carries through. I can't tell if it's uniquely Russian, but I don't know any Russians my generation or older who are wasteful or spend needlessly.

Interestingly, Russians are considered fatalistic. It's so prevalent that people have written papers about it. Having witnessed that approach to life firsthand, that is actually something I'm working NOT to pass on—nature vs. nurture.

Q: DID YOU TEACH YOUR KIDS RUSSIAN?

I did not. My mom tried a little bit. Interestingly, French was a stronger language for me than English for a while because I spent most of my twenties in France. I had planned to raise my children bilingual, French-English (being bilingual is such a gift!), and I started out speaking only in French to my oldest when she was born. But when she was almost six months old, we got a babysitter for a couple of afternoons a week who was a native Spanish speaker. We then concluded that Spanish would be more useful, and I stopped teaching her French. But it never occurred to me to pass on the Russian language because my Russian wasn't that strong. You could drop me in Russia, and I'd be fine, although I would have an accent that would identify me as being from America. I still recall when my mom and I went back the first time after the Berlin Wall fell. The state museums were free to Russian nationals, so my mom told me to stand behind her and not talk. In other words, my Russian would give away that I wasn't a Russian national. Languages are living things, so if you don't use them regularly, and with people who speak them currently, your vocabulary descends to that of a child. Your pronunciation starts to go since different language families emphasize different muscle combinations when speaking.

I used to joke and say that my Russian vocabulary is like that of a 10-year-old because I don't know how to talk about things like technology, the Internet, and cars—things beyond you as a 10-year-old. I just don't have that vocabulary. I could pick it up, and I'm sure I have some of it from reading, but I don't have a strong enough feeling about my Russian to pass it, compared to my French. I still dream in French. My French is probably close to on par with my English, even though I don't speak it as much.

Q: HOW MANY TIMES HAVE YOU BEEN BACK TO RUSSIA SINCE YOU LEFT?

Two, maybe three. My husband and I had planned to go in 2011. But then we found out I was pregnant, and I decided that we would postpone the trip just to be safe. But then we had kids, and travel became a very different proposition. So I have not been back in a while; I think the last time was 2006 or 2007. I'm hopeful that when the kids are a little older, we can take them to show them St. Petersburg. It truly is one of the most beautiful cities in the world.

Q: DO YOU FEEL RUSSIAN ETHNIC PRIDE? DO YOU EVER ROOT FOR RUSSIA AGAINST THE U.S. IN THE OLYMPICS? WHAT IF RUSSIA IS PLAYING ANOTHER COUNTRY?

Haha, yes! 100 percent! The Olympics are a tricky one, just because of all the issues surrounding the Russian team. But international soccer matches, etc., I do root for Russia. We joke that the house splits down the middle if it's U.S. vs. Russia, but it's mostly for fun. And if Russia is playing a team other than the U.S., the kids will usually support Russia as well because it's "Mommy's team."

On a separate level, Russia today is tricky politically. But for me, and it probably actually helps that I have not been back in so long, the memories are more real than the actual country. If I'm honest, much of my pride in being Russian comes from how amazing Russia's historical contributions are to different areas, such as literature.

Q: HOW HAS YOUR RUSSIAN BACKGROUND HELPED YOU UNDERSTAND AND APPRECIATE AMERICA EVEN MORE THAN NATIVE-BORN AMERICANS?

Being from Russia, and you could say even more so being from the Soviet Union, has helped me appreciate America much more. I feel it in particular now. We live in an age of finger-pointing and chest-beating, where people are quick to criticize America for the mistakes of some and ignore all the good that this country has stood for and still stands for. I find this a little hard to swallow. It feels very divisive. Coming from a country where you basically had NOTHING, I can't help but appreciate everything we all have. ■

YULIYA SHNEYDERMAN

NOW

I am 41 years old, have two young children, and live in Brooklyn, New York. I am a community college professor, teaching public health and health education for nine years now. I initially lived in Miami and went to grad school there, but the rest of my time in the U.S. has been in New York.

I hear the Russian language everywhere I go. I've heard it in South Carolina, Colorado, Florida, Georgia, Louisiana, Illinois, New York, Prague, Vienna, Istanbul, and Tel Aviv. As a tourist, I can just hear it and let it pass most of the time. The people speaking it might be my neighbors at a restaurant, but they pass in and out of my life quickly.

We came to the U.S. when I was 11, in 1992, about a month after the Soviet Union finally broke up, and we weren't sure whether we could still leave. I remember leaving very clearly. We had slowly been selling off our things. Our house in Bykhov was bare. We had bags sewn to specifications so we could take some homey things with us—sheets, blankets, dishes, even some crystal vases (most of which ended up in splinters when we finally opened the bags at our destination). We sent a few boxes of books to my aunt and uncle, who were the ones inviting us to the U.S. We wore more jewelry than usual because we could only bring a certain amount with us in the luggage. The lights were off, so we sat with kerosene lamps, and the soot was slowly blackening the ceiling of our home. Early in the morning, a small bus arrived, and we packed all that we had, and my mom, dad, paternal grandmother, and I got on the bus. At some point, I fell asleep and woke up close to Moscow. This was only my second visit to Moscow in my life. Several months before this, I went there with my dad to get some documents or forms.

Young Yuliya recites a poem in honor of the October Revolution under a portrait of Lenin.

We went directly to the airport and were escorted to an area for those seeking refuge in other countries. It was very hot (though it was January outside), and we were stripping off our heavy coats. I remember there were soldiers around us. My dad asked the soldiers for some water for me. What I remember the most, and even now can make me tear up if I'm not careful, is that I couldn't keep my favorite toy because it was too big to fit into a suitcase, and we were told we couldn't take it on the plane. It was a stuffed dog I slept with every night. Finally, we got on the plane and began the long journey. I remember little of the flights. I know we had to land in Germany, not where we anticipated, possibly because of bad weather. At the airport, the whole group of people who left Moscow that day all sat together waiting for our next flight. There were these beautiful green apples. I remember eating an apple and thinking how strange it was that they were just sitting there for people to take. My parents later told me that my dad was the first to take an apple, which led to others getting some too. Then, onto another plane. My next memory is running through JFK Airport in New York to make it to our next flight. The next clear memory is leaving the airport in Miami and feeling the hot, humid air. We already took off our coats but now had to take off our sweaters as well. My uncle met us and drove us to our new apartment. I remember driving by the "Welcome to Miami Beach" sign.

We came to the U.S. courtesy of HIAS, a Jewish charity that helps resettle refugees, and we had two Jewish families sponsor us here who arranged an apartment, second-hand furniture, a fridge full of food, and even the use of a car. In the next few days, we met the two families who sponsored us, and they, and my uncle and his family, were our main source of social contact for the next few months. They introduced us to their synagogue, invited us over for Passover, and introduced my cousins and me to crafting. At the same time, my parents had to find work, and we all started taking English classes, went to several agencies to get documents, food stamps, Medicaid, and various other social services. In about a month, it was time for me to go to school.

Meanwhile, we experienced cultural shock after cultural shock. In Miami, even in the winter, we could go to the beach or go to the pool on the roof of our building. The supermarkets had many different kinds of food and brands, too. The difference between them was unfathomable for me. We could only afford to shop when items were on sale, but we still got to eat foods that seemed exotic to us, like bananas and cereal. In fact, I ate so many bananas in my first years in the U.S. that I couldn't stand the smell of bananas for a long time. One way that I know I'm not quite as assimilated as I may seem is that I let my cereal get really soggy before eating it. Eating crunchy food barely dipped in milk for breakfast was always a strange thing for me. I was used to cooked kashas of various sorts or salami and bread.

My parents, both highly educated and having completed the equivalent of bachelor's degrees, had to start working for cash in whatever jobs they could. My dad parked cars for a while, and I can only imagine the terror of driving in a new country, knowing barely any English, and especially knowing the kind of terrible drivers zooming around South Beach. Then he washed dishes in a gay bar and finally got a job for the Department of Education, driving around to schools to meet with Russian immigrant kids to help them with school work. My mom first worked as a bartender at the same gay bar as my father, then as a full-time babysitter, and eventually ended up in retail, where she has remained since then, steadily making her way to fancier stores. My first paying job was as an occasional babysitter at age 12 for a woman in our apartment building.

I began school in America in seventh grade at a local public school. Luckily for me, I wasn't the only immigrant kid in middle school who was from the former Soviet Union. I was assigned a Russian-speaking buddy—a girl named Olga—to take me around classes, show me the cafeteria, gym, and introduce me to the American way of doing things. The biggest surprise came in the cafeteria—I had to pay for my lunch! Most kids and the teacher spoke Spanish in my ESOL classes (English for speakers of other languages), but I was steadily learning English anyway. I watched some cartoons, most memorably the *Teenage Mutant Ninja Turtles*, listened along with the news shows that my parents and grandma watched, and eventually, I turned to my first love, reading. The other Russian girls in my classes were welcoming, and one of them introduced me to romance novels. It was just the right timing for me since I was just starting puberty, and it followed nicely after the two books that our sponsors provided for me—*Are You There God? It's Me, Margaret* and a *Baby-Sitters Club*. After reading those several times over, I started to read books that I borrowed from Larissa, my romance-obsessed, slightly older friend.

The next big shock for us all came in August 1992, just a few months after we got to Florida and after I finished seventh grade. We started to see news reports about the first hurricane of that season coming to South Florida—Hurricane Andrew. For a few days, we kept the TV on nonstop to understand what this weather phenomenon was. Growing up in landlocked Belarus, I didn't understand how serious these natural disasters can be. My parents called their relatives as well as the sponsors and tried to understand what to do. Finally, after the evacuation order came, we loaded up the car and went north to stay with our sponsors at their parents' house. After the hurricane was over, our apartment building fared alright, but our sponsors' homes in South Miami were destroyed. As we drove back, I marveled at the giant palm trees blocking the roads, windows shattered, street signs laying on the ground or bent in half and started to understand the awesome power of these storms. We spent the next few days without air conditioning because the power was still out in our neighborhood during the hottest days of the year. We slept on the balcony as well as we could. At the time, because of my horrible scoliosis, I was wearing a plastic brace to keep my spine aligned. I had to abandon it for that time because the heat was unbearable. My second paying job was cleaning my mom's employer's yard along with my dad after the hurricane. We spent the whole day piling giant palm fronds and various debris into garbage bags.

At the beginning of eighth grade, I understood English pretty well but was still too nervous about speaking in class. Many kids knew that I was from the former Soviet Union and called me Commie or asked me ridiculous questions about my former home, like were there electric lights? Even without speaking much, I was able to excel in my classes, and the same kids who would tease or bully me, nevertheless, were comfortable asking me for help or tutoring in math and science classes, at which I was particularly good. I suspect this was partly because I was way ahead of my classmates in math and science when I was studying in Belarus. I was already doing algebra and geometry in seventh grade there but didn't get back into algebra until eighth grade and geometry in ninth grade in the U.S. Even the teachers remarked on my abilities, sometimes in front of my classmates. They were probably trying to motivate them. "Look at this immigrant girl who came here six months ago. She is already doing better than you." But it just led to more social exclusion for me.

I was used to not having a lot of friends. In Belarus, in my hometown of Bykhov, my family occupied a fairly prestigious place. My grandfather was the head of the bank, and my dad was an assistant principal at one of the schools. But my last name was clearly Jewish, and because my dad was in a position of power in the school, instead of the expected bullying, I was excluded, and kids regarded me with suspicion. I wasn't leaving a rich friend-filled life when we left, though it was still a scary prospect. In Miami, I slowly made a few friends, either Russian-speaking kids like me or other immigrants or children of immigrants. I also hung out with my cousins. They arrived in the U.S. about two years before us and were much more accustomed to American life by then. They also already had a little collection of Barbies and Disney movies, luxuries that I didn't have much access to outside of their home. Eventually, once my sister was born, we also got a collection of toys and movies that I enjoyed a bit. Our sponsors took us to Disney World, which was an amazing and dazzling experience for me. Over time it became less amazing because we could go on a day trip to Disney World occasionally. We got up very early, packed sandwiches and snacks, drove for four or five hours, spent the day in the park, and then drove straight home since we couldn't afford hotel stays. Growing up in Florida did afford me the luxury of seeing all of the Disney amusement parks.

My parents saved up some money to buy a condo, and we moved north to the city of Aventura, still in the same county, so still part of the greater Miami area. I had to switch schools quickly. First, I went to ninth grade in a high school in Miami Beach, then back to a middle school in North Miami Beach, and finally, I entered tenth grade in the high school in North Miami Beach, where I stayed until graduation. The exclusion followed me. Most of the kids in school had known each other since elementary school. They were from well-off families, and they had no time for an awkward immigrant girl, who nevertheless excelled in school. I talked to other high-achieving students but didn't make friends with most of them. I can count the number of real friends I had on one hand, though I could fit into several friend groups and did even at that time. I hung out with goths, alternative kids, nerds, and my core friend group was made up of those same immigrants and kids of immigrants. I enjoyed some of my peers' same high school experiences, like going to prom or a homecoming game. Still, my parents were adamantly against letting me stay over at people's houses, and I had a lot of babysitting duties since my sister was born shortly after we arrived in Miami. I also started to work at 14 so I could save some money for college. Of course, I was going to college. There was never a question about this among my friends and parents.

I dreamt of Columbia University in New York without ever visiting it or really knowing much about it. I applied and got in early. Only then, my dad and I visited the campus on a long road trip from Miami. I met my grandmother's first cousin Dyadya Yasha and his wife, Tetya Fanya. (In Russian, "dyadya" is like Mr. or uncle, and "tetya" is like Mrs. or aunt.) From that first visit, I stayed in touch with them until they both passed away. They were always amazingly welcoming and warm, and they treated me like a granddaughter. By their standards, I never called or came over enough, which is a common thing I heard from my paternal grandmother as well. When I did come over for a celebration or just a visit, they always fed me, asked me about my life, and told me stories of theirs. Dyadya Yasha would often pour me some vodka, I suspect so he could have some along with me. I can only wish that I'd been able to write things down that they told me. I miss that from my family. I never got to hear old stories from my grandparents. One grandfather died young, my other grandfather stayed in Belarus, and both grandmothers were strongly affected by dementia toward the end of their lives. Dyadya Yasha was the only one who stayed very lucid until the end of his life, and I truly enjoyed our visits, even after he couldn't drink vodka anymore. He had had several strokes when he was younger, so his left side was partially paralyzed. He sported prison tattoos, had a great sense of humor, a big smile, and a big heart.

My high school peers mostly resented my success. We were in quite an academically competitive and segregated school. Most students taking the advanced classes were white and mostly Jewish, while the rest of the school was mostly Black and Latino/a. While I was not in line for valedictorian, I did quite well in school. I moved up to honors classes by tenth grade, and in twelfth grade, I took all AP classes (and seven AP exams at the end of the year). Our high school GPAs were weighted, so we got one extra point for honors classes and two extra for AP. In the middle of senior year, when the GPAs were calculated for graduation, I snuck into seventh place—the seventh-highest GPA in a class of about 700 students. For a while, after the results came out, people would eye me or even ask me how I had moved up so many places. When many people's college acceptances started to come in, and people found out I was going to Columbia, they became even more resentful. But I didn't care. I was going to my dream school! My parents were very happy for me. I know they were worried about finances, but they made my dream come true by paying a lot of money and taking on loans. I also took out loans, though Columbia did also provide me some need-based grants.

By the time I got to college, I still hadn't experienced many of the

American cultural experiences that most of my peers had. My parents didn't really want me to watch TV late at night, so I missed out on the quintessential '90s shows like *Buffy*, *90210*, and *X- Files*. We didn't have money to go to the movies, though I was able to go to an occasional concert, and in my senior year, I was even able to go to a goth club once in a while. My parents let me date in my senior year, and since I was dating a nice Jewish boy for a while, they trusted him and me not to get into too much trouble. I slowly picked up a few culturally relevant movies, bands, and shows from him and a few other people, but nowhere near what the average teenager knew. We were also interested in quite nerdy pursuits, such as Dungeons & Dragons, Magic: The Gathering, sci-fi and fantasy books, and mostly alternative music. And, of course, I had missed the whole of the '80s, so I didn't know anything about the shows, movies, and music that my peers experienced growing up. In college, I felt a bit of an alien. Whenever new friends brought up these cultural touchstones, I mostly had to say I hadn't seen or heard these.

Luckily, people were fascinated by my ignorance and wanted to teach me and show me. I watched the Star Wars movies my junior year of college. I went to see movies like *The Matrix* with college buddies. I went to parties that played '80s music and had friends show me movies in their rooms, or introduce me to bands I'd never heard of. They liked to take me to restaurants so I could experience unfamiliar cuisines. At home, I had never really had Chinese food or sushi, Indian or Ethiopian food. I quickly found that I enjoyed foods with more spice than the fairly bland Russian, Belarussian, and Jewish foods I grew up eating. Slowly I gained fluency in many things I'd missed. But even now, at over 40 years of age, there are things that people bring up that I haven't experienced. Just the other day, I mentioned that I'd never read *A Wrinkle in Time*. It's still an alienating experience because the most common reaction is either incredulity or a hand waving, "You can't use being an immigrant as an excuse forever." I don't think it's possible to ever catch up on culture acquisition because so much of it requires extra time that I do not have.

When I moved to New York City for college, I finally felt at home. This might be strange for a girl coming from a small town in Belarus.

New York is possibly the opposite of my experience as a child. I am from a town of maybe 1,500 people, and I spent many of my summers living in a village with my grandparents, where there were probably five or six families. I grew up without ever really riding in a car, with cows wandering the streets of my hometown, with going to the forest to pick mushrooms and berries, with gardens and chickens. But something about New York spoke to me. The constant energy, the diversity of people, the tall buildings, the 24-hour subways. They were what I was craving, without even realizing it. It turns out I was always a city girl at heart. One experience that stands out and highlighted my final conversion to an American and a New Yorker came when I went back to Belarus at 21 for the first time. My dad and I went to visit our hometown and our remaining relatives. We visited the graves of my grandmother and grandfather. We spoke mostly Russian. And when we finally landed back at JFK Airport in New York, I felt profound relief. I was finally among my people again.

I learned a few other things later in life. I learned that many Jewish people, and especially Israelis, did not consider me Jewish. Now I know that the idea of being Jewish is matrilineal, and my mother is Belarussian and not Jewish. My dad is Jewish, and we left Belarus because of that. My Jewish side of the family is all either in the U.S. or Israel, while my Belarussian side remains in Belarus or Russia.

Growing up, I knew we were Jewish. I grew up in a small town where there was a very large Jewish cemetery as large as the one full of crosses. There was a burned-out husk of a synagogue (and a Russian Orthodox church still standing even in Soviet times). And much later, I found out from a professor that my hometown used to be a *mestechko,* or a small village, where Jewish families settled. When I went looking for more history about my town, I found that there was a massacre of most Jewish families during World War II right outside of town. I didn't know that as a kid, but I knew that there were almost no Jews left. All of the Jewish families knew each other, and we would get together for holidays sometimes. Beyond that and occasional Jewish dishes cooked by my grandmother, I had little connection with my culture and grew up an atheist. I know now that my dad couldn't get into the college he wanted to go to or get the jobs he wanted because of being Jewish and that people in town talked about our family in hush-hush tones. I was never overtly bullied but certainly excluded.

Even now, I keenly feel that I know little about being Jewish beyond questioning everything and knowing a little bit about the holidays. I have attended several Passover Seders, have been to synagogue with some friends, and know various Jewish people, but I do not feel part of it all. I want to learn more. I want to take Yiddish classes and cook Jewish recipes. I want to feel like I belong with some group. Most of my Jewish friends are very welcoming (and very Reform or atheist). My DNA test shows me 49.9 percent Ashkenazi, and I did pre-screening for genetic disorders when pregnant because of it. But this purely biological fact matters little. I feel Jewish in my heart but with no practice and understanding to show for it. I light the menorah during Hannukah and try to include various practices and ideas for my kids but do not feel authentic in my efforts.

I also learned that other Belarussians do not share my view of anti-Semitism in Belarus. I vividly remember meeting another Belarussian student in my PhD program and chatting with each other about when we came to the U.S. and why. When I mentioned that it was because of anti-Semitism, she said, "What do you mean? There was no anti-Semitism in Belarus." I was so shocked. I don't think I could respond in the moment. This after I heard recently that my hometown Jewish cemetery was vandalized by locals. I also remember visiting my cousins back in Minsk, and my dad took us to a World War II memorial. It is a depression in the earth, and there are black statues of emaciated people slowly walking into the center as if descending into hell. My cousins were completely shocked to find it in the middle of their town, and they expressed their sorrow at what happened to the Jews in World War II. I have always known about this. This is intergenerational trauma—to have your wounds forgotten by the people living in the same place as you, to have your experience denied. World War II is everywhere in Belarus. But the Jews, who were 10 percent of the population of that country before the war and less than one percent after, are forgotten.

These days, I have occasional thoughts about what might have been. What if I had never left Belarus? Where would I be now? Would I be on the streets of Minsk protesting the oppressive regime of Lukashenko?

Would I even still be alive? Over my lifetime, I have struggled with major depression, my queer identity, and my unconventional family structure. But the U.S. is a place where these struggles are validated and taken seriously, while mental health is rarely treated well in the former Soviet Union, and LGBTQIA+ people are actively repressed and legislated against. I am glad that I am here.

As an immigrant, I still do not fully fit into American culture, nor do I want to. I know that I would never have fit in back in Belarus, either. This blended identity—Belarussian, American, Jewish—just highlights the uniqueness of each individual who comes across my path. We all contain multitudes. We all struggle, especially during these pandemic times. And we all have valuable things to contribute to the world. That makes my job as a professor easier and harder. I need to allow all voices to be heard, all contributions to be valued. I can't become complacent and just teach the same thing every semester because my students are different each time, and their generous sharing of themselves makes the class infinitely better. I use these lessons from my life to try to improve others' lives as much as I can every day. ■

ANONYMOUS

NOW

I have written much of this chapter in my apartment on the Upper East Side of Manhattan overlooking the East River or at my medical practice on Fifth Avenue overlooking Central Park. Taking a step back, the events that transpired to get me here seem almost surreal. When I was eight years old, I emigrated from the former Soviet Union to the United States with my family. Now in my late 30s I have spent much time reflecting on the opportunities I was afforded—to live in the most vibrant city in the world, have a fulfilling career, achieve some semblance of self-acceptance, and allow my daughter to have an even brighter future.

MEMORIES OF THE OLD COUNTRY

What was it like living in the Soviet Union (the Soviet Socialist Republic of Belarus in particular) in the 1980s? It was great! I lived with my parents, who were both working professionals. My father was an engineer and my mother a teacher. We had a one-bedroom apartment in a complex of newly constructed buildings in the capital city of Minsk. I had toys, books, and vinyl records. I went to kindergarten and then first grade, and from what I recall, I enjoyed it. I remember my standard-issue navy blue Soviet school uniform, which I wore proudly. I vividly recall doing homework with my mom's help, mainly perfecting my cursive writing, which was apparently a big deal back then. My summers were spent visiting my grandparents, who lived in neighboring towns, and playing outside with my cousins from dusk 'til dawn. My maternal grandparents had a large yard with chickens, a garden, and a sandbox. My grandfather would tell me stories about how he and the Soviet army defeated the Nazis in a very big war, the importance of which I could not, and perhaps still cannot fully appreciate. In 1988, I wholeheartedly welcomed (from what I am told) the arrival of my baby brother.

What more could a kid ask for? I had a loving family and plenty to keep me busy. I knew nothing of the Cold War, perestroika, Chernobyl, or anti-Semitism. In fact, when my parents informed me that we were moving, I was not pleased. Why would I leave? I like it here! But *c'est la vie*. I was seven years old when my family left Belarus in November 1989, just days after the fall of the Berlin Wall.

I now have a better (yet still rudimentary) understanding of the social, cultural, political, and economic factors that led my parents and grandparents to uproot their lives and emigrate to the United States. The collapse of the Soviet Union shortly after our departure was probably the least of our problems. Unbeknownst to me, in Soviet society, my brother and I were second-class citizens. Our passports would have said "Jew," which would have closed many, if not most, doors for us in the future. Instead, my parents chose to leave their home behind to bust open every door for my brother and me.

JOURNEY TO AMERICA

My maternal grandparents accompanied my nuclear family on our journey to America. The trip got off to a rocky start. I vividly recall running for the train that was to take us from Belarus to Austria when a wheel popped off my baby brother's stroller! It was like a scene right out of a movie. We somehow made it onto the train with the broken stroller and waved goodbye to the rest of our extended family members, who were lined up behind a fence at the train station. As a child, I could not appreciate the gravity of that defining moment in our lives. Looking back, I cannot comprehend the heartbreak on both sides of that fence—a tight-knit family torn apart by geopolitical circumstances. We would not see each other again for years.

Once the train left the station, the comedy of errors continued. At some point on our journey, the conductors realized that their refugee passengers had packed very well for their journey. So well, in fact, that their luggage caused the train cars to lean to one side. This led to a frenzied attempt to stack hundreds of suitcases on the opposite side of the train car to serve as a counterweight. After restoring balance on the train and arriving in Austria, all those suitcases had to be unloaded with great haste before the train was to depart for its next destination. For my family, all the heavy lifting rested on my father's shoulders since he was traveling with his wife, a child, an infant, and two senior citizens. Thank you, Dad!

My memories of our time spent in Austria are sparse. We stayed in a cabin somewhere outside Vienna. My grandfather got to practice the German he learned when the Red Army captured Berlin. My brother celebrated his first birthday and took his first steps. And I was able to buy bubble gum using Soviet 3 Kopek coins that perfectly fit Austrian vending machines!

From there, it was back on a train, with our suitcases in tow, and off to Italy, where we would spend over two months awaiting entry into the United States. We lived in a small town called Ladispoli, which I now know was a haven for Soviet Jewish immigrants fleeing to the West. My time was spent riding a bicycle that my dad found and fixed up for me and attending a school set up for immigrant children by various charitable Jewish organizations. I celebrated my eighth birthday on Italian soil and vividly recall my present—a small Lego set that could not have had more than a few pieces but felt larger than life. Meanwhile, like many other Soviet immigrants, my parents and grandparents went into the retail business while in Italy. Since the Soviet government would not allow immigrants to leave with any substantial funds, most people spent their life savings on seemingly useless chattel that was allowed across the border (in all those heavy suitcases) and could then be sold in Austria and Italy. Like so many others, my family sold an eclectic array of Soviet toys, electronics, optical equipment, and kitchen gadgets. Apparently, it was a successful venture since we had far fewer suitcases when it came time to board the plane for America in February 1990.

EARLY YEARS IN AMERICA

The first few months in New York City were a blur. My parents and grandparents somehow rented apartments. They somehow obtained all the items one needs for daily living. They somehow navigated the American system to enroll in certain assistance programs. They somehow got jobs to help make ends meet. For example, my college-educated parents delivered newspapers and cleaned houses. They somehow enrolled in graduate programs to learn new skills. They somehow secured stable jobs within a few years of immigrating. All this while trying to learn a new language and assimilate into an unfamiliar culture. I am not discounting the fact that multiple safety nets and charitable organizations helped my parents do all this. I am also aware that all immigrants share a struggle and an uphill battle. Nonetheless, in my eyes, my parents' accomplishments in those first few years were akin to climbing Mount Everest.

My own foremost obstacle was starting school. I started third grade in the fall of 1990. I entered a New York City public elementary school knowing little to no English and none of my classmates. I recall that I was one of two Soviet immigrants in a school that had hundreds of students. I was the kid with the weird name and strange clothes, unable to communicate. Since the latest wave of Soviet immigration had not yet hit my school, there were no English as a Second Language classes. It was a bit of a sink or swim scenario, and like most kids in my situation, I swam. By the end of that academic year, I recall being quite comfortable with English, and by the fourth grade, I was doing very well academically. I made friends and remember feeling reasonably comfortable at school. In retrospect, I must acknowledge the kindness of my teachers in allowing a potentially terrible transition to go as smoothly as possible.

ASSIMILATION

As the years flew by through middle school and high school, I continued to do well academically. I finished high school near the top of my class. I was on the varsity wrestling team and thoroughly enjoyed the training, competition, and bonding with my teammates. Over the years, the student body at my respective schools became more and more diverse. There were immigrants from all over the world, making unusual names and accents not so unusual anymore. By the time I graduated high school, I felt perfectly assimilated into American culture. I never had an accent and spoke English fluently. I knew all about contemporary music, sports, and pop culture. I had a rudimentary understanding of American history and politics.

Despite all this, I could not shake a sense of "otherness" that haunted me throughout my childhood and adolescence. I always felt different from normal Americans. Interestingly, I even felt different from other immigrant groups. Perhaps it was a byproduct of the Cold War, but being from the former Soviet Union somehow created a sense of being looked down upon and ostracized by American society. And as a kid, all I wanted to do was fit in, fly below the radar, and not draw any attention to how I was different. This was often a challenge. While I acted, dressed, and spoke like most of my "normal" peers at school, I came home to a different culture, language, and view of the world. Trying to balance these two worlds was difficult at times and often led me to maintain strict boundaries between them. Not surprisingly, many of my early childhood friends, who remain some of my closest friends today, come from a similar background. Perhaps being around people who fully understood and accepted both of my worlds was comforting during those formative years.

College and graduate school brought significantly more acceptance of my origin and its role in my identity, possibly due to a deeper appreciation for my own family and close friends who bestowed it upon me. I became less concerned with trying to fit in. I developed deep and lasting friendships with peers from diverse backgrounds and was no longer afraid to share my ethnicity with them. My post-graduate medical training led to an even greater sense of inclusion.

The shared experiences of rigorous on-call schedules, dying patients, and demanding academic expectations create a sense of togetherness.

CURRENT RELATIONSHIP TO MY BACKGROUND

The past decade of my life has led to a sense of self-acceptance and pride with regard to my background. Perhaps this is a normal phenomenon as people of our generation seem to "come into their own" in their late 20s and 30s. Or perhaps it's simply a function of having more important things to worry about as an adult. Nonetheless, I now appreciate where I come from and how it has shaped who I am.

However, while I have come to accept my identity as a Soviet immigrant, I would not say that I've embraced it. I have met other people with similar stories who are immensely proud of their countries of origin. They loudly espouse the great achievements of the people and adore the culture. They feel a bond with the "homeland" and often reminisce about its virtues. I simply cannot relate to this mentality and find myself at the opposite end of the spectrum on this issue. Don't get me wrong. I enjoy and appreciate certain Russian foods, music, and movies. I have fond memories and remain sentimental about the celebration of New Year's Eve, which was the most popular holiday in the former Soviet Union. But any positive feelings I have toward my country of origin end there. I resent a political machine that considered people who fought for their homeland expendable and those who expressed dissenting opinions criminals. I question the backward economic policies that prevented hardworking, brilliant people from reaching their full potential. I deplore the open and accepted anti-Semitism. But mostly, I lament how all of this affected my family and other families with similar backgrounds and stories. In the end, while I do not wish ill upon my country of origin, you will not catch me rooting for their team at the next Olympics.

As I have spent much of my life distancing myself from my Russianness, I have simultaneously inched closer to my Jewishness. As a child in Belarus, I did not know what it meant to be Jewish. My parents had experienced their share of anti-Semitism and took the position of not "advertising" that part of who they were. After coming to the

United States, I started to hear the words and ideas thrown around at home. I recall my grandfather going to Temple quite regularly after settling in. My nuclear family did not go to Temple, observe the Sabbath, or make a big fuss over the major holidays. However, over time, we adopted certain traditions and started to celebrate Yom Kippur and Rosh Hoshana. My parents started to talk about what being Jewish meant to them, and I gained an appreciation for our heritage. I still consider myself Jew"ish." I do not go to Temple or observe any of the key commandments of the religion, but I truly feel a connection to the complex history of the Jewish people. I love many of the core tenets of the faith: belief in the sanctity of human life, focus on family, and value of education. However, I have come to realize that I am not, nor do I see myself becoming, someone who practices the Jewish religion. I consider being Jewish a cultural identity that includes certain customs, beliefs, and traditions that do not necessarily extend to religion. I hope to share my perspectives on Judaism and our family history as Jews in the former Soviet Union with my daughter, who is three years old and allow her to incorporate Judaism into her life in whatever manner she sees fit.

FINAL THOUGHTS

Ultimately, I consider my background as a Soviet Jewish immigrant an asset rather than a liability. Witnessing my parents' experiences and hardships through immigration and assimilation led me to deeply value and appreciate hard work, education, sacrifice, and resilience. Growing up in a Russian-Jewish home introduced me to a variety of wonderful customs and traditions. On a practical level, being bilingual affords me the opportunity to communicate with a wider range of people and better understand several diverse cultures. However, if I were asked to define myself today, I would say that this integration of various ethnicities, cultures, traditions, and religions can be encompassed in just one word—American. ■

YELENA SHNEYDERMAN

NOW

I am 42 years old and live in Miami with my husband and two children and two stepchildren. I am a self-employed lawyer who enjoys practicing law, and I am married to a lawyer, who immigrated from Ukraine when he was 12 years old.

THE PRELUDE: THE SOVIET YEARS

I spent the first decade of my life in the 1980s growing up in Minsk, Belarus, located in the former Soviet Union. Our apartment was located on the first floor of a postwar building, which was unremarkable in that it resembled all of the other four-story gray apartment buildings on our street. There was an outdoor playground, which had a sandbox, swings, and a seesaw. The neighbor kids and I knocked on each other's doors when we were sent outside by our parents, and we would run to the playground without any parents hovering over us, although I knew that my mom always kept a watchful eye from our kitchen window while she cooked. We jumped endlessly over what I now know to be Chinese jump rope, inventing new patterns, new jumps, and new games, played dodgeball, soccer, hopscotch, and any other game we could think of.

Although our apartment was located on the first floor, we still had to navigate two flights of stairs. First, the outside stairs were covered with snow and ice during the cold winter months when we gingerly held on to the railings because the stairway was so slippery. We then walked up the interior flight of stairs inside the building, which was usually dark, damp, and cold, usually smelling of urine due to the neighborhood drunks who sometimes took shelter in the building's basement when they were too drunk to find their way home. My mom grew up in that apartment and lived there with my grandparents from age four until we moved to America. When she married my dad in March of 1979, he moved into that apartment with her and my grandparents. All of the neighbors had also lived in our building their entire lives since the government provided these apartments in the 1960s as part of the country's socialist policies. If we had not moved to America, I probably would have lived there my entire life.

The apartment was a 350-square-foot space with a tiny bedroom where my younger sister and I slept on bunk beds and a living room with a sleeper sofa, which my parents folded out to sleep on at night. Until I was four years old, my grandparents lived with us too, which meant that my parents slept on the sleeper sofa in the bedroom, with my baby sister and me in the same room. We also had an upright

Third grade in Minsk. Yelena (top left), circa 1988.

piano, which my mom played for hours. To this very day, I cannot comprehend how we fit all of our clothes, which included winter fur coats and boots for our entire family of six, in the two armoires inside our apartment. The concept of closets did not enter our imagination until many years later, when we immigrated to America. We had a small black and white tube TV with a rotary dial. It had three channels, which played an endless loop of Soviet propaganda and movies about World War II and the Russian Revolution, sprinkled with very sparse kids' programs on the weekends. We also had a rotary phone, which our neighbors came to use sometimes because most of them did not have phones. Since my paternal grandparents and other extended family members lived in different towns and long-distance phone calls were very expensive, we sometimes walked to the post office, from which we sent them telegrams on birthdays, holidays, or to express condolences.

In 1994, as part of Gorbachev's perestroika reforms to allow private sector enterprise, my grandparents were able to purchase a cooperative studio apartment with the savings they had socked away literally under the mattress and with a generous contribution from my parents. It cost approximately 4,000 rubles, which was the equivalent of four years of salary at the time. Their studio apartment was probably 200 square feet but always felt spacious, warm, and welcoming. My sister and I spent many nights there playing checkers and cards with my grandparents, walking with them to the bakery for fresh bread and playing outside. My grandparents spoke Yiddish with each other inside their home, and I vividly remember my grandma lovingly calling me "shayna maidel" and "shayna punim" which I understood even then. However, I did not understand why my grandparents spoke another language in a place of complete homogeneity. Almost 30 years later, I named my firstborn daughter Shayna in honor of my grandmother's memory.

My dad went to work very early every day. Before he married my mom, he was a history teacher and moved to Minsk but could not find a similar job in Minsk because there were no vacancies, especially not for a Jew. He worked as an electrician installing alarm systems in commercial businesses. My mom was a brilliant musician who had a perfect pitch and practiced piano for hours a day on our upright piano. She also studied in the conservatory and constantly listened to music, studied music theory books, and took notes to prepare for her exams. She also worked as a teacher of solfege in a high school with a music magnet and devoted the rest of her time to her conservatory studies and taking care of us. Because music was always my mom's priority, we had a beautiful record player where, in addition to playing classical music records, my mom had a small collection of American music. We listened to the Beatles, the Rolling Stones, and even Gloria Gaynor. My parents always turned the volume down low when we listened to this "international" music because they were worried about disturbing the neighbors who would have probably thought that we were also being anti-Soviet in addition to being Jews. My mom took great care to handle the record player's needle lightly and only with clean fingertips because it was nearly impossible to find a needle replacement, and my mom could not fathom living without music.

My mom enrolled me in music school before I began regular school. She wanted me to become a musician because my career prospects as a Jewish female were very limited, especially since my parents were not members of the Communist Party and did not indoctrinate me with the communist ideals. Since we did not own a car—nor did anyone else for that matter—we walked to a nearby bus stop and boarded the city bus to get to the music school where I had piano lessons, solfege, and choir.

When I started regular school in 1986, my parents decided not to enroll me in my home school, which was across the street from us, but a school in a better neighborhood, a math magnet school with higher caliber teachers and gifted students. My parents believed that this might limit my exposure to anti-Semitism. My dad woke me before the sun rose to leave enough time for breakfast, and then a long walk to the bus stop where our boots creaked on the snowy walking paths toward the bus stop, which glistened first from the stars and then from the rising sun. There are school photos of me from that time, with my Lenin's star pinned to my uniform, looking somber into the camera because smiling for no reason was judged as being insincere and a sign of foolishness.

By that time, I was keenly aware of being Jewish. My parents had made a conscious decision to raise my sister and me with the understanding that we were Jewish, which had the intended result of us being unashamed of our ethnicity, although we never gratuitously disclosed it. We even had matzah delivered to our house discreetly during Pesach (Passover) in a nondescript box, from which my grandmother made matzah ball soup, which was accompanied by homemade gefilte fish and tzimmes so we could enjoy a holiday dinner. That was the extent of my knowledge of Pesach.

Although I don't recall my parents explaining anti-Semitism, I was keenly aware of being different even before my firsthand experience with anti-Semitism, which I believe I encountered later than my Jewish contemporaries because my teacher tried to protect me from it. Every morning, during roll call, my beloved teacher called out in alphabetical order the last names of my classmates—Gribovsky, Hilchenko, Ivanov, Medvedev—who would respond "present." However, when she reached my last name, she simply called out "Lena." This avoided my difficult-to-pronounce foreign-sounding last name from being blasted all over the classroom on a daily basis.

In second grade, however, while I was walking with my best friend from school enjoying her company, she told me nonchalantly that her father, whom I had never met, was wondering why the other Jews and I don't just move out of the Soviet Union and go live in our "Jew land." I was very surprised by this question and the dark feeling that began to descend into the pit of my stomach when I started to realize that I was unwanted in my own country. The very same day, I asked my mom whether, in fact, it was true that there was a land for Jews and recounted my conversation. To my great surprise, she told me about Israel and America, where Jews were welcomed and lived without fear from anti-Semites (like my friend's father) who wanted us to leave. She added, "You know, Lenochka, maybe we will, one day!" Although this was my most memorable encounter with anti-Semitism because it involved someone I considered a friend, there were many more instances of being called "zhidovka," a derogatory term for a Jewish female, which always left me wondering, "How do they know?" I did not, after all, have any of the physical features that Russians commonly believed were stereotypically Jewish—a large nose with a bump, unruly curly hair, or glasses, for example. I even remember my mom receiving a "compliment" one day from someone who was so shocked to learn that she was Jewish by telling my mom that she could "pass" because she was too attractive to resemble a Jew.

IMMIGRATION

After I completed third grade in the summer of 1989, my parents told me that we were leaving for America, a country routinely vilified by Soviet propaganda. They even told me that we were moving to a city called Miami, which was so foreign sounding that we might as well have been moving to the moon, especially after I learned that there were no winters in Miami and that it was like an island because it was surrounded by the Atlantic Ocean and the Gulf of Mexico. This news was exciting, and the thought of our new exotic home was almost impossible to contain inside me. However, my parents were very serious when they told me not to share this news with anyone. They were worried that we might get robbed or attacked for being perceived as Jewish traitors.

The preparations for our journey began in the summer of 1989. Since receiving an Israeli visa by mail was impossible, we were given one by hand through an underground network. My dad took the visa to the immigration center in our local police department, which was miraculously stamped for further processing even after the employee asked why the envelope in which it supposedly arrived was not presented. Somehow, we got by.

At that time, everyday food items were becoming scarce, and the grocery stores appeared emptier than usual. Ration cards were being used for items like salt and sugar. The lines to purchase poultry and meat were endless, and there were limitations on how many items each person could purchase. Sometimes an old lady who was in line alone would ask to borrow my sister or me as they approached the front of the line so they could pass us off as their grandkids and thereby be allowed to purchase food for two or three people rather than one. Then my sister and I would walk back unnoticed through the throngs of people to find my parents still in line. On one occasion, my dad purchased rolls of toilet paper, which were strung through a long twine and hung around his neck like beads while he walked home with me. Almost everyone stopped us to ask him where he was fortunate enough to find the toilet paper and whether there was any more left.

In preparation for our departure, my parents took a number of trips to Moscow to visit with the Soviet immigration authorities. They were required to give up their Soviet passports two months prior to departure, at which time we were no longer citizens of any land. We were only allowed to take two suitcases per person with us and ship a wooden shipping container of a particular size and weight of our personal belongings to Miami prior to our departure. The remaining contents of our apartment, including our toys, my mom's piano that she had since she was five years old, books, crystal, furniture, and clothes, were either sold or given away. My parents either hosted goodbye parties at our home or went out to dinner with their friends for the last time.

In the early hours of August 28, 1989, under the cover of darkness, we boarded two taxi cabs with our suitcases and drove to the bus station. There, we were met by our grandparents and a few of my parents' Jewish friends, who came to say goodbye again. Although at that time, these friends intended to remain in the Soviet Union, they left within a year after we left and currently reside in Israel and the U.S. and are still in our lives. My uncle accompanied us to Brest and then returned home to his family, only to join us in Miami two years later.

We began our immigration journey by boarding two buses with eight other Jewish families, and we rode for four hours to Brest, which was located on the border of Belarus and Poland. In Brest, we had to go through customs and immigration and board a new set of buses and were driven to Ostrowiec, Poland, which was our first time crossing the border of the Soviet Union. At that time, which was still the time of the Cold War, nobody but politicians could cross the borders of the Soviet Union without permission. We spent the night in a lovely hotel in Ostrowiec, where we had dinner in their dining room. Our next stop was in Bratislava, in Czechoslovakia (now the capital of Slovakia). There, the bus drivers told us to step off the buses and remove our things because another set of buses would take us to our next destination—Vienna. When the new set of buses arrived, the drivers engaged in a shakedown, demanding additional money for our transport, even though it was all prepaid. Everyone began to protest the injustice of this blackmail, but we were alone with the other families at a deserted bus station at dusk, surrounded by the only possessions that we had, and the cash in our pockets was supposed to cover our entire journey to the United States. Our only forms of identification were our visas, which my dad was holding in his inside pockets. We were refugees. We were stateless, homeless, and jobless, and we were standing at night in a deserted bus station in a foreign country whose language we did not speak.

Soon, the kids began to whimper. My grandmother began to panic, crying, "This reminds me of evacuation." *Evacuation* was a term that referred to the migration of Soviet citizens eastward to areas like Kazakhstan during World War II, when the Germans began to invade the Soviet Union in 1941, making their way through Poland into Belarus. My grandmother was 25 years old at that time. She and her toddler son and her younger sister were part of the evacuation when they were forced to flee Minsk as it was being bombed by the Germans and relocated to Kazakhstan, where they were resettled as evacuees and given food rations, housing, and a factory job. My grandmother hardly talked about her life during the war. However, on this day, as we and other multi-generational Jewish families were standing alone at the bus station with our only possessions and visas that labeled us "refugees," she likened our departure from the Soviet Union in 1989 to her escape from Minsk during World War II. Ultimately, the majority decided that it was best to pay the extorted amounts in order to get to Vienna rather than protest on account of justice and fairness and risk our trip West.

VIENNA

Eventually, we made our way to Vienna in the late evening, only to learn that due to our delay, the person who was waiting for us to drive everyone to their accommodations had left. The train station was closed. However, the Austrian police unlocked a train to allow the kids and women to get some rest. The seats were folded horizontally into beds, and my sister and I slept while the armed police officers were kind enough to stand outside our trains to ensure our security. The irony that armed Austrian authorities were keeping the Jewish refugees safe did not escape us.

The next day, we were driven to a building with communal bathrooms and a kitchen, which we shared with other Russian-Jewish refugees. The kids spent their days running through the common areas and playing with the only toys that we brought, while our parents worriedly went to their appointments with the American and Israeli Embassies and paid for expenses that we owed for housing and transportation. Although we did not get to explore Vienna as tourists would during our two-week stay, it was still memorable for its outdoor farmers market, which had an infinite supply of fruits and vegetables, especially after the empty storefronts that we left behind. We also walked past many storefronts that had an overabundance of shoes, clothes, toys, coffee shops, restaurants, and lounges, in contrast to the empty stores we had left behind. It was all a bewildering sight to a 10-year-old who had never been outside of the Soviet Union.

ITALY

After Vienna, we arrived by train in Rome, Italy, which provided a brief preview of the beauty we would later find in Miami. It was still warm in September, and we had the good fortune to be randomly placed to live in a resort on the Mediterranean Sea in Santa Severa, while my parents had to find a more permanent apartment for the two or three months that we expected to remain there. Again, with great surprise, we found ourselves living in an airy two-bedroom apartment in Santa Marinella, only a few blocks away from the sea. My grandparents occupied one bedroom and my parents the other, while my sister and I slept on a Murphy bed and couch in the spacious living room. Up to that point, this was the largest apartment we had ever seen, and it had a large patio that led into a grassy green yard. We lived in Italy for two months, waiting for our visa applications to America to be processed and approved.

Despite the stress of the unknown that my parents experienced, they made sure to take us to the beach at the Mediterranean Sea. They also hosted dinners for their refugee friends, who brought their kids and gelato and "fiascos" of red wine, large bottles of wine with a fat round body and a large bottom, partially wrapped in a straw basket. We celebrated my father's 35th birthday surrounded by our new friends. My parents, who were—incredibly—younger than I am now, seemed so mature, wise, and confident, even though I now understand how uncertain and stressed they must have felt. They did not speak Italian or English, for that matter. They were citizens of no land. They only had a limited amount of cash, no bank accounts, no credit cards, and no home. They also had elderly parents and small children to feed and care for with zero employment prospects. While some Soviet immigrant families sold various Soviet trinkets they had packed in the suitcases at the flea market for extra cash, my parents did not have a single entrepreneurial bone in their bodies.

Every night, we went to a designated outdoor square for a gathering along with approximately 1,000 other Russian Jews awaiting their future in Italy. At this gathering, the refugees' last names were called when their interviews at the embassies were scheduled and, subsequently, when their visa applications to America, Canada, or Australia had been processed. Those who chose to go to Israel or those who would have liked to go to America but had no family in America had flown to Israel directly from Vienna. This was the *first* time everyone's last name sounded foreign, and ours did not stand out—Sherman, Kaplan, Goldman, Abramov. Everyone looked around when the names were called to see whom they belonged to, but nobody laughed at the foreign sound of the name. We were finally starting to feel at home.

Our name was finally called, and we ultimately learned that our visa applications to Miami had been approved. Miami was our final destination because of a campaign by the Hebrew Immigrant Aid Society (HIAS) to encourage American Jews to invite their Soviet relatives to join them in the United States. At that time, my uncle's second wife had an aunt who lived in Miami and completed the necessary documents to "invite" them to America while they "invited" us. In short, a complete stranger was ultimately instrumental in our ability to exit the Soviet Union and resettle in Miami.

WELCOME TO AMERICA

Finally, our turn came to leave what felt like paradise and catch a Pan Am flight to JFK Airport in New York, from which we transferred to a flight to Miami. On October 28, 1989, exactly two months after we left our home country, we stepped outside of Miami International Airport. It was impossible to believe that it was warmer outside than it was inside the airport. A person we had never met until that moment, but who was instrumental in our final destination being Miami, picked us up from the airport and drove us to a one-bedroom apartment in Miami Beach. We drove through well-manicured tree-lined streets and bridges surrounded by water on roads that felt smooth as butter. Outside of our building, coconuts were blooming on palms, and the Atlantic Ocean was only a half-mile away.

Our apartment was subsidized by the Jewish Federation, which paid a deposit to the landlord and for the first three months of rent. During these first three months, my parents and the other Jewish refugees needed to find work. They attended daily English classes at the Jewish Federation and were given leads on various job vacancies. My grandparents took care of my sister and me while we watched American cartoons and played with other refugee kids in our building.

My mom, always eager to learn new things, enrolled in Miami-Dade Community College and learned English fairly quickly. She then began working at a Jewish daycare associated with a Conservative temple, and my dad drove the school bus for this temple. The rabbi was intent on making new Jewish families feel welcome in his temple, and because my mom was so amazing with children and began to conduct music classes, he asked her to sing in the temple's choir during services. The rabbi's family and my parents developed a friendship, and the rabbi decided that the Soviet Jewish families would enjoy gathering for an authentic Jewish chuppah. He asked my parents to have a Jewish wedding and invited all of the newly arrived Jewish refugees.

Although my parents had been married to each other for almost 11 years by that time, they never actually had a wedding. One of the temple members lent my mom a striking white wedding dress, and my sister and I got all dressed up into the best clothes that we had packed with us from Minsk. I was so giddy to attend my own parents' wedding! The wedding story, including photos of my parents saying their vows, was published in the local newspaper. Both the temple members and the newly arrived Jews attended the wedding, which featured a translator so the officiating and the rabbi's sermon did not get lost, and banquet-style kosher food and an open bar.

My parents enrolled me in a Jewish elementary day school, which charitably opened a handful of spots for Soviet-Jewish children. This was the first time the school was extending charity to underprivileged children, and the pity was palpable. I was only 10 years old, without any concept of social status and only a few words of English in my arsenal, and yet the feeling of being a charity case was inescapable. I could sense my classmates looking me over as "other," as not belonging to their privileged group of wealthy American Jews. Thankfully, the students wore uniforms, but even with everyone wearing the same clothing, my shoes were not Keds, which were popular at that time, and my hair was not tied into scrunchies. At that time, my parents saved every penny that they earned at their minimum-wage jobs and purchased nothing but necessities. Even though we were not accepted as Jews in the Soviet Union, I had never felt as much an outsider as I did in that school. Again, my name was difficult to pronounce and was constantly mispronounced as "Helen, Helena, Elen, Elena, Jelena, and Yolanda," while my last name was usually too difficult to even attempt due to its complicated spelling.

Yelena's parents' American-Jewish wedding, circa 1990.

We did not begin the process of assimilation until several months after our arrival when we were matched with an American Jewish family who, through a temple project, wanted to meet a Soviet-Jewish family. Along with other Soviet Jews, our family was driven to dinner at a temple in South Miami, where we were seated at a table with an American Jewish family with kids similar in age to my sister and me. My parents were very hesitant to strike up a friendship and be viewed as a charity case, but this American family was so persistent in their attempts at getting to know us that my parents finally gave in and accepted their invitation to come to their house. Somehow, despite my parents' poor English at that time, we became fast friends with the other family and spent all the Jewish holidays at their home. We learned how to conduct a Seder, the traditional foods eaten during Pesach, the

Yom Kippur fast, and breaking the fast with bagels and lox. We ate delicious Rosh Hashanah meals, attended temple with them, joined them for Thanksgiving and the Hanukkah gift exchanges, and spent carefree afternoons at their pool during the summer months. Their kids introduced us to Nintendo, and their parents gifted us with Nintendo Game Boys, Keds, Barbie dolls, crayons, stickers, and so many toys that were beyond our imagination. Although I remained friendly with their kids, we never truly connected. However, our parents are still close to this day.

After graduating from the Jewish day school in sixth grade, I went to a public middle school and high school where I still struggled to make friends for a few years due to my still fledgling English and my feeling of not belonging, which I could not shake off after the Jewish day school experience.

In high school, I was able to blend in with various groups of kids who were also born in other countries, albeit in South America. I still struggled with my identity and my confidence. Again, teachers and kids struggled with pronouncing my name, not because it was Jewish, but because it was foreign and spelled in a manner unfamiliar in America. The soft "L" sound of my first name is not an English sound, and to this day, whenever I have to provide a name for a restaurant reservation, I provide my husband's name, who legally changed his name from Igor to Gary, in order to assimilate.

During the first few years of our arrival, the question of "Where are you from?" was answered with "Soviet Union." During that time of late 1989 and the early '90s, almost everyone in America had heard of the Soviet Union. The question that inevitably followed was, "What part?" and became very annoying over time because very few people were familiar with the various republics of the Soviet Union and even fewer people had heard of Minsk, Belarus. So, I began to change my answer to the second question to "Russia." Over time, I changed my response to the first question to "The *former* Soviet Union," since the Soviet Union had ceased to exist in 1991. Recently, however, when I say that I'm from Belarus, I'm no longer met with blank stares, in part due to the political unrest in Belarus that has made its way into the American media. However, I'm not actually from Belarus since that's not my birth country, and I'm not ethnically Belarussian. But since my birth country does not exist, being from Belarus seems like the correct answer.

Even though I don't identify with my birth country anymore and still feel like an impostor among American Jews and other Americans, I now have the courage to correct people when they mispronounce my name. I host Pesach Seders at my house, hiding my feelings of Jewish inadequacy by preparing some of my favorite Pesach dishes, and have my family take turns reading from the Haggadah. My kids, who are nine and three years old, attend a Jewish Sunday school and accompany me to temple on the high holy days. One of my biggest assimilation feats is smiling on cue for photos as if I have no care in the world. I don't think anyone could possibly guess that neither I nor any Soviet would be caught dead smiling on camera for no reason in our Soviet days, not because we were unhappy, but because we would be judged as being simple. Mercifully, my kids have no fear of being judged for displaying their happiness and enjoy spending their free time hamming it up for our iPhone cameras and making TikTok dances.

NOW

We tragically lost my mom to a rare lung carcinoid two years ago, which developed out of nowhere despite being a nonsmoker and taking her health very seriously. Sometimes I wonder whether it was caused by Chernobyl or her early childhood spent in very poor living conditions in wooden barracks with very little heat before the government issued my grandparents the apartment in Minsk where I grew up. Although my parents worked very hard in America without feeling spiritually or financially fulfilled, they have seen their own children make strides.

I live with my family in Miami, only a few miles from my father, who still lives in the condo where I grew up. Although I believed that I would move out of Florida after graduating from college, I ended up in law school at the University of Florida. Then I passed the Florida bar, which led me to find a job in Miami.

I am now 42 years old, married, with two children and two stepchildren. My youngest daughter is in preschool, which may surprise a lot of Soviets, who became grandmothers at my age. In fact, my mother was only 40 years old when I graduated from high school. My oldest daughter is in fourth grade and cannot imagine changing schools, much less moving across the world to a new country.

I am a self-employed lawyer who enjoys the practice of law, and I am married to a lawyer, who immigrated from Ukraine when he was 12 years old. I live in an affluent part of northeast Dade County, in a neighborhood with single-family homes, the majority of which are owned and occupied by Jews from South America, Israel, and Russia. The street directly outside of my community is lined with a handful of synagogues to which my neighbors walk with their kids on Friday evenings and Saturdays. Even though I consider myself a Reform Jew, I love being surrounded by religious Jews and living in a city densely populated by Jews. It is a scene that I would not even dream of in the place where I was born.

I enjoy running outdoors, going to the beach, reading, and traveling. I feel very fortunate to live a privileged life, where I do not have to hide who I am and to be able to provide it for my kids (who take it for granted). I remain forever indebted to my parents' sacrifice of their home, friends, and comfort so that I would not have to be afraid to be myself. ■

ALEX KASDAN

NOW

I am 55 years old. At present, I co-head a media company, Expert Webcast, and am an investment banker in Los Angeles. Previously, I worked as a banker and corporate lawyer in New York and Europe. I have a family and young children.

I was born and grew up in St. Petersburg (then Leningrad), Russia, and left the Soviet Union with my family at age 14 in May 1980, on the eve of the Summer Olympics boycott. My family believes that the Soviet government let us go after having denied our exit visa for quite a while, along with many other "refuseniks" in an effort to avoid any possible confrontation between foreigners visiting the Olympic Games and "disloyal" citizens or traitors to the Motherland. In any case, we were lucky.

I do not have any negative memories of growing up in Russia. We had a comfortable life in the center of the city, right on Nevsky Prospect, a summer house on a lake where I used to love to spend my summers and dream about fishing there to this day. I knew that I was a Jew, but I had a very vague idea of what that meant, other than my grandmother always said that as a Jew, you had to work twice as hard as everyone else to succeed. I also always knew that if someone made derogatory remarks about Jews, you had to fight back. Being Jewish had nothing to do with religion in my mind. It was a nationality, just like being Russian, Polish, or Italian, but Jews in Russia were not considered Russian. Interestingly enough, we became "Russian" when we arrived in America.

Also, growing up in Russia, even children led a double life. What you did, said, or heard at home was not to be repeated in public. My brother, who was then seven, did not mention a word of our planning to leave the Soviet Union to anyone, although my parents never explicitly told him not to. Somehow, he knew. It was the same with me.

Growing up in the '70s and '80s, World War II, or the Great Patriotic War, as it was called, was not all that far behind us in memory or public life. We all grew up on war movies, stories, books, and war games. One of my grandfathers was killed in the war. The other was a pilot who made it all the way to Berlin in 1945. When I think of it now, most people in Russia at the time, who were younger than I am now, had been in the war. As kids, we were always told not to pull on wires sticking out of the ground for fear of hidden bombs that might not have detonated.

Immigration was exciting. I remember waking up super early to go to the airport for our flight to Vienna. I knew that we were never coming back. I have snippets of memories of leaving, such as going through passport control, customs, and boarding the plane. My brother had a stuffed teddy bear with him that he had always carried around as a toddler. The customs agents, whom I remember as extremely nasty, cut it open, looking for hidden contraband items.

I really liked Vienna when we got there. What struck me the most was how clean and colorful it was. I remember walking into a food store looking at the selection of colorful yogurt bottles that I had never seen before. I also remember going to the famous Vienna Opera House with my parents. We bought the least expensive tickets, standing way up in the nosebleed section. Halfway through the performance, I tripped on the stairs, and a few coins in my pocket fell out, creating quite a bit of noise, much to the consternation of everyone in the theater.

Everything was new, and everything was different. It was exciting as a child, but I have always wondered how scary the unknown that lay ahead must have been for my parents. They were in their early 40s, and it's amazing for me to think about the fact that they were much younger than I am today and yet had the courage to take their family across the ocean to an unknown new world with very uncertain prospects. I have always admired this choice and the courage behind it.

After two weeks or so, we traveled from Vienna to Rome. I remember the long train ride in the middle of the night and being unloaded from the train right before it arrived at the Rome train station by a bunch of young Italian guys in leather jackets. All of us were "stateless," without visas to Austria or Italy or a place to call home or go back to.

We were taken to Castel Gandolfo, a beautiful suburb of Rome, which also happens to be the pope's summer residence. After a few days, we went to Ladispoli, where we stayed for the next few months, awaiting a visa to the United States. Ladispoli, a beach town on the Mediterranean, was great. We went to the beach almost every day, took bus tours to Rome and around Italy. My parents made friends with an Italian man, Vincenzo, who wanted to learn Russian and was proud to share his love of Italy and all things Italian.

As all Soviet immigrants, we had very little money, as families were only allowed to take $45 per person out of the U.S.S.R. We, as a family, took a job cleaning a summer house. My dad and I got a job picking grapes at a vineyard with a large Italian family. I also honed my Italian language skills in the *mercato* selling some of the things Russian immigrants were allowed to take out of Russia, such as a camera and Russian souvenirs. None of this was a hardship. It was all new and exciting, the beginning of a new beginning.

After about five months, we were given an American visa and flew to New York. We settled in Stamford, Connecticut, about an hour away from New York City. There were not many Russian immigrants in Stamford, but the people who were our mentors from the Jewish community were extremely nice and helpful. We remained friends with them for a very long time.

Ninth-grade school picture, first year in the U.S.

I started ninth grade in the middle of a school year. It was tough at first. One really wants to fit in as a teenager, but it is very difficult if one doesn't know what the "in" is. I had studied English in Russia and could communicate, but my knowledge of colloquial American English was zero, as was my knowledge of American popular culture. The world was very different in 1980, and most American kids knew very little about Russia or Europe in general. On my first day in school, one of my classmates asked me if I spoke German. I was perplexed and asked him why he thought I should speak German. He said, "Didn't the Germans beat the Russians in the war?" Interestingly, I also found that despite having grown up in Russia, behind the Iron Curtain, I had a much more rounded perspective and knowledge of history, geography, and literature than many American kids my age.

High school graduation.

Our stay in Stamford was not very long. My father, an electrical engineer, received three job offers, one in San Francisco, another in Pittsburgh, and the third in Cleveland. We went to Cleveland, which is a very nice city but very different from the New York area. Another new cultural experience all over again! We settled in Ohio and bought our first American house. My mother, who is a concert pianist, had many music students and gave several concerts. I made quite a few friends and got my driver's license, which was a big deal, as I did not have to depend on my parents and friends to drive me around anymore.

After two years in Cleveland, my father got a new job offer in New Jersey, and we moved the summer before I was about to start my senior year in high school. Although I missed my friends, living close to the beach on the Jersey Shore, an hour train ride from New York City, was great.

Having applied to a number of colleges and universities, I chose Middlebury College in Vermont. I was the only Russian student on campus. College life was great, and I got to spend my junior year abroad in Florence, Italy, attending the Universita di Firenze and studying international law and economics. Studying at a European university was a very different experience than college back home. One's entire course grade was based on one oral exam one-on-one with a professor at the end of the year. As I learned later at Columbia, my University of Florence professor, Antonio Cassese, was a world-renowned authority on international law.

Florence was wonderful. I learned to speak Italian like a native and made many Italian friends with whom I am in touch to this day. I think having a Russian background and language made it much easier to learn Italian and fit into the Italian culture. Coming back to Italy as an American brought back memories of having seen it just a few weeks after leaving Russia. This was a very different experience. It no longer felt like being an outside observer.

After Middlebury, I graduated from law school at Columbia University and spent several years practicing as a corporate and private equity lawyer in New York. The rest of my career has been as an investment banker in New York, Europe, and California, as well as a corporate counsel at Schlumberger. About 10 years ago, I co-founded a company called Expert Webcast, www.expertwebcast.com, a professional media company and thought leadership platform hosting roundtables on law and finance with leading law, accounting, and consulting firms and corporations. I moderate many of the programs.

While working at Credit Suisse First Boston in the '90s I spent about a year working for the Moscow office. Not having many ties to Russia or any desire to go back, working there was a very different and interesting experience. We banked just about every freewheeling oligarch one read about in the newspapers. Transactions ranged from oil company IPOs to gold mine privatizations to sales of television networks. The work was interesting, yet culturally the country and the people had not changed much, and in the long run, I preferred being in the West.

America has changed greatly in the 40 or so years since I arrived here, mostly for the better. This is definitely home and a place where I have lived most of my life.

I am glad to have a Russian-American dual identity, which has broadened my horizons and allowed me to have a different point of reference on many things, academically, professionally, and socially. Having said that, most of my friends have always been non-Russian, my wife is a Russian immigrant, and my kids do not speak any Russian.

For the most part, once my family came to America, we always wanted to be American and build a new life around that, without being a Russian transplant.

Being Jewish has always been an ethnic, cultural, or national characteristic for me, not religious. That really has not changed much.

I have always had a vision of America as a place where people can put a stake in the land in the wilderness and succeed through their perseverance, regardless of where they come from, a place where people can realize their dreams and provide a better life for themselves and their children through hard work and perseverance. Although from time to time I am skeptical as to how much of this ideal still holds true, having traveled and lived extensively all over the world, I am always happy to come back and call the U.S. home. ■

IRENE FISHER

NOW

I am 56 years old, happily married, with two fabulous boys. My older son is finishing his last year of law school in New York City, while my younger son is a banker in Boston. After attending Yale University and Harvard Law School, I started my legal career at a big Wall Street law firm. After four years and seemingly countless billable hours, I went in-house and became a general counsel of several multinational companies. I now split my time between Florida and New York, enjoying spending time with my husband and my family, as I continue to work as a general counsel and now minority owner of a health and wellness company. In my spare time, I enjoy the beach, tennis, and cooking.

I vividly remember the cold morning in 1976 when my grandfather, God rest his soul, walked me to school, and kissed me goodbye. I didn't know if I would ever see him again. My family is Jewish, and at that time, anti-Semitism was prevalent throughout Russia. Jews were regularly denied entrance to universities, better jobs, etc. So, my grandparents, aunt, uncle (God rest his soul), and cousin were all leaving my hometown of Odessa later that day to find a better future. Almost all my family was going to the United States, leaving behind me and my mother and father. My immediate family was very small. I am an only child. My mother has one sister, and she has one son. For the entirety of my life, until that fateful day, we all lived together—

eight of us in a small apartment. And now five were going to be gone. For how long? No one knew. Would I ever see them again? No one knew. We worried that our goodbyes might be forever.

I was 10 at the time, so off to school I went, trying to hold back my tears and fears. I came home to an apartment that never felt emptier. But I hugged my mom and told her it would all be OK. Or so I hoped.

The next year or so was very tough. We didn't talk much about whether we would ever be together again. We just tried to hang on. I went to school between my trips to other Eastern bloc countries and cities as a member of the Soviet Union Olympic reserve chess team. My dad taught me to play when I was nine, and I immediately excelled. Shortly after learning to play, I had a coach and studied hours a day. Then I would play on the weekends, most often against people in their 30s or older. Chess was my salvation. My mom went to work as a piano teacher, being strong as she always is. My dad went to work as a molder, going to as many of my matches as he could attend, given his work schedule.

After what seemed like an eternity, but was less than a year, my grandparents finally settled in Newark, New Jersey, and were able to send us an invitation to come to America. The path to leaving was not easy for my dad, as he worked for the government. So the moment we applied to emigrate, my dad lost his job and was seen as a traitor. He quickly found a menial job working in a food store to keep us afloat financially. One day I was very sick with a fever and stomach pain, and my dad brought home a bag of oranges that smelled delicious. But I couldn't eat them because I was sick. Those few treats from the store were lovely respites to an otherwise very difficult time waiting to see if we would be permitted to leave. My mom helped to make ends meet by teaching piano privately and remaining strong.

Somehow I was still allowed to go to school, perhaps because I played chess so well at such a young age. I'm not really sure, but no one called me a traitor or an ungrateful Jew, as they did to my parents.

Finally, we were allowed to leave without the few things we had amassed over time. My father carefully and painstakingly packed a few pieces of clothing and personal belongings into a single suitcase for each of us. (My dad is the best packer in the world and has lovingly taught my kids to do the same.)

We boarded a train in Odessa. The train was on its way to Austria. We were three scared people with no country, no rights—just a dream to rejoin their family and to be free to practice our religion. Several times during that seemingly endless few days journey, Russian soldiers and inspectors would come in, sometimes searching us under the guise of making sure we weren't taking precious "government secrets" with us. We were told such things would happen, and my dad was prepared—as he always is. Before leaving Russia, with the few rubles that we had to our name, he bought several bottles of vodka. And each time Russian soldiers came, my dad would offer the vodka in the hopes we would be left alone. I had never been so scared in my life. I was always very good at math, and I kept calculating when we would have to stop giving a bottle to each soldier and start giving one bottle to several of them. Even then, at what point would we run out? Those questions and calculations kept spinning in my head until I would fall asleep, praying that we would reach our destination soon.

Finally, we arrived in Vienna. I had never been to Austria and vividly remember thinking how fast-paced everything seemed. People walked and spoke so quickly. I was scared by the newness of it all, but that fear was different from the petrifying fear on that train. It had a glimpse of hope. I don't recall much of the time in Vienna, which was a few days staying in the hotel, waiting for the next stop on our journey.

A little town on the outskirts of Rome called Ostia Lida was the next stop on my journey, where we stayed for almost three months until we were granted permission to enter the United States. I picked up a decent amount of Italian as I listened to people all around me. My dad got a job working in a pizzeria so we could feel like we had a few pennies, or lira, in our pocket. I remember playing video games with my dad and having pizza, anxiously waiting for the freedom to come. My mom and I also went to see Pompeii with some other Russian immigrants in Italy—a treat that was larger than life to me. To this day, I wished my dad could have joined us, but he insisted on trying to earn extra money so we would feel less stressed.

Finally, that fateful day came in June 1977 when we boarded a huge plane for a very long flight to Newark, New Jersey. It was my first ever time on an airplane. I was scared but also excited to see the family members that I hadn't seen in two years. I couldn't wait. When we landed, I was never so happy but still scared. What I thought was fast-paced in Vienna was multiplied by hundreds as we walked past people at the airport. Finally, after never-ending paperwork submissions, we cleared customs, and I was overjoyed to see the excited faces of my family. Indescribable happiness had overcome us all. I remember going to my aunt and uncle's apartment in Newark, where many of my family friends from Russia had gathered to celebrate our arrival. I went to bed feeling exhausted and so happy.

With the help of HIAS, a Jewish organization that supports Soviet Jews in their fight for freedom, we got a small apartment in a low income subsidized housing complex, also then known as "the projects," in Newark, on the same floor as my grandparents, aunt and uncle. We were together again. My father worked as a molder and my mother as a bookkeeper to put food on the table and buy some bare necessities. They would both be learning English on the job.

It was summer. Every morning I would watch cartoons with my grandfather and learn English by doing so. I was excited by the many possibilities that seemed available to me. My dad still wanted me to pursue my chess career, so I started looking at any tournaments that I could enter with a fee we could afford. I entered and won a few tournaments and was highly ranked. But we couldn't afford a coach. Driving to see a coach was expensive, and chess in the U.S. was not the cool, hip, and trendy sport it was in Russia. So after a few months, I stopped.

In September, I went to Solomon Schechter Day School, a Jewish school, which made my grandfather quite happy because we were unable to practice our Jewish religion in the USSR. I learned to read Hebrew, as well as a lot about Jewish history and practices. But school wasn't easy. While I picked up some English, learning on the fly came with many embarrassing moments. To this day, the first day of school sticks out vividly in my mind. I was waiting outside the classroom, and a student asked me how long I had been waiting there. I misunderstood and thought she had asked me how long I had been in this country. So I said, "Three months," and she looked at me like I was so strange. When she walked away, I realized that I had made a mistake and felt deeply embarrassed.

I began school by enrolling in sixth grade to learn English better, even though I was eligible for seventh grade. The strategy seemed to pay off. I picked up English pretty quickly and ended up skipping seventh grade to be in eighth grade. I did well in school and even made some lifelong friends (like my friend David, who still remembers that I was the first person to speak to him on the bus). Math was my strong suit—not surprising since it is the subject that the Soviet Union pushes. And, for chess players, math is like breathing. I also liked learning about Jewish culture and Jewish religion and history—something that I would never be able to do in Russia.

I matured quickly, as the circumstances dictated. When we came to the U.S., I was the only one in the family who read and understood English. So as mail would come in, I would often help my parents deal with whatever issues had arisen. That made me grow up pretty quickly.

I was also pretty driven as a child. I wanted to succeed—fairly typical for immigrants. I also wanted to do all that I could to help my parents, as they sacrificed everything to come to America and give me a better life.

After several years, my parents saved up some money and bought what was called a mother-daughter house in White Meadow Lake, New Jersey. It was a quiet community that used to be a summer cottage village until people started adding heating systems and living there year round. We lived in this home with my grandparents. My mom, dad, and I lived on the walk-in level, and my grandparents lived on the second floor. The home was modest, but I did have my own small room and a separate room that I would use to study. While we never had much money growing up in America, my parents always made the best of it, and I never felt poor.

After we moved into our home, I transferred out of Solomon Schechter Day School as the commute was too long. So I started a new school as a junior in high school and was again the new kid. But I was enrolled in all the AP classes being offered and quickly found a group of Jewish kids who shared my desire to get ahead.

Life was simple. I went to school, studied hard, and listened to music in my spare time. My dad taught me to dance when I was invited to my first party at Solomon Schechter School. I worked on weekends at my grandfather's deli store to save some money, which my parents painstakingly saved for me. I remained focused on getting into the best school that I could.

I had my heart set on Yale. I applied to Yale, Harvard, Princeton (my parents' favorite since it was nearby), Brown (because it was an Ivy League university, but it was too far to visit and couldn't spare the time or the money to go), Cornell, Dartmouth, and the University of Pennsylvania. I didn't apply to Columbia as I believed it was too leftist and communist in its leanings. Northwestern was my safety school—again, never went to visit. The University of Pennsylvania was the first to admit me, as it did when I applied to law school there. Oddly, Northwestern, my safety school, waitlisted me! I guess not going to visit gave them a hint. Harvard rejected me, which relieved me since I did not enjoy my visit to the school. So I was running to the mailbox every day, waiting for what I hoped was a big envelope. I remember my dad saying that we've been in America for five years, and I got into the fifth best school in America, the University of Pennsylvania, so I should have been happy. But I yearned for Yale. Finally, the day came. Yale was the last to respond, and it accepted me.

I was elated. Then came the worries of how I was going to afford it. Yale offered financial aid, but it was not generous. I had to borrow money using student loans, but interest rates were 12 to 15 percent in those days. No matter. I went to the local bank and signed countless documents. My parents' tuition payments strapped them very tight. Years later, I learned that sometimes they didn't know how to put food on the table and make the payments. My dad took a second job cleaning the local Catholic high school for extra money. I got a job at Yale, working for Professor Nordhaus in the economics department, running errands, making copies, whatever it took. I was determined to succeed.

And succeed, I did. I got past freshman year, which was a struggle. I came from a public school and was competing with prep schools like Exeter and Andover—the best of the best. They read the books that we were reading at Yale when they were in their prep schools. So I found a wonderful tutor at Saybrook, my residential college, who helped me fine-tune my writing skills. I worked hard and took advantage of every opportunity. When I found out that Yale offered simultaneous bachelor's and master's degrees, I jumped at the chance. That meant reading hundreds and sometimes even thousands of pages each week in my political science major. But I was determined, so I found an Evelyn Wood speed-reading class and took it to help me handle the workload.

I did very well at Yale, graduating summa cum laude with a very high GPA. I had worked hard, made wonderful friends, and learned to live on my own. I have a few favorite memories. First, my parents visiting me every week in the beginning, driving up and just sitting with me in the car as there wasn't much we could afford to do. Money was tight, but my parents were very proud and never complained. I would initially speak to my parents twice a week and always tell them how hard it was for me—especially freshman year. As a mother now, I realize how hard it must have been for my parents to hear my complaints all the time. Second, becoming involved in politics and coming home to argue with my parents about my views. My dad would say that I would change my views once I started to work and make money. He was right. Third, I remember all the wonderful Yale traditions that stay with you for life. Lastly, after being recruited by the CIA, I recall my dad telling me that if I accepted the job, they would send me to Russia, where I could get killed.

While at Yale, I applied to law school, as I had always intended to be a corporate attorney. I had my sights set on Harvard Law School and was thrilled beyond words when I got in. More student loans followed, and more belt tightening for my parents. But I got to Harvard, where I did very well. To help with finances, I got a job as soon as I got to law school. I worked as a research assistant for Professor Abe Chayes, who took me with him to the international world court in The Hague in the Netherlands, as he helped to argue a case there. The excitement of that first semester soon took a tumble, as my dad had a massive heart attack. I studied for my first semester finals in the hospital. But thankfully, my dad recovered, and with the help of my mom's watchful eye and strict diet, my dad got better. He, unfortunately, needed open heart surgery in my last semester at law school. So I studied for the bar exam as my dad recovered. I took the bar exam and passed, which goes to show that what doesn't kill you makes you stronger.

As I look back on those tumultuous times, I am forever grateful for the strong support from my parents and husband, who have been my guideposts and rock. I am deeply thankful to my grandparents, who were visionaries in their thirst for freedom, including religious freedom, and instilled in me the sense of fighting for what you believe in and having a long-term strategic plan to accomplish your goals. Being a first-generation immigrant made me tough and fiercely independent very early on in my life. Not having anything of financial value makes you hungry to achieve and succeed, only to ultimately realize, as I do every day, that material things—while a necessity—are not the true source of happiness, which comes from having love and support in your life.

IGOR KIRMAN

NOW:

Igor Kirman, 50, lives in New York City with his wife, Galina, and their two kids, Ariel (18), the author, and Shaye (15). He is a corporate lawyer with a passion (some might say obsession) for ping pong. He could not be more proud of his daughter for bringing this book to life.

LEGACY

I often refer to myself as Russian (or a Russian Jew from Ukraine), but I was born in Kharkov, Ukraine's second largest city, back when it was part of the U.S.S.R. Now it's spelled Kharkiv, and Ukraine is a separate country embroiled in a frozen conflict with Russia. But back then, they were one country, and my city was culturally and linguistically Russian. I sometimes point out that the first time I heard Ukrainian spoken was on the streets of the East Village in New York. Kharkov is an industrial city known for its factories and World War II tank battles. But for me, it will always be my first home. I had a happy and warm childhood. We lived in a one-bedroom apartment. I remember the apartment quite well. It seemed spacious at the time, yet it's odd for me to even imagine how four adults—my parents and my maternal grandparents—and two kids (my sister Anna was born in 1977) could live in a space that small. I remember at least one bed and one couch, and my sister slept in a crib. We were happy, and maybe even lucky, to have the apartment. I remember a rug hanging on the wall and a small ventilation window in the kitchen called a "fortochka." We spent a lot of time in the kitchen watching my grandma cook. I also remember the bathroom, which doubled as my father's photography darkroom. I remember the newspaper cutouts that substituted for toilet paper some days. But we had a car and a telephone, which no doubt caused some envy across the hallway. On the other hand, we lived on the uppermost floor (the fifth) of a building with no elevator, which surely caused no envy. I don't know how my mother got her two kids up those stairs.

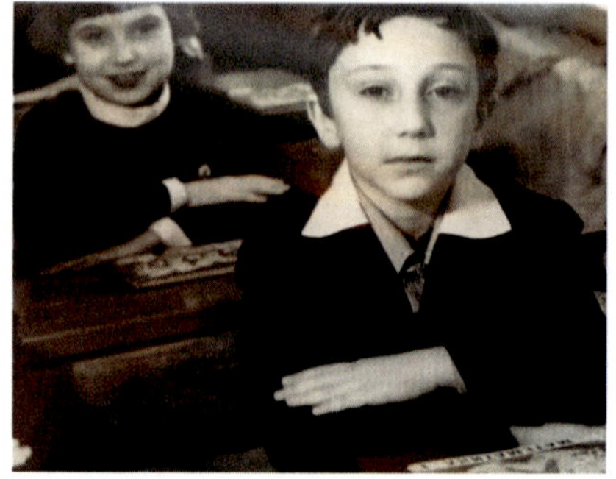
In first grade, there was only one permitted way to raise one's hand: at a 90-degree angle.

I was old enough to make it through a few months of first grade before we left. I remember the first day being a big deal. Kids brought flowers for teachers! We sat at desks with one boy and one girl per desk, sitting with hands folded in front.

My father was a factory manager who fortunately managed to avoid being drafted into the Communist Party through some tortured efforts, which he delights in retelling to this day. My mother worked as a trained economist in some department. (Everyone "worked for the government," and everything was "a department.") In fact, it was one of my mother's prior job searches that pushed our family to leave the U.S.S.R. My mother, fresh out of school, went looking for a job. It was hard for Jews to find jobs, even after university graduation. At one prospective department, the man interviewing her instead asked to step outside to speak with my father. He explained that he wanted to tell my dad "man to man" that my mother would not be hired, that they had already met the informal Jewish quota. My father accepted the news in stride. He knew the ways of the world and had seen anti-Semitism often. He grew up with it in school, in the army, and the workplace. Anti-Semitism was the "in your face" variety, sometimes literally. He tells the story of how one day when he finally bought his first car and picked it up, he swerved to avoid an oncoming driver. After the two drivers got out of their cars to complain of the near-miss, the other driver took one look at him and said, "Zhidovskaya morda" (kike face), a highly insulting but common slur. My dad decked him and proceeded with his maiden voyage. But somehow, at my mother's job interview, he had decided that enough was enough. He did not want this life for his children and would be applying for an exit.

Igor with his dad Vladimir. Formal photography was popular in the U.S.S.R.

Seeking emigration for Jews was no small matter, and there were risks involved. For one, merely making the request meant the loss of a job in most cases. My mom and grandma were cautious and opposed the move. When my sister was born in the fall of 1977, the risk seemed to grow. But my dad and his surprising ally, my usually very cautious grandfather, were determined and prevailed. After months of cajoling and paperwork, my family had an exit visa. We said our goodbyes to the remaining family (my father's mother and his brother), and on a snowy night in January 1979, we and our belongings boarded a Soviet express to Vienna by way of Warsaw. I would never see the Soviet Union again.

PASSAGE TO THE WEST

In those years, immigration was no simple journey. In later years, people boarded a plane in Moscow and 10 hours later landed in New York. For us, it was an adventure, even if we didn't know it at the time. I still remember the train journey that took us beyond Soviet borders. While in Poland, en route to Vienna, soldiers with machine guns boarded the train. To an eight-year-old boy, this was equal parts scary and exhilarating. I had only seen machine guns in picture books and my imagination. To my parents, I suspect this experience probably lacked all entertainment value. Then 10 days in Vienna in January 1979, our first taste of the West. I have only two memories of Vienna, and both are seared in my brain. The first was in what I might now call a stationery/convenience store. I had begun collecting bubble gum wrappers the year before we emigrated. My father used all his connections to obtain a few for me. I think my treasured collection totaled four or five. But here I was, in a humble stationery/convenience store staring at row after row of more gum varieties than I could imagine. The proverbial kid in a candy store! Except, of course, we couldn't afford any of them. My second memory is of my first Western supermarket. I remember two things that jumped out at me because I didn't quite understand them. First, was the idea of bread sitting on shelves, wrapped in cellophane. Ukraine had terrific bread (after all, it is the "bread basket of Europe"). But it showed up on a truck, and we queued up to receive it while it was still hot. There was no reason to preserve it for shelf life. The second was the juice containers of different types, sizes, shapes, and flavors. In Ukraine, I remember just a glass bottle, but here were yellow containers and green ones, big and small, wide and narrow, and some shaped like figurines. I'm not sure I understood that they were different types of juice, most of which weren't even sold in Ukraine.

ITALY: LIVING THE MEDITERRANEAN DREAM

Then came our three-month sojourn to Italy. In those years, Soviet Jews were allowed to leave the U.S.S.R. under international pressure. But the Soviets gave exit visas only to Israel, ostensibly for religious reasons, even though they knew that virtually everyone in those years was headed for America. After all, Soviet pride could not admit that anyone would want to leave the Soviet Eden to go to the main enemy, which Soviet propaganda painted as a cesspool of racism, poverty, and exploitation. Even though Soviet authorities understood where immigrants were really going, everyone had to play along. Act one was for us to request exit visas to Israel. Act two was for the Soviets to let us leave for Israel. Act three was to request asylum while in transit and redirect to the United States. To do this, the U.S. government, together with a variety of Jewish agencies, such as HIAS, JDC, and ORT, set up an asylum processing operation outside of Rome, and most Soviet immigrants, like us, settled for the approximately three-month wait (this was the age of paper and mail applications!) in one of several suburbs outside of Rome.

We moved to an apartment in Ostia Lido, a suburb of Rome. Compared to our previous home in Ukraine, it felt like a palace, but I suspect that if I were to see it now, I would be shocked at how small it truly was. My memories are patchy but, in some cases, very distinct. After all, it was my first prolonged taste of the West. Our family seemed busy, and we were friends with a number of other immigrant families, including a few who had originally hailed from the same small village in which my father grew up. (In fact, it was remarkable how many people from that village eventually made their way to America.) My wife and her family were also in Ostia Lido at the same time, so we could have met as kids! I remember taking a train to visit one out further in the suburbs, where I marveled at the fact that they had rented a full house, not an apartment like us. One enduring memory is of the outdoor market in Rome, where every weekend, Soviet immigrants would sell their wares to supplement their living allowance—Soviet linen; cameras; wooden lacquered boxes; and matryoshkas, those nested dolls much beloved by tourists—and whatever else they had brought in the suitcases we lugged across the Iron Curtain. I joined my parents as we stood outside, yelling out "Una mila, una pezzo" (one mila, one piece), hawking these wares. How did we even know to bring them? Everyone seemed to have similar stuff, as if some unwritten code was passed down the immigration chain. And I still don't know how these Soviet-made goods could compete with the offerings available in Rome. Probably some combination of curiosity and the right price. We were grateful for the extra money and dutifully made the half-hour trip by train every weekend.

Italy is also where I found out that I was Jewish. I had heard the word once before. I must have been five or so, and my family decided to take a vacation to the Black Sea. My mother and I went ahead, my father to join us later when his job permitted. There were no hotels, of course. The usual way to find lodging was to walk house to house in the seaside town until someone would rent a room "off the books." My mother and I carried our suitcases from house to house, asking for availability. I remember one old woman—a babushka—asked us if we were Jewish. When my mom said yes, the babushka apologized but said that she could not rent to Jews. "What is a Jew?" I asked my mom as we turned to leave.

"That's just who we are," she said, and we moved on. But now, at age eight in Italy, the mystery was unlocked. It was Passover, and we were celebrating with a traditional Seder ritual and meal. Full-on prayers, kosher food, the works. My family explained my religion to me for the first time. To say that I was curious is to severely understate my level of excitement that night. My mind was racing. What's more, I learned that my family had conducted a Seder every year of my life. How was it that I had never seen it? That turned out to be no coincidence. My family would wait until I went to sleep before starting the multi-hour celebration (dinner at midnight?). It was too dangerous to practice the religion, and they were afraid that I might inadvertently blab to a friend.

Practicing for the New York cousins.

We did some touristy things in Rome, seeing the big sights with my parents while my grandparents stayed put with my infant sister. Then my dad and I took a bus trip north to Florence, Venice, and Pisa. We could only afford one ticket, so he and I went, and I sat on his lap on the bus. The north was beautiful, and to this day, the memories of that trip are most often what I recall of Italy.

Meanwhile, while I was running around playing soccer on the streets of Ostia Lido, my parents were busy attending to the serious task of getting us to America. Trip after trip to Rome to conduct interviews, fill out paperwork, start learning a few words of English. Most of all, there was the bureaucracy and the waiting. (At the time, it seemed insufferable, but now, I'm grateful for my extended Italian stay.) My family could choose to go to Australia or America. And once we chose America, we had the choice of New York or Des Moine, Iowa. The Jewish community in Des Moines was looking to shore up its ranks. My dad was tempted by dreams of owning his own farmland, something he could not do in the collectivist U.S.S.R. But in the end, he chose New York. I often wonder how different my life would have been had we chosen Des Moines (or Australia).

FIRST STEPS IN AMERICA: WHAT A COUNTRY!

It was nighttime when the plane from Rome to New York's JFK Airport touched down. We waited for the transport bus, and being so tired from the journey, I fell asleep standing up. We ended up staying in a Brooklyn hotel on Clark Street for the first two weeks. The hotel catered to immigrants and had a strip club on the first floor. I made lots of friends, and I remember soccer in a nearby park. I also promptly got sick with measles and ended up being introduced to the New York subways, which is how my mom and I made our way to Coney Island Hospital. After a few days, I was circumcised —yes, at age eight years, not eight days! A Hasidic group was in charge of the ritual, which took place in a common room in the hotel. I remember taking a few sips of wine—not enough—as I did feel a lot of pain! It was a rough way to enter the Jewish covenant, to be sure. And it was just a foretaste of the many ways in which Russian Jews like us were disadvantaged compared to our American-born brethren.

We had no relatives in America. My parents knew a few other immigrant families, and one of them had been a few weeks ahead of us in the immigration journey. These pioneers had found an apartment in Queens, and we followed them there. The building, at the crossroad of three neighborhoods—Forest Hills, Corona, and LeFrak City—was a veritable depository of immigrants from all over the world. Outside of Brooklyn's "Little Odessa" in Brighton Beach, it was probably the area with the highest concentration of Russian immigrants in New York (and the U.S.). We had not one, but two, Russian delis on the main drag (108th Street) to remind us of old tastes. Seeing elderly Russians congregating in parks near building entrances was a common sight. But the Russian community was still an island in the larger sea of other immigrants and the native-born.

We ended up with two apartments in our extended family—a one-bedroom for my parents, my sister, and me on the fourth floor and a separate studio apartment two floors up for my grandparents. (My parents were offered a two-bedroom instead of a one-bedroom, but they deemed it too expensive at $340 per month instead of $315.) I would spend a lot of time running up and down the staircase between the two. I slept on the living room couch, and the others shared the single bedroom. My sister, who was less than two at the time, never had a crib in the U.S. My parents put some chairs around her bed to make sure she would not roll over. (Ironically, she actually had a crib in the U.S.S.R.) The roach infestation (unfortunately in both apartments, so there was no escape) is still a source of bad memories, but we were happy to have the space. We furnished it through handouts and by carefully watching the garbage pile in the back of our building. Long before dumpster diving became hip, we competed with other immigrants to grab whatever table, couch, or lamp made its way to the trash. The sanitation workers servicing our building must have wondered why they never saw discarded furniture from a building that size. We got our first table from a synagogue that had decided to discard it with a missing leg. Problem? For people accustomed to the Soviet kludge method, this was no problem. We found a pile of bricks, and one of our table legs simply became sturdier than the others!

Across the street was what I then thought of as a park, but it was really a parking lot for an elder living facility. I spent many days and evenings in the empty space between the cars, mastering my new love—baseball! We played with all the other immigrant kids and a few American ones most nights until it was too dark to see the ball. We also let our energy out running up and down the hallways, playing tag and (multi-floor) hide and seek.

We were dirt poor. We received assistance from a number of Jewish resettlement organizations, including the New York Association for New Americans (NYANA), which helped Soviet refugees. We also got food stamps. My mother's food budget for our family was $30 weekly, and we bought only the most discounted offerings (I remember the local Fine Fare supermarket, and clipping coupons was a family sport). My parents still talk with pride about how they would never buy a can of Coke, even on a sweltering summer day. Even in later years, when we indulged and went out to celebrate an occasion, a restaurant outing meant a fast food place. Burger King, Roy Rogers, and Pizza Hut were our favorites. I don't think I saw a tablecloth in a restaurant until college.

My father went straight to work, first working for $3 an hour as a machinist, but quickly moved over to driving a taxi, a popular but hard job for Russian immigrants in those years. It was only many years later, in 1996, that he bought an auto repair shop called VIP Auto Repair.

The stories he tells of his struggles in the early years of the job bring forth both shock and laughter. In the pre-GPS era, he got lost countless times in the streets of a city he did not know and could not ask his way out of trouble because he barely spoke English. One time he got lost driving Japanese tourists, who themselves did not speak English, for hours from JFK Airport to Manhattan. Surely, a classic case of the one-eyed leading the blind. Now he laughs about that story, but I can only imagine the terror he felt going out every morning without a safety net. Yet his courage and determination to provide for his family drove him forward, and he worked 16 hour days, six and sometimes seven days a week. (Years later, he had saved up enough to buy himself a taxi "medallion" and thus became a taxi owner, driving for himself.) At one point, I remember my family counting its savings, which totaled $7.50. And yet, the hard times did not change his values. One day early on, he discovered an entire satchel of jewelry in the backseat of the taxi, left behind by a passenger. He suspected it might have been a passenger he had picked up at a particular hotel, so he left his number with the doorman there in case someone called. Sure enough, a grateful woman located him a few days later. It was an inheritance with sentimental value that she could never replace. She gave him a small reward and a box of chocolate candy. Many of his taxi-driving friends told him that he was an idiot for returning the jewelry. But he came home beaming and remains proud of that story to this day.

SCHOOL

Then there was school. I was sent to a Jewish day school, known as a yeshiva (Yeshiva Dov Revel in Forest Hills), no doubt at the suggestion of one of the Jewish groups helping us resettle. My mother (and later my grandmother) had to work once a week serving food in the lunchroom to keep tuition reasonable. I recall the terror of my first day. The third-grade teacher walked me into a full classroom in the middle of the day, all eyes on the new kid. She then handed me a piece of paper, an assignment of some kind. I remember seeing the word "Name" at the top, with a blank line next to it. I had started learning a few English words during our immigration journey, and I understood that I was supposed to fill in my name. But I had a problem. I knew my name, but I did not know how to write it in English. I sat there staring at her, not knowing how to express my dilemma. This blessed woman somehow figured it out and wrote my name on the blackboard for me. I joked later that had she written my name as "Egor," maybe I would be spelling it that way now.

School was at once a culture shock and a culture bridge. It presented a double challenge at first. I knew next to no English and even less Judaism and Hebrew. I was thrown into the deep end and had to learn fast. Thankfully third grade is still a time when even native-born kids are learning vocabulary. I remember for one assignment, we had to take a list of 10 words the teacher gave us and write a sentence for each. The point for most kids was to learn each of those 10 vocabulary words while writing the sentences. For me, the task was harder. I sat there late into the night, with my mother and my dictionary at hand, and looked up practically every word of every sentence. I guess you can say I was learning a lot more than my classmates! Between doing that and watching TV, I started picking up the language. For my parents, it was much slower going.

School was a vector for Judaism. I learned to read Hebrew (and became one of the fastest readers in the class), ate kosher food in school, and brought home a request for our family to keep "kosher for Passover." Even now, while my parents do not keep kosher or the Jewish Sabbath, they still keep those old Passover habits, keeping separate dishes for Passover and eating only kosher for Passover food. I think we were expected to go to synagogue at least on the holidays, and I remember going many times. They were all Orthodox synagogues, with separate seating for men and women. Soon my grandfather found a small synagogue near our house where he became very active. He had a beautiful singing voice, and he used it there to good effect. I had a bar mitzvah ceremony and party, but we did it in the Russian style in one of Brooklyn's Russian restaurants/nightclubs.

Baba Nina and sister Anna, starting our American Seder (no need to hide!).

In fifth grade, I transferred to the Hebrew Academy of West Queens

(HAWQ), which required a yellow bus commute. After a year there, I transferred to my local elementary school for sixth grade (PS. 220) and then attended my local junior high school (Halsey) for seventh and eighth grades. The public schools were diverse in a way that the Jewish day schools had not been. Now I was truly surrounded by immigrants and Americans of every color and creed. In the Jewish schools, I was the oddity—Jewish like everyone, but also different. Here my differences were obscured by a sea of diversity. There were Russians, and many of us were friends, but many of my best friends were Indian, Pakistani, Korean, and Colombian immigrants too.

Sixth-grade graduation with proud sister Anna.

CULTURE: THE ORIGINAL TV BINGE

It might be an exaggeration, but not a huge one, to say that I became an American by watching TV. I still recall the very first show I saw. *The Six Million Dollar Man* was playing on TV in the home of a family we were visiting. It caught my eye, I was dazzled by the story and the special effects, and then ... it stopped. Or rather, it switched to something totally incongruous, which made no sense to me. It was a commercial, of course, but the concept was utterly alien to me back then. (Ironically, the idea of commercials is becoming alien again in today's media environment.) Why would a great story be interrupted, just as it was getting to the good part, only to then show me advertisements for a cola product or a car? I had a lot to learn about capitalism, but that was a start.

I threw myself into TV watching long before there was binge-watching. I watched cartoons—*Tom and Jerry, The Flintstones, Scooby-Doo, Smurfs,* and a dozen others. I watched cop shows—*The Dukes of Hazzard, Magnum P.I., Miami Vice, Barnaby Jones,* and others. I watched dramas—*The Little House on the Prairie, Dallas, Dynasty,* and *Knots Landing*. I also watched tons of sitcoms—*Three's Company, The Jeffersons, What's Happening?, All in the Family, Who's the Boss?, Family Ties, The Cosby Show, Happy Days,*

WKRP in Cincinnati, among many others. These shows helped me learn the lingo and the jokes, but they also taught me how to act in America.

LATER YEARS: BECOMING AMERICAN

Year by year, we became more American, but each of us at different speeds. For my sister Anna and me, the process moved at light speed. We loved the new country and wanted to drink it all in. We could not wait to make all the new sights, sounds, and colors all our own. I learned English as quickly as I could so that I could rush into this new world. I learned new words and lost one accent while picking up another (a hybrid Queens/Russian one that some with a good ear can detect even now, though in attenuated form). Even so, there was no escaping my immigrant status. In school, some kids would never let me forget it. The Cold War was still raging, and taunts of "Commie" and "Better dead than red" in school were mixed with "Dirty Russian" or "Stinking Jew" on the playground. But this was Queens, perhaps the most diverse area on the planet, and everyone was from somewhere or had something that could be made fun of. As we played soccer (on concrete, I might add), handball, stickball, and touch football, we grew tough skin and learned to let these taunts roll off us. And we gave as good as we got. We were as ethnically and religiously diverse as you get, but it all felt perfectly natural as we did battle on those concrete playing fields.

In many ways, I did not fully fit in. First, it was the clothes. We bought American-made clothes, but they had a certain cheap look that marked me for sartorial sneers among schoolmates. We purchased everything on deep sale—the cheapest t-shirts, shorts, and sneakers. I wore the cheap knockoffs of the latest brands of the day. Nothing matched.

Then, there were the cultural gaps. I was watching the current cartoons and sitcoms but didn't know the old ones that other kids had grown up on. I hadn't read any nursery rhymes or children's stories, and I didn't really know the words to any classic American songs. ("The Star-Spangled Banner" became the patriotic exception to the rule.) And the way I talked was different. I was working harder than my American counterparts to learn vocabulary, but there were still a lot of basic phrases and idioms that I didn't know. And of course, no matter how much I learned and tried to pass myself off as an American, my very Russian-sounding name (Igor) would always expose me as a newcomer, or so I thought. I thought about changing it at various points to Eric, Alec, Gary, and even Ike, but never did.

Igor with his mom and sister Anna.
At least the wristband matched!

My parents and grandparents loved America but had a harder time integrating. For my grandparents, well into their 60s and in retirement, the language was a tough gatekeeper. My grandfather would go the next two decades holding the same dog-eared copy of his English vocabulary book, but he never did manage to speak more than some scattered phrases here and there. The transition was tough for my parents, who were 30 at the time of immigration. On the one hand, it helped that they were both working, which meant they were dealing with Americans in English. But my dad drove a taxi, so the dialogue was more limited. After some classes (English, technical drafting, computer skills), my mother also went to work, finding a position as a clerk in the American Kennel Club in NYC. The office environment allowed her to practice her English. To this day, she remembers how the three words "smile," "smell," and "smoke" were particularly hard for her to distinguish correctly, but they were far from the only ones. American names such as John, Jane, and Michael seemed utterly alien and bewildering to them, just as Vladimir, Vladislav, and Mikhail might to American speakers. Their social circle was entirely Russian-speaking, so they were never thrown into the cultural deep waters and forced to swim. My wife's Russian immigrant parents, who lived in suburban New Jersey and worked in office environments, were forced to speak English more and had an easier time. My parents and I spoke mostly Russian, but I noticed that English words kept creeping into my side of the conversation. (For my sister, who was much younger and never learned Russian in school, this became even more frequent.) Even navigating the subway systems for my parents was a nightmare, with its frequent stops and required changes. Trying to understand a conductor speaking through the faulty loudspeaker system of those days was a challenge for everyone. Often, you took your chances and followed the crowd. One story my mom tells is about their experience opening their very first bank account. They walked into a bank, waited their turn to speak to a bank officer, but when it was their turn, they didn't know what to say. They were saved by a minor miracle, as a man waiting nearby overheard their awkward attempts to teach Russian to the bank officer and came to the rescue. I find it hard to imagine them resolving to even give this a try, knowing they did know how to express themselves. But try they did, and somehow they always managed to get things done.

My parents were devoted to Anna's and my futures. That, after all, is why they left. I'm sure they found it frustrating not to be able to navigate the new American world as our guides. The language, culture, and new electronics were all easier for us to assimilate than for them. In many ways, we became their guides, their teachers. But their essential roles of parents always remained, and they taught us deep values. They also understood enough about America to teach us the big picture, even if they could not navigate the particulars. I still remember when I first decided I wanted to become a lawyer. My dad and I were riding in his yellow cab under the bridge in Long Island City, and he told me his dream was for me to be a lawyer. When I asked why, he told me that "In this country, lawyers are educated, respected, and make good money." I'm not sure I even knew what a lawyer was, at least not beyond what I had seen on *Matlock* or *L.A. Law*, but that day launched me on my way. The author of *Le Petit Prince* supposedly once said that "If you wish to build a ship, do not divide the men into teams and send them to the forest to cut wood. Instead, teach them to long for the vast and endless sea." That was how my parents taught us the American dream.

SUMMERS IN THE CATSKILLS

One indulgence in those early years was summer in the Catskills. It became fashionable in the Russian immigrant community to send their children, with grandparents, to the "bungalow colonies" in upstate New York. For $700 or so for the entire summer, we could rent a small bungalow with one or two small bedrooms and have access to green grass playing fields, a swimming pool, some swings, and mostly each other.

It was a camp of sorts, with no bunk beds, and our counselors were our grandparents. For us, that was Ski Bungalow Colony in Wurtsboro, New York, about 17 miles from Monticello (Exit 113 on NY-17). Owned by a Polish family from Brooklyn, it had a clubhouse with a pool table and a jukebox (the song that ate the most quarters was G3 on the jukebox, Blondie's "Heart of Glass"), a tennis wall, a basketball half-court, swings, and of course an amazing pool. I had been to a few summers of day camp in Queens, but this was a different level of fun.

Fun in the Catskills was not just on land!

Year after year, many of the same families rented in the same place, but with some turnover bringing in new blood. It wasn't 100 percent Russian immigrants, but the American visitors came for a weekend or a week, not the whole summer as we did. We lived there with our grandparents, and on Friday nights or Saturday mornings, we waited anxiously as our parents made their way from New York City to visit for the weekend. The excitement was enhanced by the knowledge that they would be bringing shopping bags of groceries (some from the Russian delicatessens in Forest Hills) to replenish week-old supplies. I'm sure there were other things in those brown bags, but what I remember most is the potato chips! By the end of the weekend, half the supply was gone. These summers were among the happiest memories I have from childhood, probably for the same reason that many kids enjoy overnight camp. It was a time for fun, sports, and growth. At first, it was just us Russian immigrant kids hanging out with each other. But as we got into the middle teenage years, we made friends with the "townies." A popular hangout was "behind the statue," in the church parking lot right next to our bungalow colony, where the forested location next to a creek gave us ample space to build nightly fires and be hidden from the world.

BECOMING MORE FULLY AMERICAN

My race to become an American continued uninterrupted through the high school years. We bought a townhouse in Kew Garden Hills when I was in eighth grade, and I became a double bus commuter to school. Our new neighborhood was less of an immigrant enclave, so that was a sea change. Between commuting and more schoolwork, I had less time to hang out across the street, a pattern that continued when I started commuting—one and a half hours each way—to lower Manhattan to attend Stuyvesant High School, a school full of immigrants then and now. We still visited the old neighborhood because my grandparents lived there, and of course, the Russian delicatessens were there. And my parents still socialized "the Russian way," with a table full of guests, family-style food that seemed to always be coming, and lots of vodka toasts. I think I learned public speaking and the art of thinking on my feet while watching and eventually making those toasts!

I went to Yale for college in the fall of 1989, and this was a big cultural step for me. I was excited beyond belief but was also anxious. It's one thing to adjust to a social scene in New York schools full of immigrants, but I was now imagining trying to fit into Dink Stover's Yale. Visions of J Press-clad students with their secret handshake that I did not know wearing their New England prep school ties dominated my imagination. I was intimidated before I even set foot in New Haven. I remember making a trip to the downtown Manhattan Brooks Brothers to buy two heavy striped sweaters—one blue and one green (no doubt sale items)—which I kept for way too many years. Of course, by then, I probably looked foolish, and the people I was trying to imitate looked nothing like the stereotypes I had imagined.

My immigrant past manifested in a few other ways too. I decided to study Russian as my foreign language in college. I had been so busy running away from it, focusing only on English, it was now time to try to understand my native tongue. My intuitive understanding of the language was passable, but my knowledge of grammar was nonexistent. I still recall the observation my first Russian teacher made when she met me after I had taken my placement test: "You are the worst kind of student I can imagine," she began. "You think you know the language, but you don't. You should consider tutoring." And this was before class

Igor, his mom, sister, and Baba Nina and Deda Senya at Yale. Only one of them is trying to "fit in" with his clothes.

began! I did fine, without tutoring, and even took a Russian literature course, reading Gogol and Dostoevsky in the original. Along with two like-minded friends, I organized our own "Russian table." We had gone to the official Wednesday language table that the Russian department hosted but found them too American. Where was the constant food? The toasting? So we decided to invite a fun-seeking bunch of Russian-language students to our own version. Every Friday evening, we raced to grab private alcove dining room in my friend Steve's residential college. We snuck in a bottle (sometimes two) of cheap vodka and sat for hours, eating round after round of dining room food while making toasts. We had strict rules for toasting—the proceedings always began with our first two traditional Russian Table toasts, "Za Nas" (to us) and "Za Vstrechoo Pod stolom" (to meeting under the table), and toasting proceeded clockwise from the president, without skipping anyone. Everyone had to drink to every toast, no matter how distasteful. For years to come (and to this day), I exported this tradition to all sorts of other social gatherings.

I briefly considered some detours from my law school path, at one point considering using my Russian language skills to work for the CIA, but I eventually decided to stick to the original plan (hatched in that long-ago taxi drive with my dad) and went to law school next at Columbia. There I met my wife, Galina, also a Russian immigrant from Ukraine who followed a very similar path to mine. Our common cultural heritage and shared immigrant story (we were in Italy at the same time but did not know each other) no doubt contributed to our coming together, whether we were conscious of it or not.

REFLECTIONS ON MY RUSSIAN-AMERICAN IDENTITY

For years, I used to track the ratio of time spent in America compared to the U.S.S.R. I remember when I reached the 50-50 point, sometime in 1987, when I had spent half my life here. It was a major milestone. Was I finally an American? Or if not then, when? I don't know that there was ever such a dividing point—Russian here, American there. For a long while now, to most people, I'm indistinguishable from the native-born, even though I know the project of becoming an American may still be ongoing at the edges. Sure, a few with a sharp ear have told me they detect just a hint of an accent, but I tell them it's more likely to be a Queens accent than a Russian one. Once in a while, I mispronounce a word or miss an old cultural reference (the new ones I miss for an entirely different reason). But it is infinitely easier for me to speak English than Russian, which I do haltingly, and do so mostly with my parents (and sometimes with my Russian-immigrant wife, when we don't want our kids to understand, now that spelling words out is not an option). I've gotten more than an earful, in fact, about the decision not to teach our kids Russian. The food I eat is American (even if that often means Italian or Chinese). The TV shows and movies I watch are American (even though I love watching foreign shows with subtitles, including Russian ones). My increasingly overloaded information life, including books, articles, and so on, are all written in English. And I have grown a separate Jewish identity, courtesy of America, that had only at best a latent existence in the old country.

And yet, my Russian identity is still with me and most likely always will be. I sometimes wonder how much of that is due to my memories of the old country and how much to growing up in its shadow as an immigrant. I tend to lean toward the latter explanation. My memories of Ukraine are important to me. Most adults don't have such clear lines of demarcation. How many can really remember the difference between age seven and nine? To me, those memories are isolated and worlds apart. I remember running around with friends, trying to catch butterflies and, foolishly, bees with a matchbook in front of our building in Ukraine. I remember the smell of the pool where I first tried to learn to swim (Russian-style, being thrown into the deep end), the first day of school, uniform on and flowers (for teacher) in hand, sitting straight up with hands neatly folded in the prescribed manner on my desk. I remember playing with an electric train by our New Year's tree, playing ping pong with my uncle when visiting him in Belarussia (now Belarus), and being bitten by a wild cat—right through my heavy socks and pants—as I stepped on its tail in the middle of a catfight (and the trip to the hospital to get tetanus shots for it). I remember also being in the hospital to remove my tonsils and adenoids, staring at the pan filling with my blood because I had been given only local anesthesia. I remember parties at home and with relatives and streets and parades and vacation trips, and much more.

But even more important to my hyphenated identity were the stories, the mores, and the values, which nurtured me in those early years after arrival in America. I learned a lot about Russian culture and the Soviet regime, listening to hours upon hours of adult conversation during many drink-soaked dinners and celebrations. Every occasion was an opportunity for my parents and their friends to toast something about America or tell stories and "anekdoty" (anecdotes) about how "the system" worked (and was circumvented) in the old country. I learned a lot about the Soviet mind, including hard-edged values such as suspicion of motives, superstition, and distrust of power. Many Soviet immigrants kissed the American ground they walked on but often also thought many Americans to be hopelessly naive about how the world really worked "out there." I didn't simply adopt this gloomy mindset, but I was certainly exposed to it.

It is clear that my immigration journey played a part, and in some cases, a decisive part in my choices. I can still "think" (and also feel) in Russian, and therefore can look at things—even things having nothing to do with immigration—from a different and sometimes outsider's perspective. Being an outsider has made me also appreciate things that many Americans probably take for granted. The vast majority of my friends are not Russian-born, but a surprising number of my closest ones are. I didn't plan it that way, but I wonder whether my background, and theirs, provided a gravitational pull of sorts. Then there's my wife and soul mate, also a Russian immigrant. I can't say that I was specifically looking for a Russian background in a girlfriend. But perhaps subconsciously it helped, and our common background and journey have certainly provided a lot of glue in the years to come. When our kids were born, we did not choose to teach them Russian. How much of this was a deliberate choice (I recall some rationales), and how much was just sheer inertia, I don't fully know, but my guess is that it was some of each. But we have taught our kids "immigrant values," teaching them to appreciate hard work, outsider status, and not taking things for granted. And it was important for us to have our kids grow up to be close to their grandparents, and we took every opportunity to make that happen. The idea that we could ever move to another city and separate the grandparents from their grandkids was a non-starter. We no longer lived together in a Soviet-sized one-bedroom apartment, but the idea of family proximity didn't die altogether.

I've been back to Russia (not to Ukraine) twice as of this writing. Once in 1995, when I was in law school and on an exchange program. Communism had recently fallen, and it was exciting to see the new Russia. I took another trip a few years ago to speak at a legal conference. I enjoyed the trips. They felt far more personal than just a vacation would. It was great to be in a "foreign" country but have the native language and social tools to get by. But it was also clear that Russia itself had changed, that it was only partially the country we knew in its Soviet days. I guess in some ways, countries, like people, can evolve mixed identities as they age.

When the plane landed in JFK after my last trip, there was no question I was home. ■

ACKNOWLEDGMENTS

An anthology is, by necessity, a group project, and while I had the privilege of conceiving and editing this book, my first thanks must go to the group of 20 immigrants profiled here. Writing and sharing with the public on a personal topic is no easy matter, as I discovered when some would-be contributors found the task too emotional and dropped out. For each contributor, the immigration journey has most likely been the defining pivot in their lives. I know it can be delicate to write about such a personal topic—about one's struggles, fears, and family circumstances. I am grateful to this cohort for teaching me a lot about a topic that continues to fascinate me, even more than when I started.

I also want to thank my parents, Galina and Igor Kirman, who were my inspiration for the book and helped guide me along the way. They lived the tales described here and taught them to my brother Shaye and me from an early age. I know how hard they have worked to succeed and also to ensure that the best of "immigrant values" are passed on to my brother and me. Thank you, Shaye, also for being my co-conspirator and helping me "decode" our parents' secret Russian sayings from time to time.

I want to thank my publisher, Kristin Mitchell, and my proofreader, Shannon Booth, both of whom were terrific in every way. They worked quickly and with good cheer. I can't wait to write another book with you!

I also want to thank Barry Nalebuff, whose daughter's anthology book was a helpful inspiration for this project, for his helpful comments on my introduction. ■

APPENDIX: QUESTION GUIDE

The catalog of questions below is a general guide for you as you write your narrative. The questions are intended to stimulate thought and bring back memories of things you can choose to write about. They are not intended to be a paint-by-number guide to writing your memoir. While I expect that many memoirs will cover a fair number of these large topics, no memoir will cover them all. Every story is different, and I suspect you will choose to highlight the things that matter to you. Use these questions as a menu. Create your own questions. Do whatever it takes to bring your story to life.

In terms of presentation, I expect that most people will write a narrative with chapter breaks organized by themes. But feel free to write in a different style if it better captures your narrative. If it's easier for you to add question breaks into your writing, so it looks like an interview, do that. I will work with you to edit this, so focus on the story itself.

QUESTIONS

NOW

Tell me about yourself in 100 words or less. Where do you live? What do you do? Age? Married? Children? What is your passion? It would be great to add a photo, especially of you as a young immigrant.

LEGACY/ BACKGROUND

Describe your family's life in the old country. Do you have any special memories or circumstances? How did your family decide to leave for America? Below are some questions you can consider asking:

How old were you when you immigrated?

Tell me about your family in Russia. Where did they live? What did your parents do? Describe the economic situation (e.g., car, telephone, stories of privation, etc.).

Did your mother work? If yes, who took care of you at home?

Describe your parents (e.g., drinking/gender roles, Russian attitudes, etc.).

Did you live with your grandparents?

Do you remember your apartment, school, etc.? What was it like?

What are your most vivid memories of the old country? Did you have friends? Were you aware of any privations or problems, or did your parents shield you?

Why did your family leave? Was anti-Semitism an issue? Economic opportunity? Did your parents talk about it? Who came with you?

What happened to your parents when they requested to leave? Were they ever denied? Were they fired?

What did your parents tell you about America?

Did your grandparents come with you? If so, what role did they play?

If Jewish, did you experience any anti-Semitism? Did you know you were Jewish? What stories have you heard from your parents about anti-Semitism?

THE JOURNEY

Describe the immigration process throughout your journey to America.

Do you remember the immigration journey? Your first taste of the West?

Did you seek refugee status? Exit visas to Israel? Do you see yourself as a refugee or an immigrant?

If you stopped in Italy:

What was your impression of Italy when you arrived? Did you experience a shock? Where did you stay?

Do you remember selling wares at the market? What else do you remember from this time?

Did you have a choice of where to go—Israel, U.S.? If so, which city did you choose?

AMERICA: EARLY YEARS (FIRST STEPS IN AMERICA)

What was your first memory of America? What was your impression of living conditions? Stores, food, clothing, etc.? Was it a culture shock?

LIVING

Where did you move to? How did your family make that choice?

Did you live in an ethnic enclave?

Did you have relatives or friends here?

Describe your apartment/living conditions.

Describe the first years. What were the challenges you most remember?

What did your parents do when they arrived? Were they able to work in their prior profession?

Was their loss of professional status hard for them/you? What motivated you to succeed? Compare their job here to their job/status in the old country.

Did you help your parents? If so, how?

Did you get help from Jewish or welfare organizations? Did any individuals help you?

How did America compare to the stereotypes you knew about (e.g., capitalism, treatment of minorities, etc.)?

Did your family have money troubles? Tell me some stories of how your family saved money.

SCHOOL

What stereotypes of Russian immigrants did you deal with?

What kind of school did you attend? Was it overwhelming? What was it like socially? Did you make friends?

Describe the first day of school. What was your first impression of the school?

If you attended a yeshiva, did your parents accept the religious customs you brought home? How did it make you feel toward Judaism? Are you more Jewish today because of it? Do you have any resentment?

Can you share any embarrassing stories due to a lack of culture or language?

How well did you do academically? Was it harder for you than non-immigrants?

Did immigration provide motivation?

ACCULTURATION

Share some stories of hardship—something you had to overcome.

How long did it take you to learn English? How did you do it? What role did TV play?

What language was spoken most at home?

Were you worried about not fitting in socially or not understanding cultural/TV references?

Did you ever consider a name change? Did your name sound too Russian?

When growing up, did you celebrate American holidays like Thanksgiving?

How was America different from what you expected? What was surprising? Did you expect it to be a paradise with streets paved with gold? Was life harder/less rich than you expected?

What American attitudes took adjusting to—openness, freedom, kindness from strangers?

Who were your friends? Did you have Russian friends or other immigrant friends?

Did you experience discrimination? Did you get called "Commie," "Red," "Dirty Jew"? Did people make fun of you for the way you dressed, sounded, etc.?

Did your parents put pressure on you to succeed (e.g., "We did this for you … don't blow it.")? Did this pressure limit your ability to study non-professional subjects in school or encourage you to pick certain careers (doctor, engineer, lawyer, etc.)?

Did you go to camp? If so, was it a Jewish camp?

In what ways was your childhood different from that of American children?

BECOMING AMERICAN: LATER YEARS

Tell me about your family's income in the early and later years. Did you live in poverty?

How did your parents adjust to becoming American? In what ways have they retained the old country habits/mores? What American habit/lifestyle did your parents disapprove of?

Tell me about your schooling. Were you a good student? Were you encouraged to go to college?

If you went to college, tell me about your experience. Where did you go? How did you choose it? What did you study? Did you gravitate to ethnic friends? Other immigrants?

Where did you choose to live after college? Was it important to live near your parents? If so, is this a legacy of immigration/old country values?

How did you pick your profession/job? Were your parents or immigrant status an influence?

What portion of your social circle is immigrants/Russian?

Tell me about your later life (e.g., job, dating/marriage, kids). How has immigration affected these?

JUDAISM (IF JEWISH)

How was your Jewish identity affected by your immigration experience/status? (This does not need to be its own section but can be sprinkled through other narratives.)

Tell me about your Judaism. Did you know you were Jewish in Russia? What level of observance did your family have? Did you become more Jewish over time in America? What about your parents?

Did you experience any anti-Semtisim in the U.S.S.R.? Did it affect your experience in the U.S. (e.g., willingness to engage with the Jewish community)?

What is Judaism to you? Is it mostly a religion? An ethnicity, a nationality, or both?

Were you proud to be Jewish in America? Were there any visible displays like a Magen David?

Were you circumcised? Did you have a bar/bat mitzvah? Was it different from the bar/bat mitzvahs that American kids had?

Describe your Jewish education. Did you go to a Jewish day school, Hebrew school, a camp, or JCC programs? Did you feel the Jewish community tried to brainwash you?

How did the Jewish community welcome you? Did you feel comfortable in synagogues or like an outsider?

Did you marry Jewish and raise your kids Jewish?

Is your Jewish identity or your Russian identity more important to you?

Did your parents pressure you to marry Jewish or Russian? If so, did you?

IDENTITY/REFLECTIONS

Talk about your identity, especially to what extent it is a dual identity shaped both by your Russian past and your American present. What does the process of "becoming American" mean to you?

What are your thoughts about the phrase "Only in America"?

Would you say you are Russian-American? What does the hyphen mean to you? How do you compare to the stereotype of Russian-American?

Some immigrants are ambivalent about Russia, while some are deeply Russian. Do you have a love-hate relationship?

Did your parents ever become fully American?

How has your Russian background helped you understand and appreciate America even more than Americans? Which parts of America?

What is the best/favorite story about the old country you remember hearing growing up?

Which Russian values would you want to pass on to your children?

What part of Russian culture do you still partake in (e.g, food, drink, music, books, etc.)?

Did more Russian immigrants, who spoke Russian, ever look down on you for being too American or for not being "a real Russian" (e.g., you chose to speak English and not Russian).

When you speak Russian, is it "Americanized"? Do you have a Russian accent?

When did you first think of yourself as primarily American?

With all the struggles and hardship that immigration presented, would you do it again? Would you rather be an immigrant, or would you rather be native-born?

How did your immigration experience, being an immigrant, affect your political views?

How are Russian immigrants from your era different from today's immigrants? Is the process of assimilation similar?

Do you ever catch yourself translating words from Russian to English or vice versa in your head? Can you think in Russian? What's your favorite Russian word that lacks an English equivalent?

Do you ever feel Russian ethnic pride? Do you ever root for Russia against the U.S. in the Olympics? What if Russia is playing another country (e.g., France)?

Have you sought out to deepen your connection to Russia? If yes, in what way?

Have you gone back to visit? If so, how did you feel? Was it what you imagined? Did it change the way you view your identity? Is it important that your kids visit?

If you have kids, did you teach them Russian? Would you want them to marry Russian? If your kids could learn only Russian or Hebrew, what would you want them to know?

Are you still becoming more American? Or has that stopped? Will you ever feel 100 percent American? In what ways can you never be 100 percent American?

If you can give new immigrants (immigrant children) one piece of advice, what would it be?

Printed in the United States
by Baker & Taylor Publisher Services